In the
NAGA'S
WAKE

In the
NAGA'S
WAKE

MICK O'SHEA

ALLEN&UNWIN

First published in Australia in 2006
Copyright © Michael O'Shea 2006

Allen & Unwin
83 Alexander Street
Crows Nest NSW 2065
Australia
Phone: (61 2) 8425 0100
Fax: (61 2) 9906 2218
Email: info@allenandunwin.com
Web: www.allenandunwin.com

National Library of Australia
Cataloguing-in-Publication entry:

O'Shea, Mick, 1975– .
    In the Naga's Wake : the first man to kayak the Mekong,
    from Tibet to the South China Sea.

    ISBN 978 1 74114 869 5.
    ISBN 1 74114 869 3.

    1. O'Shea, Mick, 1975– . 2. Kayaking – China. I. Title.

797.1224092

Set in 11.5/15 pt Dante by Midland Typesetters, Australia
Printed by McPherson's Printing Group, Australia

10 9 8 7 6 5 4 3 2 1

Contents

To my grandparents, Frank and Daphne Kennedy, who taught me that warmth of heart is the greatest possession a person can have.

To the diverse people of the Mekong, whose kindness, generosity and goodwill never fail to inspire me.

Preface

This book traces the most challenging and rewarding journey of my life to date. A journey along the entire length of the Mekong River, from its frozen source on the Tibetan Plateau to the tropical South China Sea; a distance of four thousand nine hundred and nine kilometres.

The events, people and places depicted herewith are real and have been described as I experienced them. Freedom of expression is severely restricted in several Mekong nations. In certain circumstances, the names of individuals have been altered in order to protect their identities.

The Mekong First Descent Project (MFDP) was made possible by the support and generosity of a long list of people and organisations to whom I remain eternally grateful. I would like to point out, however, that, as the sole author of this book, the thoughts, views, experiences and realisations expressed within are mine and mine alone, and are not those held by project supporters or third parties associated with the MFDP.

The expedition took me through dozens of language realms; I have not attempted to adhere to any rigid transliteration system. The transcriptions simply reflect the way I speak or hear the languages.

The Mekong descent entailed some extreme challenges both on and off the river and some situations spiralled unexpectedly out of control, to the point where they threatened not only the survival of the project but also my life. Indeed, when writing this book I was tempted not to include some of the less savoury events through a desire to focus more attention on what I perceived as the constructive experiences of the journey. After giving the matter considerable thought I realised that above all else it is my goal to recount the entire expedition as it occurred and not a version that glosses over major events for the sake of convenience.

In the Naga's Wake is my honest account of the Mekong First Descent: the trials, tribulations, challenges and amazement of a world-first journey from a river's source to the sea.

Mick O'Shea
September 2006

Map 1 Course of Mekong   ix

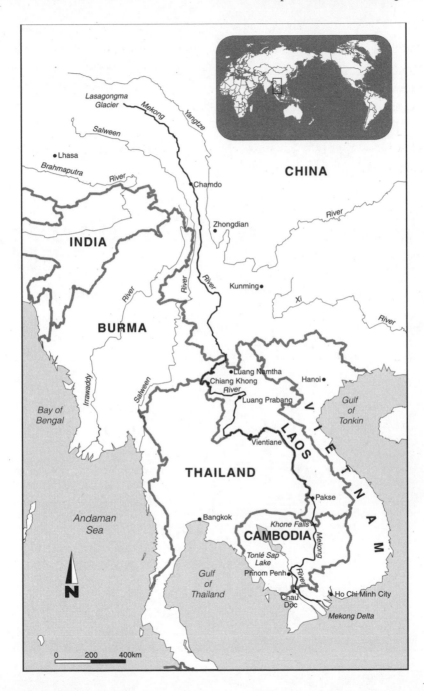

1   Inspiration and the Mekong

I dug deep to rally the strength needed to pull my heavily laden kayak onto the rock. I fell back against the gorge wall exhausted, coughing and gasping for air. The previous section of the river had taken its toll and I felt humbled and weak. My lungs burned as I coughed up water, shivering with cold. I pulled my 'pogies' [neoprene paddle mitts] *off the paddle and put them on to my shaking hands, then stuffed my hands under my armpits in an effort to keep myself warm. The rapid roared below me as if outraged that I had narrowly escaped its embrace. As I recovered, I reflected on just how close I had come to being turned into fish food. I also needed to work out how much trouble I was in.*

From my vantage point on the tiny island sanctuary of rock and rubble, the remnants of an avalanche, it became clear that I was cornered by the river with my back literally against the wall. There was no safe line of passage out of the gorge, which was studded with powerful 'keeper holes' [usually formed behind rocks where the water flows over the rock or a submerged object, causing water downstream to flow back over the top of the water rushing over the submerged object and creating a type of violent washing-machine effect that can fatally trap a kayaker]. *I scanned for a route to climb my way around the dangerous section of river, but sheer-sided canyon walls hemmed me in. Powerful currents ensured there was no way back upstream. Beyond the heart of the heaving violence of the hole was a long line of powerful boils and whirlpools all the way to the next bend.*

The whirlpools were so strong that I would almost certainly drown if I was forced out of the kayak by the holes. What was even more intimidating was what might be around the next bend. A nine-metre waterfall with no place to stop above it? The steadily increasing gradient drop or 'steepness' of the river made me think that this was a strong possibility. Yet because no one had ever navigated through the region before the only way to find out was to paddle blindly around the corner and hope for the best.

I pulled out the satellite phone, my only way of communicating with the outside world, but there was no signal. With my nearest support team member over two thousand kilometres away as the crow flies and with no access by land, help would not arrive in time anyway but somehow the sat. phone not working compounded my sense of isolation.

I took out the laminated maps from my dry suit chest pocket to help me work out how long the river might continue like this and if there were any potential exit routes. Nothing. There didn't seem to be any visible exit routes, and the contour lines on the map, which indicated the extreme steepness of the terrain, looked pretty much the same for the next one hundred and thirty kilometres. The river was rising by between ten to fifteen centimetres a day, which meant that the rocks I stood on would be part of the rapid within a few days. There was also the ever-present threat of flash flooding playing on my mind since I entered this constricted and extremely steep section of the river. I was cold, tired, shaken by the rapidly deteriorating conditions, darkness was looming and there was nowhere to sleep.

*'F**k this!' I spat out my frustration. 'This is just too much,' I thought to myself. 'For Christ's sake, just give me some options.' My expeditionary career in Asia spanned almost a decade, and I had always felt I could get myself out of every situation. This was an entirely new experience. I was in deep, way over my head, and to continue around the next bend would not only be foolish but possibly fatal.*

With the conditions getting more treacherous by the hour, there was no other option but to continue on alone into the longest unexplored and most treacherous section of the entire Mekong River.

An unfamiliar veil of despair came over me as I realised that I would have to play Russian roulette with the next bend and probably many others in order to have a chance of making it out alive. I knew there only had to be one significant waterfall in one of the sheer-sided canyons to permanently end my journey. My research on previous exploratory river expeditions through the region had made me acutely aware that the nearby Yangtze, Tsangpo and Yellow rivers, which make similar descents to the Mekong off the Tibetan plateau, each had their own 'super extreme' stretches in their most remote inner sanctums. These extreme portions had claimed dozens of river pioneers' lives in the past two decades and the geographical indicators hinted that I was entering the Mekong's own 'super extreme' stretch with no way out except via the river.

I sat on my rock island for several minutes, trying to gather my composure. For one long moment I felt an intense loneliness and a yearning to live. I thought back to the conversation I'd had the previous evening by sat. phone with my fiancée Yuta and found myself praying, with all my heart, to the naga, revered protector and destroyer of all life on the Mekong, to at least give me a fighting chance and let me see her again. I started to pull myself together.

I scanned downstream again to find a way out through the surging violence. I began conjuring up visions of my kayak narrowly skirting the most perilous features of the next part of the river and visualised the precise life-saving manoeuvres I would need to actuate in order to make it through the wild rapid. I struggled to ignore my subconscious, which was warning me that the constantly changing dynamics of the rapid put my chances of avoiding the keeper holes at around fifty/fifty. I breathed deeply three times to oxygenate my blood, and with a flick of my hip released the friction of kayak plastic on rock and slid into the heaving surges of water to test my fate.

Journal entry, 6 June 2004

The Mekong gorges of Tibet, through which I struggled for survival in June 2004, represent a small portion of one of the world's greatest rivers, known in English-speaking nations as the Mekong.

About fifty-five million years ago, one of the most magnificent geological events in the Earth's history occurred when the India tectonic plate collided with Asia, lifting up the sea floor thousands of metres above sea level to create the largest existing mountain range on the planet: the Himalaya. Amongst this upheaval, the Tibetan plateau, with an average elevation of over four thousand metres, was also created. It is from this point, often referred to as 'the roof of the world', that the great Mekong River trickles from a glacial spring at an altitude of five thousand two hundred and twenty-seven metres.

Oblivious to man-made political boundaries and ideology, the Mekong Basin provides sustenance for some seventy million people from over one hundred different ethnic groups from a vast swathe of Asia. The Mekong flows predominantly along a north–south axis for four thousand nine hundred and nine kilometres from the barren grasslands and glaciers of the Tibetan Plateau to the humid tropics of the Vietnam delta. This unique longitudinal range ensures that the Mekong spans an unparalleled variety of climatic realms and associated natural environments that in turn support a biodiversity surpassed by few regions on Earth.

'Mekong' is an English abbreviation of the Thai name for the river, Mae Nam Khong, which loosely translates to the English, 'Kong, Mother (of) Water'. This name, steeped in respect and reverence reserved for a nurturing mother, best symbolises the connection that most of the basin's peoples have with their river in either practical or spiritual terms. For more than six thousand years, a myriad of ethnic groups have shaped their existence around the cycles in the river's ecology and, above all else, the availability of the water, silt and fisheries that the system provides.

This connection to the Mekong River transcends the notions that people from the world's most developed nations have of their own country's rivers, such as recreation, generating electricity and material survival, and is manifested in a spiritual and cultural foundation of the different social groups found along the Mekong's banks. Numerous festivals, rituals, folk tales, poems, proverbs, songs, art and dance found throughout the length and breadth of the basin stand as testimony to the incredible role this river system plays in its peoples' lives.

Even as globalisation takes an uncompromising toll on the traditional regions of Asia, there is no doubt that for tens of millions of the Mekong's people, the river permeates every aspect of their existence and to this day continues to be a major force that turns 'the wheel of life'.

The first reference to a section of the Mekong in the western world came via Marco Polo, who crossed a suspension bridge spanning a wild portion of the river in Yunnan in 1283. Father Gasper da Cruz of Portugal made the first 'recorded ascent' of a significant stretch of the river in 1555. Over the next four-and-a-half centuries dozens of incredible journeys, with motivations as diverse as the conversion of souls to dreams of colonial domination and the unravelling of scientific curiosities, took place along much of the river.

These epic western adventures of conquest, struggles and dreams shaped the political destiny of much of mainland South-East Asia, yet more often than not ended in failure and tragedy. Incredibly, by 2004 over seven hundred and twenty years after the first westerner stood on the banks of the river, significant sections of the Mekong mainstream remained neither navigated nor explored at ground level by locals or foreigners.

My first encounter with the Mekong happened when I was a twenty-year-old traveller from Western Australia on my first overseas trip. While travelling through Asia en route to Europe I stumbled upon the shimmering red river in northeastern Thailand in 1995. I approached the Mother of Water on foot through a sleepy hamlet of rustic teakwood stilt houses, finally reaching a broad expanse of water fringed with hundreds of swaying coconut palms. Coming up over a flood embankment I was immediately struck by the size and tranquil beauty of the largest waterway I had ever seen.

At that point my knowledge of the river did not extend far beyond some general facts, such as that the Mekong's delta extends through southern Vietnam, where a bloody war of attrition had taken place during most of the sixties and seventies, and that the river also passed through Laos, Thailand and Cambodia. I knew it was a big river but not that it was arguably the eighth longest in the world. (I have since found out that historically the Mekong was believed to be the twelfth longest river, yet more recent scientific analysis of the river's length, taking into account the correct location of the source, which was pinpointed by a Sino–Japanese team in 1994 and confirmed by the Chinese academy of sciences in 1999, controversially places the Mekong's length at four thousand nine hundred and nine kilometres, making it the eighth longest river.) The Mekong also has the tenth greatest volume of water of all the world's rivers. I knew that it had significant biodiversity, but not that it was one of the planet's most intense biological hotspots, playing second fiddle only to the Amazon and Nile basins in terms of natural diversity.

I spent ten days relaxing on the river's banks, travelling to several small towns and villages where naked children frolicked in the shallows and fishermen cast their throw nets below riverside temples glimmering with golden tributes to the Thai version of the *naga*. This dragon-like creature from Hindu and Buddhist mythology is endowed with powers of life and death over all creatures on and below the water's surface. According to ancient legends that are depicted in temple murals in northeastern Thailand, the *naga* created the river with its immense body as it made its way south, leaving a channel of life-giving water in its wake. The *naga* seemed to be watching over the river from the balustrades of every village temple, observing the passing of time and the miracle of light dancing off the water's surface. The pace of rural life in the laidback Isarn province of Thailand mirrored the Mekong's timeless flow.

Since that impressionable first time, several amazing rafting and trekking expeditions into the remote Mekong tributaries and tribal areas of northern Laos between 1997 and '99 left me yearning for more. In 2000 I moved to Malaysia to work as a centre manager for a whitewater rafting company. I ended up spending seven months working on highland rivers with the Malaysian aboriginals, the 'Orang Asli', who taught me about the forests and their way of life.

Carl Traeholt and Rubin Ghan, my employers and Asian river exploration mentors, introduced me to the range of exploratory opportunities that still existed in the region by encouraging me to take part in first descents of rivers in peninsular Malaysia, Borneo and Sumatra. In late 2000 I established a consultancy company developing off-the-beaten-track adventures going into new regions of Laos. During the first two years that I lived in Laos, I spent about half my time in the provinces exploring riverways, caves and mountain trails while training locals to make a living from taking foreigners into their backyards. Before I knew it five years had passed and my work expanded from Laos into Thailand, Cambodia and Vietnam and throughout much of the lower Mekong Basin.

The Mekong River technically forms a thin meandering line from its birthplace at the base of Lasagongma Glacier on the Qinghai Tibet plateau to the point where it releases into the South China Sea some four thousand nine hundred and nine kilometres downstream. Yet this slither is merely the central artery of an immense interconnected water network that incorporates every stream, pond, lake, ground water resource and reservoir that is ultimately connected to the Mekong mainstream by the forces of gravity. This extremely complex living and evolving network of life is known as the Mekong Basin and incorporates a land area of some seven hundred and ninety-five thousand square kilometres, including around eighty-five per cent of the Lao and Cambodian national territories respectively, thirty-seven per cent of Thailand's national territory, twenty per cent of Vietnam's, almost four per cent of Burma's and less than two per cent of China's.

My natural instincts have always forced me off the standard tourist routes and into remote natural and cultural regions while travelling and it was always here, where few others had the will to venture, that I found the most rewarding experiences.

In order to work within the regions that inspired me I began researching and developing nature/culture-based, multi-sports travel programs throughout the Mekong Basin and beyond. My goal was to provide the conscientious traveller with access to the same regions that inspired me while simultaneously benefitting the local peoples and environments that formed the attraction. By mixing kayaking, rafting, cycling, trekking and village stays I was able to provide naturally and culturally sensitive people with access to rarely visited areas, on programs that were designed to actively benefit the peoples and environments we visited. As time passed I increasingly found the travel medium of the adventures I created moving away from the roads and trails that are so rapidly being paved towards the river systems. I also found that I was increasingly drawn to explore more of the Mekong Basin's waterways, both within the context of work and recreationally.

The ecological diversity of the Mekong Basin is prolific along the rivers, lakes, streams and wetlands, and it is these river arteries that also provide an efficient way of gaining access to remote areas of the basin via kayaks, rafts and canoes. A day of kayaking or rafting can cover the same amount of area you would travel during two to five days' walking in the mountainous and heavily forested terrain. You can also carry more supplies and thus spend more time in the wilds.

Being able to silently travel through old-growth forests on natural river currents increased the number of wildlife sightings. Travelling on the waterways enabled me to see parts of South-East Asia that hadn't changed for centuries, and gave me a glimpse into little known cultures and ecological environments.

Discovering the unknown sections of rivers became a passion. No two rivers have the same character and every exploratory adventure uncovers something new. Travelling between steep-sided canyons to paddling through caves that were up to eight kilometres long, and even finding semi-nomadic tribal villages that local governments did not know existed, I realised I had found my calling. This type of existence was what I was born to.

Over the years I came to know many of the river peoples of the lower Mekong Basin personally and I still find an endless source of fascination in the close relationships these people share with their environments. These days my own lifestyle has also become connected with the cycles of the river system and the people who live within its cycle. Between 1997 and 2004, I remember visiting at least sixty villages in the lower Mekong Basin where the elders I spoke with claimed that they had not had a foreigner stay in their village before. These peoples were from some twenty-two different ethnic groups within Laos, Cambodia, Vietnam and Burma, yet they all had at least two things in common: their lives were all intimately tied to the cycles of the Mekong River system and they all shared a simple and genuine hospitality.

After three years of developing adventure travel in the Mekong Basin I gradually found my inspiration waning, despite the satisfaction of starting up a new environmentally friendly and sustainable adventure travel company. The immediate demands of managing the daily operations and employees of the company meant that exploration and development were often placed on the backburner. My life was slowly becoming one of mundane routine, something I had always sworn to avoid at all costs. It was time to reignite my passion for adventure. It was simply a matter of working out how best to do it.

In 2001 and 2002, I was living in Laos in a house that had panoramic views across the Mekong River to Thailand. I would often wake in the morning and enjoy a rich Lao coffee on the balcony, watching the river and the people come to life. As housewives tended their riverside vegetable gardens and children skipped to school along red dirt roads, I wondered what the furthest point of the light brown-coloured river would look like on the Tibetan Plateau several thousand kilometres to the north and started to do some research.

To my surprise, in an age where the greatest mountains had been climbed dozens if not hundreds of times, the continents traversed and the oceans crossed by almost every vessel imaginable, I discovered that the Mekong had never been fully navigated or explored at ground level. It occurred to me that this was just the type of challenge I needed. I knew with my accumulated experience in exploring Asian rivers, combined with existing contacts throughout the basin, that it was a challenge I could probably achieve. Not only did it have the potential to reinvigorate my life with the true sense of adventure that I needed but it also offered an avenue to address an issue which had been eating at my subconscious for years.

The river system that has captivated my imagination for years with its boundless beauty and diversity was facing one of the most significant ecological crises of its fifty million-year history and I was all too aware that by and large, the world had not noticed. Somehow the enormous issues facing the Mekong Basin had been overlooked by the global community and I was both distressed and frustrated to silently lay witness to events that I deeply felt were unjust. The largest engineering project in world history was well underway nearby the Mekong in China. Most people were aware of the infamous Three Gorges dam project on the Yangtze River, which attracted widespread condemnation from the world when it was revealed that the lives of millions of Chinese and a priceless natural treasure would be destroyed by Beijing's energy policy. Yet I, like many experts, academics, researchers and informed observers throughout the lower Mekong Basin, realised that it was the slightly smaller Chinese project currently underway on the Mekong River that had the potential to eclipse the Three Gorges dam in terms of overall environmental and socio-cultural impacts and I felt a steadily increasing desire to let the world know why.

The seeds for the first descent of the Mekong River were sown. My exploration of the Mekong River would be the perfect project to get the message out to others by using the descent to create informative documentaries and print media articles. Throughout 2002 I restructured my company to free up more time and by early 2003 I was working on the Mekong descent concept almost full-time.

2 The challenge

The enormous amount of research I needed to do to get the first descent of the Mekong River up and running hit home as soon as I started to work my way through gigabytes of web information, maps, books and my address book with eight years' worth of contacts in the Mekong region. I was on the look out for titbits of information that would be useful for a first descent. I would be passing through some of the most desolate and remote environments on Earth, as well as travelling through a complex tapestry of geographic, ecological, cultural, political and historic environments. All of these factors needed to be researched thoroughly to make sure that exploration of the Mekong River was actually viable.

My primary goal was to identify the major obstacles that I would come across on the journey and work out the solutions to overcome each of them. Identifying the greatest obstacles was a time-consuming and often frustrating process due to the fact that no one had tried to tackle the Mekong from source to sea before; this also meant information was limited. As the list of obstacles grew day by day, the solutions became ever more difficult to conceptualise. Some of the more challenging tasks on the 'to do' list were daunting.

~ Find out if navigation is even possible through the steeper sections of the river in Tibet and Yunnan, checking maps, satellite imagery and actual surveys.
~ Try to obtain or access tightly restricted military maps of restricted travel regions.

~ Obtain permission to cross borders at places where foreigners don't usually cross.

~ Work out the approximate stretch of the river that would be frozen in April/May.

~ Identify viable re-supply points in regions where there are no marked roads.

~ Get filming authorisations in politically insular nations.

~ Ask if we can be accompanied by police or military escorts through regions controlled by Burmese rebels or armed remnants of the disbanded Khmer Rouge.

~ Try to procure sponsorship for the one hundred and thirty-two items on the 'essential equipment' list.

~ Set up evacuation plans, taking into account our extremely limited local information available.

~ Put in place a viable sponsorship plan for securing the US$315 000 we estimate as the minimum required to take a team of four people and support/film crew of three down the Mekong to produce the planned documentaries.

And there were another seventy or so points on top of these.

Four months after starting intensive research on the project I discussed my ideas with my friend Alan Boatman, founder of Geo Systems International and an environmental research impact assessment scientist based in Vientiane, Laos. He was intrigued and keen to participate as the support team leader, putting his logistics skills to the test, as well as gathering scientific information on the river system that fascinated him. Alan's extensive knowledge of the Mekong Basin's geography and environmental issues were an invaluable resource and his insights helped to clarify many of the awareness-building goals that would form the foundation of the project.

With so many questions unanswered after months of research, we decided to speed things up by making a two-week field survey to the steepest sections of the river in Yunnan province of China in July 2003. In August of 2003 the Mekong First Descent Project opened its doors based out of Alan's office just one hundred and fifty metres from the river.

Towards the end of 2003 we found out about several expedition teams that would be competing with our project. The last real attempt to explore the entire Mekong River's course had been the French Mekong Expedition of 1866–68, led by Ernest Doudart de Lagrée and Francis Garnier, which travelled from Saigon to Yunnan and ended with the loss of Lagrée's life. By astounding coincidence, in 2004 and 2005 three separate expeditionary teams representing Japan, China and New Zealand, in addition to my own, all planned to complete full descents of the Mekong.

The Japanese team was led by Masayuki Kitamura of the Tokyo University of Agriculture. Masayuki was the team leader of the expedition that discovered in 1994 that the Mekong source is located at the base of Lasagongma Glacier in Eastern Tibet. In 1994 and again in 2002 Masayuki led rafting teams who successfully completed first navigational descent expeditions along two separate stretches of the Mekong River, totalling over eight hundred kilometres. The Japanese planned to complete their goal of full Mekong exploration by making further expeditions, in 2004 and 2005, that would take them down the remaining four thousand one hundred kilometres of the river—if successful they would complete the Mekong descent in four stages.

We also learned from several sources that a Chinese team, reportedly led by an experienced veteran of the historic first descent of the Yangtze River, Mr Song Yipin, had the support of the Chinese government and also planned to take on the river in 2005. Like me, the Chinese planned a one-shot run from source to sea to claim the title. However, before starting from the top they intended to undertake some shorter descents of the river in preparation for the whole hog.

The third team was from New Zealand and were sponsored by the Sir Edmund Hillary Trust, an official project supported by the New Zealand government. Their goal was to make the first man-powered descent in one shot through the entire Mekong Valley using a mixture of trekking, mountain biking and kayaking. Although the New Zealand team's expedition would not require them to challenge the Mekong's most extreme environments (due to the fact that they would ride on man-made roads around the most perilous rapids, gorges and natural obstacles) theoretically, at least, they could claim the first complete man-powered descent of the Mekong Valley if not the first descent of the Mekong River. Even though the challenges associated with our respective descents were very different, I realised that the general public probably wouldn't bother differentiating between the descents, so I made it a goal to beat them to the South China Sea if I could.

We later became aware that the Japanese and Chinese teams had decided to join forces with another whitewater team, led by a veteran explorer of greater Tibet's rivers, American Pete Winn, in an attempt to navigate and explore the steepest and most remote stretch of the entire Mekong, a portion we referred to as the Mekong gorges of Tibet. The Mekong gorges in the southern half of eastern Tibet are characterised by steep-sided, inaccessible and apparently uninhabited canyons that possess large volumes of water and an extremely steep gradient drop (steepness) of as much as twenty-nine feet per mile over its steepest one hundred-mile stretch. By comparison the steepest portions of the Grand Canyon, internationally renowned as being one of North America's wildest big water runs, descends at just seven feet per mile on its steepest one-hundred-mile stretch. The Mekong gorges of Tibet possess similar volumes of water yet are around four times steeper—an extreme section of river to explore by any standards. With the Mekong gorges of Tibet section explored, one of the river's major obstacles would be removed, helping to clear the way for both the Japanese and Chinese to achieve their goals.

Towards the end of 2003 it became clear that we were struggling to raise the funds required to mount our expedition. Alan and I decided to contact the international team via Pete Winn to see if there was interest in mounting a combined attempt on the entire river in 2004, thus reducing the costs for everyone. The response was pretty concise. The Chinese said they would only challenge the entire river with an all-Chinese team, Pete had no interest whatsoever and there was no direct response from the Japanese. We decided if we couldn't join them, we had to beat them and continued with our original plans.

I set a departure date for March 2004 and accepted that I would probably be descending through the gorges of Tibet at about the same time as the joint international expedition and the entire river at the same time as the New Zealanders, with the option to race the latter to the finish line if it was deemed necessary.

As the departure date loomed, it became clear that the secured sponsorship funds were significantly less than the budget needed to support the project. This meant we had to make major adjustments to the structure of our expedition if it was to go ahead. Alan and I could not afford to pay for the production team or the sponsored professional paddlers that we had wanted to join us as part of the descent.

Work commitments, the heavy financial burden of funding the MFDP and the uncertainty of gaining access to the Tibet Autonomous Region (TAR) of the Mekong forced Alan to withdraw his involvement from the project. To keep to the plan and the schedule it was now up to me, which meant I would have to go into considerable personal debt. Failure would not only be personally devastating but it could wipe me out financially. The luxury of waiting another year to raise money was simply not an option.

It wasn't just about taking the trophy for the first exploration and navigation of the Mekong. I couldn't put my consultancy company on hold any longer as it would mean my staff would probably end up losing their jobs while I spent another year working out the logistics and funding for the expedition. It was a price I was not willing to pay.

There were some long days filled with doubt after Alan left. Would it really be worth risking my company, my life and all my worldly possessions in order to chase a dream that had a significant likelihood of failure?

A passage from the book *Wanderer*, by Sterling Hayden, a Hollywood film actor who had followed his dream and run away to sail to Tahiti, helped me answer that question, reminding me of the personal realisations that had led me to start a life of adventure in Asia in the first place:

> *What does a man need—really need? A few pounds of food each day, heat and shelter, six feet to lie down in—and some form of working activity that will yield a sense of accomplishment. That's all—in the material sense, and we know it. But we are brainwashed by our economic system until we end up in a tomb beneath a pyramid of time payments, mortgages, preposterous gadgetry, playthings that divert our attention for the sheer idiocy of the charade.*
>
> *The years thunder by. The dreams of youth grow dim where they lie caked in dust on the shelves of patience. Before we know it, the tomb is sealed.*
>
> *Where, then, lies the answer?*
>
> *In choice . . .!*
>
> *Which shall it be: bankruptcy of purse or bankruptcy of life . . .?*

I decided to put everything on the line to make the project fly with the resources I had, plus those that were scheduled to come in as the descent proceeded. The limited budget required slashing costs, and this was done by deciding to do the descent solo with a film and photographic team of three following and filming the descent where possible from roads, riverside trails and on the river.

This change in plan opened up an intriguing possibility. Several of the world's greatest rivers had already been fully navigated by 2004, but all of the first complete descents were done by teams of expert paddlers pooling their skills and resources. If I was successful the Mekong would become the only one of the world's ten greatest rivers to be fully navigated and explored for the first time in history by a solo adventurer. I liked the idea of breaking new ground.

3 Preparation, departure and the recipe for disaster

The loss of Alan's contribution dramatically increased my workload leading up to the final months before starting the expedition. Fortunately I had people around me who were willing to take on some of this work. My Thai fiancée Yuta, who happened to be born in a house overlooking the Mekong in Nongkhai, came to my assistance, and despite having a full-time job managed to spend every other waking moment helping. Hoopy, a friend of mine and Yuta's, volunteered her services, and my ever-reliable mother in Australia also came on-board to assist with publicity and locating sponsors. With our combined efforts and the help of some staff from my company, getting the project off the ground was still a possibility.

During the four- to five-month journey down the river I planned to produce two documentaries and a photographic book on the Mekong Basin. My original plan was to team up with professional adventure documentary-makers that I had previously worked with. I knew it was important to have people I knew and trusted along for the ride, so in the early stages I contacted qualified friends to see if they were interested.

The problem, at this stage, was that we didn't even know if we would be successful in getting enough sponsorship to fund the trek. When I finally committed myself to a departure date for the expedition, the original budget had been reduced dramatically, and three months before heading out my original choices were already booked in for other projects. With such short notice I had to put together a team of people I had not worked with before.

A recommendation from a friend in Vientiane led me to Nicolas Suaret, a petite, softly spoken, twenty-four-year-old Frenchman. Nico had recently finished film school in Paris and was producing short films for aid agencies, government and non-government organisations.

Abe was a Lao citizen who had worked for Lao National TV for several years. He agreed to work with me as the assistant cameraman and grip. Abe was fit, easygoing and highly motivated. His English language skills were limited, but both Nico and I knew enough Lao to communicate with him.

Stanislas Fradelizi, another Frenchman, was a freelance photographer and friend of Alan's. Stan had been very helpful in the lead-up to the expedition, particularly in the last few weeks when I needed all the help I could get. Stan had lived and worked in Asia for several years, working from a 250cc XR trail bike, touring the regions of the lower Mekong and capturing landscapes and portraits of rural environments and people. He was just back from a two-month journey along the Ho Chi Minh Trail. He seemed keen to further develop his career in adventure photography.

Three weeks before our departure Lara Jones, an Australian photojournalist, flew into Vientiane on the project budget to work as the media liaison and PR person. I had met Lara by chance several months earlier when she wandered into my office for travel information. It turned out that Lara had done a lot of photography in the Tibetan regions of China and was keen to be involved in the expedition as a photojournalist. As Stan was already booked in as our photographer, she took on the PR role.

Alan mentioned he had some misgivings about Lara due to previous dealings he had had with her. I was keen to get the project moving and was impressed because Lara had sidelined other work to make herself available for the next five months. I gave her the benefit of the doubt. For the first few weeks leading up to the expedition

Lara worked hard to attract media interest and generate revenue for the project by arranging the sale of photos and articles.

The few days before the start of the expedition were extremely hectic with Lara, Yuta, Stan, my company staff and myself all working long hours to get everything done. There were logistical problems running right up to the time the team were ready to head off on the expedition, such as government red tape stalling the release of funds from a sponsorship grant provided by the Tourism Authority of Thailand and problems procuring filming equipment. Money was extremely tight as we all tried to stick to the available expedition budget.

Everyone's nerves were at breaking point as the tension of working to the deadline started testing our resolve. It became clear to Yuta and I that Lara was not handling the stress well when one day she suddenly started hurling verbal abuse at me for not having the petty cash immediately at hand to pay her hotel bill. As there were so many things to get done before departure I didn't have time to dwell on the confrontation and initially put it down to the stress everyone was under. After encountering more surly attitude from Lara I discussed the matter with Yuta on the morning of departure and both of our instincts told us to cut our losses and get rid of Lara as we felt there would probably be further trouble if she stayed on. But on the practical side we also knew we needed media coverage to promote the expedition and generate much needed income from the sale of photos and stories to keep the expedition going. With departure on the doorstep there was simply no time for alternatives.

Stan, Nico, Abe, Lara and I flew out on a sponsored Lao Airlines flight to Kunming, the capital of Yunnan province located to the northeast of Vietnam, a town famous for being the gateway to the celebrated southern branch of the Silk Road. We were met by James Shenton, an expatriate operating a travel agency from

Kunming. James was responsible for getting the permit to paddle and film within the Tibet Autonomous Region (TAR).

After three days of delays in Kunming, we finally departed in a Beijing jeep, the Chinese equivalent of a Landrover, and started the long drive north to Zongjian, a small city rather optimistically promoted by the Yunnan Tourism Board as the Shangri-la described in the James Hilton classic *Lost Horizons*. Set on the southeastern steppes of the Tibetan Plateau, Zongjian, like so many small cities of western China, is experiencing a Beijing-style sprucing up complete with cloned rows of uninspired shopfronts decorated with some superficially painted facades in the local ethnic style, which in Zongjian happens to be Tibetan. Zongjian marked the official setting-off point for our quest to the source of the Mekong.

Considering that we were about to set out on a major expedition, the camaraderie of the team seemed surprisingly low. I tried to bring the group together over a meal and a few beers but there was an edginess surrounding the group that I couldn't quite put my finger on. The situation was certainly not helped by the silent conflict that persisted between Lara and me. My gut instincts had alarm bells ringing.

Soon my worst fears about the fate of the expedition surfaced. We had been in China for just over a week and were nearly ready to leave Zongjian. James called a meeting with the field team, which consisted of Nico, Stan, Abe and myself, stating that he had some serious matters to discuss. James believed that morale was low and that the way to deal with bringing the group together was by increasing the financial benefits for each team member. I was so committed to the expedition that I somehow assumed others shared the same enthusiasm for what we were trying to achieve. I was shocked to see how James and Nico began angling for an increase in benefits. I struggled to come to terms with the fact that these two had decided to wait until after we had been in China for a week to renegotiate their fees when they knew it was now too late for me to make alternative arrangements if I did not agree with their new terms. With the budget already tight their demands threatened the viability of the entire project.

Tense negotiations went on throughout the night. With the implied threat of a team walkout, which would have resulted in the cancellation of our permits into Tibet and the documentary losing a director, we hammered out a new set of terms for the expedition. I realised that I was now paying the price for recruiting strangers whose motivations and tactics I had failed to anticipate or prepare for.

To add fuel to the fire, we were also faced with an unexpected shortage of cash, albeit short term, due to sponsorship and donation funds not arriving on time. Despite the setback, I decided to push onwards in the hope that the tactics, which to my mind bordered on extortion, would be finished with once and for all now that new terms had been reached.

Nico, Stan, Lara, Abe, myself and our half-Tibetan half-Chinese driver, Nongboo, headed north out of Zongjian towards the Mekong's source on 9 April 2004. The scenery was magnificent as we travelled from the verdant valleys and karst outcrops of Zongjian county into the eroding landscapes and avalanche littered slopes of the Yangtze Valley. We climbed on switchbacks across the soaring snow capped mountains of Sichuan en route to the Qinghai Tibet plateau. Our Beijing jeep rattled delicately along precipitous, white-knuckle inducing mountain roads that stretched between classic Tibetan mud-walled huts.

An age-old Tibetan folk law that is common knowledge throughout much of Sichuan dictates that it is bad luck to build dwellings with right angles as construction features. So as not to break with tradition the Tibetans of the region build all structural features of their houses at slightly offset angles. Walls, doors, window frames and roofs are all constructed to be slightly narrower at the top than the bottom, providing a slightly oblique perspective and a uniquely Tibetan style. The ornately decorated multistorey buildings are generally decorated with vibrant painted colours, complete with detailed geometric patterns around windows, doors and eves. Some of the dwellings we encountered were so beautifully presented that if I didn't know better I probably could have thought them places of worship rather than humble abodes of simple farmer folk. Lush valleys of pine gave way to gushing clear water streams and waterfalls that tumbled in steps for hundreds of metres down to the valley floors, where they joined forces with other streams to continue their relentless quest towards the sea. So many picture postcard settings were encountered each day as we proceeded that I simply lost track of all the places I mentally earmarked to revisit. I felt alive and could hardly wait to arrive at the trek's starting point, to get out there amongst it.

The stares of Tibetans, dressed in sheepskin jackets or yak leather overcoats, who tirelessly tended fields of barley or herded flocks of yaks and sheep, were testimony to how few foreigners passed this way. I was surprised by the low-population density in this dramatic part of the world's most populated nation.

Every now and then the widely spaced Tibetan farmers' dwellings, which seemed to merge perfectly with the surrounding landscape, were replaced by cramped, drab-looking white tiled and blue stained-glass buildings that stood in stark contrast to the magnificent landscape, and I knew we had arrived at one of the small district centres that are becoming increasingly inundated with Han Chinese migrants from the lowland areas. The settlers, who originate primarily from the densely populated eastern regions of China, are encouraged by the government to relocate into the regions once controlled by the nation of Tibet.

Stan, Nico and Abe stopped at many locations to get familiar with the new equipment and to work out communication techniques using two-way radios to coordinate the footage captures. Lara started taking more and more of her own photos using the professional equipment. This concerned Stan, as he felt she was taking over his role as team photographer, so he asked me to intervene.

We pulled up in a steep-sided valley that was blanketed in old growth spruce. The setting was spectacular and the camera team got out to take advantage of the warm afternoon light. As Lara pulled her camera gear out of a well-padded touring bag I took the opportunity to discreetly try to make it clear that Stan felt she was overstepping a professional mark. Our discussion heated up, to put it mildly. I decided not to continue with the conversation until things had calmed down a little.

Eventually when things had settled we drove to the next town, where Stan and I tried to resolve the issue of the photographs with Lara in a restaurant. Lara refused to give in and this time Stan lost his temper. He stood up abruptly and stormed out of the restaurant. That afternoon I asked Nico and Stan to decide whether they still wanted Lara to join us on the trek to the source and it was unanimously agreed she should not. Lara was given some money to backtrack to Zongjian, where she would wait for our dispatches from the trek.

Even with Lara temporarily out of the picture, the prospects of building the trust and camaraderie so important to an effective expedition field team had taken a battering in Zongjian because of the benefit negotiations, and we hadn't even properly started the trek yet.

I struggled to forget the past events and get the team bonding by keeping a sense of humour and sparking up random conversations. As we approached the trek start point, instead of getting the feeling of a focused, motivated and united team, I sensed a growing apprehension, distrust and uncertainty. The expedition seemed to be starting on very shaky ground.

4   A river is born

It is visions of stunning environments and of regions steeped in ancient culture that dominate my memories of the five-day, four-wheel-drive ride across China and Tibet to reach our trek starting point. We drove for hour after hour on rough and tumble dirt and rubble mountain roads that were almost completely devoid of motorised traffic. At times, hours passed between sightings of farmers' homesteads and as I traced our progress, millimetre by millimetre, across our one-metre-squared map I slowly started to come to terms with the sheer scale of the plateau we were ascending.

We passed through the town of Litang in eastern Sichuan, which at over four-thousand metres above sea level is one of the highest permanent towns in the world. We pushed on for a further fourteen bouncy hours to the tiny speck on the map called Serxu, which marked the final settlement we would encounter before departing Sichuan and entering Qinghai, a Chinese province made up largely of lands once governed by Tibet. The southern half of the province is almost completely Tibetan in ethnic make up, excluding a smattering of Han and Hui (Chinese Muslim), who tend to reside in the region's larger towns. It was near Serxu that we fully crested the Tibetan Plateau for the last time after several days of climbing to within reach of its broad open expanses, only to dip back down into and along the deep river valleys that characterise the edge of the plateau.

The environmental change as we crossed the clearly visible tree line was dramatic. Within metres, pine trees, that had been the dominant feature for great distances suddenly vanished and were replaced with undulating grasslands and rugged outcrops of rock and snow. After so many hours in the car it was a relief to realise that we were finally closing in on our destination, and it became clear that we had entered a distinct new cultural realm, a region dominated by semi-nomadic herders.

On the barren undulating plains of the plateau, between three and a half thousand and five thousand metres above sea level, where little more than hardy grasses, mosses, lichens and seasonal flowers can survive, semi-nomadic herders continue to live as they have for centuries. During the coldest months of winter, when temperatures can drop below minus forty degrees Celsius, they shelter in simple, permanently built mud-walled dwellings outside of which can be seen long walls constructed from yak dung, which provides the critical source of fuel for warmth and cooking during the winter. As the winter's permafrost begins to melt around April each year and new grass shoots begin to replace the grasses that died from the cold, the herders abandon their permanent residences in favour of transportable tents woven from yak hair. These provide them with mobility to seek out the best pasture lands, which are urgently required to fatten up their ailing livestock in time for the next long, cold winter.

As we drove by many herders were just starting to erect their tents. Dressed in animal hide clothing, similar to the ones that have kept their kin warm for countless generations, their rugged yet warm demeanour gave me the impression of an extremely proud race of people. In days gone by, the fearless horse-riding warriors of Tibet swelled the ranks of Genghis Khan's armies and shot fear into the hearts of Han Chinese emperors as far away as Beijing and Shanghai. Even the emperors of Persia to the distant west were forced to yield to the great armies that hailed from the wild lands of the Tibetan Plateau. To this day the horsemen of eastern Tibet still carry small sabres, referred to as *grai*, which are always fastened to their hip, ready for any situation that may arise. When a rugged bunch of nomadic herders, with leathery faces from a hard winter, rode towards me at a canter one afternoon with *grai* dangling at their sides, it didn't take a great deal of imagination to understand why the Chinese were inspired, through fear, to build the Great Wall in a futile effort to keep the 'Barbarian' warriors at bay.

While it is true that the Chinese have an active policy of making the Tibetans a minority people on their own lands, through Han Chinese migration into Tibet, the migrants as a general rule tend to move almost exclusively to the small towns and district capitals, leaving the countryside to the Tibetans. Hopefully the Tibetans will always remain masters of their own plains.

In all the world's continents there are three massive storage areas of fresh water that make up over seventy per cent of the Earth's vital liquid, most of it stored as glaciers. These three crucial storage centres are the Antarctic, the Greenland ice caps, and the Tibetan Plateau. All three of them are rapidly melting due to the effects of global warming and the effect on humanity during the next century, as temperatures steadily increase, could induce a global catastrophe much sooner than many people realise.

The Tibetan Plateau includes almost all of the world's territory higher than four thousand metres. Its southern rim, the Himalaya –Karakoram complex, contains not just Mount Everest and all thirteen other peaks higher than 8000 metres, but hundreds of seven-thousand-metre peaks higher than anywhere else. It seemed strange to drive along a relatively flat, undulating plain and realise that we were often travelling at well over four thousand metres above sea level.

Zato now lay approximately twelve-hours' drive due west of Serxu and as we rattled across the broad open expanses of the plateau and crossed numerous crystal-clear streams I pondered on the fact that six of the world's largest river systems drained from this very high plain. As testimony to the incredible natural bounty that these basins sustain, over half of the world's human population and a similar percentage of the planet's biodiversity live within the drainage areas of the Mekong, Indus, Yangtze, Yellow, Salween and Brahmaputra (which later becomes the Ganges) rivers. I felt honoured to be able to travel across the regions that give rise to river systems that ultimately sustain most of the planet's land-based life.

Before long we encountered a powerful blizzard, which reminded us all of the risks we would face. The snow came down so thick and fast that our jeep was actually forced to a standstill due to a lack of visibility. Just as quickly as the blizzard arrived it disappeared into thin air, leaving nothing but a blanket of snow. What surprised me the most, as we travelled day after day along mainly dirt roads, was just how remote and desolate the region was. We would often drive for hours without seeing a permanent settlement or human life of any kind. Considering we were officially driving through China, a lack of people is not usually the first thing that comes to mind.

We pressed on and passed through some dramatic gorges carved out by the tributaries of the Mekong before the adolescent river, known locally as the Zaqu, came into view. She meandered swiftly through sheer-sided gorges of oxidised rock (rocks that have been exposed to and chemically affected by the elements). Even in her infancy, the Mekong had a slightly reddish tinge because of the clay and sediment suspended in the water. Large ice packs could be seen clinging to the bank, confirming our expectation that the spring thaw had some way to go. It was clear that the water temperature would be only marginally above zero degrees Celsius and I felt a distinct shudder down my spine as I considered the thought of that water splashing up onto my face before being further cooled by the brisk winds that would no doubt blow through the gorges.

Occasionally we would pull up in small towns and settlements where we would grab a bite to eat in simple Tibetan or Han Chinese restaurants that were typically warmed by yak dung-fired iron stoves located in the middle of the room and surrounded by gruff looking locals who could hardly contain their surprise at encountering for-eigners. Entering these dwellings was always achieved by pushing our way through thick blankets that were draped across the doorways in an attempt to keep some of the highly appreciated warmth indoors. After several days of extremely oily food we were all keen to eat a meal that had less than twenty per cent animal fat. Abe took to the challenge by commandeering kitchens in several of the restaurants we visited. He would whip up tasty Lao-style stir-fries in a matter of minutes. As Abe displayed his culinary flair, skilfully tossing the contents of the frying pan into the air while simultaneously reaching for an array of sauces, Nico would fastidiously clean and re-clean his camera and Stan would snap away at anything or anyone that moved in a remotely interesting way.

After five days on the road, and to the relief of our collective back-sides, we arrived in Zato, a bustling frontier town located where the road stops on most maps of Qinghai, on 15 April 2004. We had trav-elled around one thousand kilometres from Zongjian, averaging just twenty-five kilometres per hour.

Zato marked the launching point for our quest for the Mekong source. Its population is composed of a mixture of Khampa Tibetan semi-nomadic herders, Tibetan traders and the occasional Han merchant family. The Khampa Tibetans are historically known as a fierce warrior clan from the eastern regions of Tibet, who through-out history have maintained a staunchly independent nature often at odds even with the national leadership in Lhasa. When the Chinese communists invaded Tibet in the late 1950s it was the Khampa Tibetans who put up the most sustained resistance, which was never-theless crushed by the overwhelmingly powerful Chinese Peoples Liberation Army. More than any other place we visited, Zato had the feel of the Wild West. Dust blows through the semi-paved streets, while local folk and nomadic visitors go about their daily business. To the northwest of Zato, where the Mekong source lies, the Tibetan Plateau unfolds for thousands of square kilometres, devoid of sizable settlements of any description. It is one of the few regions in Asia where it is possible to drive for days on end and not encounter a single town that deserves mention on a map.

The rugged men of the high plateau don't try to come across as cowboys as they ride into Zato on stout ponies, sporting tailored suits and broad-brimmed hats, to do a brisk trade in yak carcass—they just are. The proud sun- and wind-burnt highlanders are significantly taller than their Chinese neighbours and have a masculine yet refined disposition that is heavily influenced by their Buddhist beliefs, which is physically manifested by the presence of intricately worked silver and soapstone religious jewellery such as prayer beads, necklaces and rings. The clichéd six-shooter once sported by their western counter-parts is replaced by the artistically decorated Tibetan *grai*, with six- to eighteen-inch blades. The 'Yak Boys' of eastern Tibet are indeed the real thing and if Hollywood's directors grow tired of scouring the pages of history to resurrect stories of man in the wild frontiers then I can honestly say there's no shortage of genuine cowboys to be found in the back country of Qinghai.

It's hardly surprising that when the American CIA decided to foster insurrection within Tibetan areas annexed by communist China in the 1950s and 1960s they chose to recruit and train the Kham horsemen from eastern Tibet in their secret bases in the Pacific. Unfortunately, the once-feared yet hopelessly outnumbered warriors of Kham proved ineffective against modern weaponry and bomber planes and all resistance was ruthlessly crushed by the Red Army. For decades millions of herders were forced into an alien existence of collectivisation during the communist party's fanatical and failed attempt to replicate Chairman Mao's utopian dreams.

While the Red Army ruthlessly stamped out the remaining armed resistance in Tibet, the Cultural Revolution reared its ugly head to systematically destroy approximately ninety-five per cent of all Tibet's religious architecture and a long period of religious and cultural persecution followed. The courage the Tibetan people have displayed, by enduring such hardship while proudly maintaining their rich cultural identity, is a remarkable testament to the strength of their culture and ancient traditions. It is also a credit to the current Chinese leadership that they are finally allowing the Tibetans to rebuild their monasteries throughout the region and one can only hope that this positive start will be followed by many more progressive steps that will help to increase Tibetan self-determination.

As we pulled into Zato, no less than forty curious characters crowded around the car to peer in through the windows at the 'round eyes'. Our every movement became a matter of great public interest and discussion. In Zato we met Jimmy, a Khampa Tibetan with fair skin and hair flowing down to his shoulders. He would be our translator for this leg of the journey and he was soon joined by Doujie, a short, imposing man dressed in an impeccable black suit. Doujie had guided some of the scientific expeditions to the Mekong source in the preceding years. After going over maps, strategies and costs we set a game plan. After a day of layover, so that Doujie could tie up his affairs, we set out at 9 a.m. on 16 April 2004. My previous travels along lengthy and heart-stopping road journeys on sketchy Himalayan paths in India, Pakistan, Nepal and Yunnan had tempered my fear of being in a vehicle that drove dangerously close to precipices; but at times the road north of Zato took this fear factor to a new level and I spent several long minutes sitting with my hand on the door handle, ready to fling it open and launch myself out to safety should my worst fears evolve and the jeep careen off the edge to its doom.

Within an hour of leaving town, as we were trying to move a four-wheel drive along a track that barely passed as a mountain goat trail, the jeep popped a hub lock and we had to limp back to Zato for repairs. For the cost of fuel and a tip, Doujie managed to find another jeep and we headed out again.

Three hours of treacherous driving took us to the settlement of Zarching, located on a flat plain sitting between snow-covered peaks. Doujie invited us inside a plain mud-walled dwelling to warm ourselves over a cup of hot yak butter tea with some locals. Inside the hut we were invited to rest on a wooden bench draped with sheepskins and blankets to form a type of Tibetan-style sofa, in front of which sat a low coffee table-like settee that was soon straining under the weight of a twenty-kilogram slab of raw yak carcass, kindly plonked down by the lady of the house. Smoke filled the room as it billowed from the freshly stoked yak dung stove and two *grais* were stabbed into the carcass. We were instructed to help ourselves to a meal of raw flesh. Nico, Stan, Abe and I all looked at one another and I think we were all waiting for someone else to go first when Doujie casually sliced off a chunk of semi-frozen flesh and started chewing on it. I went next and found that the flesh tasted far better than I expected. Before long I found myself going back for second and third helpings.

We took the opportunity to chat with the herders, who extracted a living from the incredibly harsh environments of the plains. We heard of how wolves had taken seven sheep the previous night and that bears would periodically come down from the mountains after their winter hibernation to terrorise locals and take livestock. With April being the end of the Tibetan winter I suddenly felt a little less paranoid about bringing a fourteen-inch machete for the lonely nights spent in the wilderness.

It was at Zarching, located about three hours' drive north from Zato, that I had the opportunity to meet Buong, a curly-haired, thirty-four-year-old local who told us about the powerful spirits associated with a nearby mountain referred to as Black Horseman Mountain. Buong claimed that everyone in the area knew the mountain had a powerful *xida* protecting it (*xida* are spirits that Tibetans believe reside in certain natural features such as mountains, rivers, lakes and old trees), and that great respect had to be shown by all so as to not upset these spirits. In days gone by, non-believers had tried to hunt around Black Horseman Mountain without requesting the permission of the *xida* and all had faced untimely deaths. Buong and his companions believed that it is only when a man and his family are threatened with starvation that the *xida* will offer clemency to those who poach the natural bounty surrounding the mountain.

I was struck by the sincerity and seriousness of Buong and his friends. They were not merely reciting the stories of their parents and grandparents for the interest of foreigners. These young men had a thorough knowledge and belief in the folklore of old and I was honoured that they felt they could be so open with us.

I looked forward to talking with the locals who lived closer to the Mekong source, several valleys away to the northwest, to see how their stories and lives were connected to the river. After thanking the herders for their time and the copious amounts of slightly rancid yak butter tea we pushed on. Just as the sun sank behind distant mountains we arrived at a herders' winter settlement on a vast plain covered in snow.

As was the custom in all settlements we visited, we were met by vicious mastiff dogs that were fortunately restrained by chains. Steam and saliva flew from their mouths as they hurled the full weight of their muscular bodies toward us until the chain would jolt them back with an equally alarming force. I was glad the chains were thick! The herders were busy weaving lengths of yak hair into long rolls of coarse fabric, which are then sewn together to make the dark summer tents that were an important part of their semi-nomadic existence. Without a second thought they offered us an empty hut for the night and proceeded to fire up the yak-dung stove to keep us warm.

That night the temperature plummeted below minus fourteen degrees Celsius. We rose early to find the radiator in our jeep was frozen solid and six pots of boiling water failed to sufficiently warm up the situation. Nongboo, our Chinese-Tibetan driver, came up with his own unique solution. He disconnected the radiator, pulled it out from the car, then poured kerosene over it before setting it on fire. His improvised mechanical skills saved the day because after a couple of more radiator bonfires we were again rattling our way across the plateau towards the trek starting point.

We persevered through the frozen creeks, snowstorms and rugged terrain at more than four thousand metres above sea level. The countryside was crawling with marmots; their furry little behinds could be seen darting into burrows as we passed by. Eagles carved circles overhead and could occasionally be seen making a stealthy swoop to pick up breakfast or lunch. Snow cats and foxes would go about their business undisturbed by our presence until we stopped for a photo; they displayed a remarkable ability to disappear very quickly.

By about 3 p.m. we had arrived at the furthest point the road could take us: Huze homestead, some nine-hours' drive from Zato. As we walked in, we were welcomed with yak butter tea and another raw carcass to hack in to, and we realised that these special treats were the Tibetan equivalent of tea and biscuits. At the entrance of the dimly lit mud-walled hut I noticed the carcass of a young yak sprawled across the landing. When I asked about it I was told that wild dogs had made a mess of the poor beast the previous night. My machete was now clearly etched into my mind as an essential piece of camping equipment. We spent the afternoon at Huze while word was sent to Bussr, an old herder and horseman who was said to know the Mekong headwaters area like the back of his hand.

By 10 a.m. the following morning, Bussr had made his way to Huze with eleven horses and his feisty mastiff dog that Doujie called 'Mekong', because he was thought to be the only dog to have stood at the Mekong source. As the most experienced rider amongst the foreigners I was given the most spirited horse, who I called 'Red', due to his healthy tan-coloured coat. The short, stocky Tibetan horses have a larger lung capacity than normal horses and are able to cope with the high altitudes and thin air of the plateau. Red was strong, fast and generally quite responsive. I had the feeling we would get along just fine.

Finally on 18 April, a full two weeks after touching down in China, we were at the horse trek start point. After loading the horses we set off around lunchtime. As we climbed higher and higher I kept an eye out for any signs of altitude sickness. Nico and Stan started to complain of headaches. Abe seemed to be faring quite well. Physically I felt great and buzzed with energy, excited to finally be on my way without motorised help towards the river's source.

As time went by I noticed Nico becoming increasingly lethargic and he was getting his camera out less and less often, despite my subtle prompts for him to take advantage of the dramatic landscapes and periods of good light for filming. After many stops to readjust the loads on the horses, we pushed on into the evening and at 8.20 p.m. arrived at a large herders' tent perched on a windswept hill sitting at four thousand two hundred metres in elevation. We were all quite travel-weary and I set about cooking a dinner of noodles with ham chunks.

No sooner had I taken the steaming broth off the cooking flame than news arrived about a man in the neighbouring herder's camp who had been gored in the face by a yak. Nico, who was formerly an emergency officer for the French fire service, Jimmy and I decided to see if we could help. We grabbed our hefty first-aid kit, housed in two, ten-litre, airtight containers, and trudged for thirty minutes across the grasslands in freezing conditions to a bunch of yak-hair tents on the side of another hill.

As we entered the tent the smell of blood filled our nostrils and the seriousness of the situation immediately became apparent. Apparently the yak's horn had gone through the man's left cheek and up towards his brain, about fifteen centimetres. The man, called Doozeh, had lost litres of blood and was having trouble remaining upright. He was a herdsman in his thirties and he lay on his back, his face caked with clotted blood. The wound was about eleven hours' old. Doozeh's eyes were swollen shut. Fresh blood oozed from his mouth and nose and his breathing was laboured.

The huge gaping wound in his left cheek had a small piece of rag protruding from it. When we asked how big the piece of rag was, with much gesturing and discussion in Tibetan via Jimmy, the answer was the size of a fist. This meant that about ninety-five per cent of the rag was packed up inside the man's skull. Nico and I checked his airways, breathing and pulse. His breathing and pulse were weak, and Doozeh was semi-coherent. We immediately cleared some of the blood clots away from his mouth and nose to open his airways, and then attached him to a saline drip.

We feared Doozeh would not survive an evacuation, which would involve at least two to three body-jarring days on a twin-horse stretcher and another three days by four-wheel drive to get to the nearest sizable hospital. We called up our expedition medical advisor, Doctor Ben Burford of the Australian Embassy Emergency Clinic in Vientiane, via satellite phone for advice. He told us that we needed to be prepared that the man would probably die if we decided to remove the rag and clean the wound to fight the inevitable infection that was developing. He also warned us that on many occasions foreigners had ended up temporarily incarcerated for any involvement in the death of a local during medical emergencies. It was a sobering thought in an already grim situation.

We called a meeting with the family and asked if they could evacuate Doozeh and they explained this was not possible. They intended to leave him where he was and hope that he improved. It was clear that Nico and I were his only chance of getting any medical treatment. We explained that the rag had to be removed and the wound thoroughly cleaned if he was to be given a decent chance of pulling through, but there was also the chance that their husband, father and friend could still die.

Before we started we needed to know that if Doozeh died we would not be blamed. After a short meeting the family agreed that we should attempt to clean the wound. We asked the family for clean water and they came back with tea. We tried again and they came back with two large pieces of snow covered in dirt. We sent runners out for fresh snow but the results were not much better. We were perched on a hill that was miles from the nearest stream and the snow had been blasted by dust. This was all the family had had access to.

The yak-hair tent was smoky and dirty, but with outside temperatures at around minus fourteen degrees Celsius, working inside was the only viable option. We boiled up the cleanest snow we could find and sterilised it with iodine. Using a large piece of gauze, tweezers and hot water we began to heat, soften and remove the thick layers of scabs and clotted blood from around Doozeh's nose, lips and mouth to make sure he could breathe properly. We sent runners to get lights and supplies. Stan came back with more gear from the other camp. He found the entire scenario just too gory to watch and soon headed back.

It was a gruesome task. I removed the clots while Nico assisted me. At one stage, while I was removing a large, slippery clot of blood from Doozeh's upper lip, I saw Nico's eyes dilate and he rocked, nearly fainting. Once the airways were cleared, we set our attention to the rag. This would be the point of no return.

After forty minutes of cleaning, we began tugging to remove the rag and suddenly realised it was not nearly as big as first declared. The yak's horn, although going through Doozeh's cheekbone, had broken his nose but had not gone through to his skull. Doozeh now had a good chance of pulling through.

By 3.30 a.m., after leaving a carefully explained course of anti-biotics and clean dressings, we were on our way back to our own camp. It looked like Doozeh would make it and a peculiar feeling of euphoria came over me. Returning to camp, we ate and then collapsed, exhausted, into a deep sleep.

After four hours of sleep it was time to refocus, and by 8 a.m. we were packing the horses, ready to leave. We began the long day's ride, climbing steadily across frozen creeks, steep-sided ridges and open valleys where dramatic Jurassic rock struts reached for the sky.

I'm not sure what happened and can only put it down to the smell of human blood that must have been on me, but Red's entire reason for living suddenly seemed to be pitching me from his back. As soon as I put one foot in the stirrup and begin to raise the other to mount him he would bolt. One foot out of the stirrup made it hard to keep balance as he jumped around like a bucking bronco. Before the day was out I had hit the deck three times. No amount of talking, stroking or readjusting his straps would change Red's mind. He would suddenly bolt in dangerous terrain and it took all my strength to restrain him.

At one point he bolted, causing another packhorse to bolt with us. As the packhorse galloped at full speed, just ten metres in front of us, a large bag fell from that horse's back, knocking Red's legs out from under him. We both hit the ground hard. Fortunately neither of us was seriously hurt. I asked Bussr if we could swap horses but he only smirked, with a look that seemed to say, 'You think I would try to ride him today? Are you nuts?'

It was a long cold day. We crossed frozen streams and rivers, and scaled steep rills of glacial gravel to cross ridges. Wildlife was abundant, and throughout the day we saw two wolves, two herds of chiru (an endangered breed of Tibetan antelope), a pack of wild horses and a wide array of birdlife, including an assortment of eagles, vultures, geese and ducks. I even saw small fish fingerlings swimming in one of the streams at an altitude of around four thousand six hundred metres. The weather conditions became increasingly unpredictable, changing from clear skies and dusty whirlwinds to snow and sleet within twenty minutes.

Our lips and noses began to blister and peel from the icy wind and sun glare. But we were fortunate enough not to encounter really severe weather that could potentially snow us in for days. Nico and Stan were still struggling with the conditions. The previous night's drama had been a wake-up call for everyone, reminding us of the dangers of our venture. Tension seemed to be growing. At one point, while crossing a frozen stream, Stan's foot punched through the ice into the shallow water, forcing him to ostrich-step across some more ice to reach dry land. Everyone laughed. Because I was closest, and probably because I also giggled earlier in the day when Stan accidentally swigged at a bottle of kerosene thinking it was water, he went off the deep end.

'Fuck you! You're always laughing at someone else's expense. I could have broken my fucking ankle, man,' he yelled in frustration.

'Stan, take a chill pill. It was funny and you're fine. Everyone thought it was funny!' I answered. Everyone else instinctively remained silent. Stan continued yelling, making me realise how much stress and anxiety he was feeling. I must admit I found it hard to relate to how he felt because from my perspective we had reasonably good weather and, although physically demanding, the trek wasn't excessively difficult, plus we had competent guides. I made a mental note not to laugh at any funny situations regarding Stan.

Although we planned to reach the source and camp slightly downstream, progress was slow and as dusk descended we were forced to
pitch camp one valley over from the source in a secluded cul-de-sac at
an elevation of nearly five thousand metres. The night was cold and
long with temperatures as low as minus sixteen degrees Celsius.

The following morning all of us felt the effects of altitude. I had a
headache coming on, as did Abe. Stan and Nico seemed to be more
severely affected and barely ate any breakfast. Nico looked to be in a
sorry state with little remaining strength. Progress remained slow
with Stan and Nico needing frequent rest breaks.

We came over a ridge to view the Mekong mainstream for the
first time. It was beautiful: a long white slither of ice extended to
the south for some ten kilometres between stark black mountains
tipped with glaciers. Nico and Stan were really struggling now and
I suggested to them that they should start descending into the valley
floor, some three hundred metres below, where they could wait with
Bussr for the rest of us to return in a few hours. But they were both
determined to try to make it.

As we made our way up the final valley, Doujie stopped and
pulled out his binoculars, gazing across to the distant mountains on
the other side. He claimed to see a bear but when I looked I only saw
a large herd of highly endangered chiru scurrying with incredible
speed and agility up the gravelly slope. I was amazed that so much
wildlife flourished this high up.

Despite my mild headache I felt fantastic and was looking
forward to the sight of Lasagongma Glacier, from where the Mekong
trickles. We tied down the horses at around four thousand nine
hundred metres, leaving Bussr with them, and trekked on foot for
forty minutes. The debilitating affects of altitude become quite acute
when one passes above five thousand metres. Every fifteen metres or
so on the uphill we were forced to stop, gasping for air, before slowly
catching breath again and proceeding. I had to shoulder Stan's photo-

graphic equipment on the final leg as he grew too weak; even Abe was starting to succumb to the altitude and the strain began showing in his face.

Finally, there was the Lasagongma Glacier right in front of us. I was ecstatic. I headed over to the base of the glacier where Doujie and Jimmy were busy prostrating in front of a large dark rock near where a small thread of water trickled from the ice. It was here that the Mekong, known by the Tibetans as Lasagongma Stream, trickled into existence. Abe pointed at the trickle and yelled out *Mae Khoay!*, Lao for 'my mother'. Abe was the first ever Laotian to see the river's source. I became the first Australian, and Nico and Stan the first Frenchmen.

We spent some time at the base of the glacier taking photos, drinking the water and resting. When I finally checked the Global Positioning System (GPS), I realised that we were at the first point from where the water is released in April, but that the designated geographical source was actually well above us, some forty metres up on a large embankment of snow. I let the guys know that we had not quite reached the source, but they had nothing left to push on with. They were exhausted. Even enthusiastic Abe decided the final leg was too difficult, deciding to wait while I climbed alone. I could see by the fatigue on the faces of Stan and Nico that they needed to descend as soon as possible. I moved fast.

The final stretch was straight up the side of the snow-covered rill through knee-deep powder. It was hard going. Gasping for breath every ten or so steps I slowly made ground. After twenty minutes and six checks of my GPS, I was there at the officially designated source of the Mekong River, 94:41:44 east longitude and 33:42:31 north latitude, five thousand two hundred and twenty-four metres above sea level.

I turned around to scan the breathtaking view of the Mekong Valley. It was rimmed by glaciated peaks and rugged limestone.

A feeling of joy and anticipation surged through my veins. A lifetime of adventure and nearly two years of dedicated work on the project had brought me here. Approximately one hundred and twenty kilometres of trekking and four thousand seven hundred and eighty kilometres of paddling lay between me and the South China Sea— it was just the beginning. This trickle at the base of the glacier I stood on was the start of a lifeline for some seventy million people from over one hundred ethnic groups. The waters of the system arguably supported as much aquatic diversity as the Amazon Basin and its environments housed a significant proportion of the world's biodiversity.

I realised it would be a great honour to become the first person to see the entire river's mainstream if I could achieve my goals. With that thought in mind, I took the first step of the descent of the Mekong mainstream, half running, half rolling down the powder that coated the glacier to where the guys were waiting. I don't think I ever felt more alive.

5 Euphoria on the roof of the world

The tiny trickle of icy water that comes from the Lasagongma Glacier is just one of millions of similar trickles that spring to life throughout the length and breadth of the river's seven hundred and ninety-five-square-kilometre basin. All of them ultimately join the Mekong River, yet none of the other streams in the river system can compete with the Lasagongma in terms of river distance from the Mekong's mouth in Vietnam—it is this simple fact that has caused the little Lasagongma Stream to attract a surprising amount of attention in recent years.

In 1994 French explorer Michel Piessel used outdated Russian maps to reach the conclusion that the Zanaqu, another small stream which emerges from a spring in the next valley over from the Lasagongma, was the most distant tributary from the river's mouth. He followed the Zanaqu to its source and announced he had discovered the source of the Mekong River. Surprisingly, without referring to more detailed satellite imagery and maps, which indicate that the Lasagongma Stream is longer than the Zanaqu, the Royal Geographic Society accepted Piessel's claim and for nearly a decade the source was officially recorded as being located in the wrong position.

While Piessel was proclaiming the source of the Mekong, a separate and simultaneous Sino–Japanese expedition took place to Lasagongma Stream; neither research team knew the other existed. The Japanese expedition, led by Masayuki Kitamura, correctly claimed that the Mekong source was located at the head of

Lasagongma Stream yet, probably due to the fact that the Japanese findings were not initially published in English and due to lack of contacts with western geographic institutions, their findings were not referenced against Piessel's nor acknowledged as being more accurate until many years later. To make matters even more confusing, after the Japanese and Piessel's expeditions located the source in 1994, two separate branches of the Chinese academy of sciences have claimed two other sources nearby, one slightly further up Lasagongma Stream than the Japanese source and another on a nearby stream called Ganasongduo.

For me, trying to figure out which source was the most accurate before embarking on the expedition proved quite a headache and for a while it looked like we would have to visit several of the disputed sources to play it safe. It was only when I stumbled upon an explanatory document, authored by Pete Winn, just weeks before departing did I finally figured out which one we would head for. The document explained that in 1999 the two branches of the Chinese academy of sciences used satellite analysis and further research trips to finally reach agreement that the source at the base of Lasagongma Glacier indeed gave birth to the longest arm of the Mekong River. The Japanese originally discovered this, but with glacial retreat occurring over the proceeding years the Chinese were able to relocate the source a few metres further up the mountain than the Japanese. With glacial retreat expected to continue into the foreseeable future it is apparent that the source will continue to move up the mountain for some time to come.

As it departs the glacier, the stream initially heads in a northwesterly direction as a thin slither of ice before angling to the left to set a course due west through a dramatic valley carved by ancient glaciers. We continued downstream for a couple of kilometres to where Bussr was waiting with the pack horses. We estimated it would be a trek downstream of one hundred and twenty kilometres before the frozen stream would defrost enough to start paddling, so we still had quite a way to go by horseback.

We followed the long trail of ice interspersed with trickles of water down a wide valley lashed with freezing winds and bouts of snow. A string of peaks, which rose to altitudes in excess of five thousand five hundred metres above sea level, lined both sides of the valley. Located close together they displayed remarkably different characteristics; some were dark, almost black-capped with glaciers, while others were brown and covered in glacial gravel.

As we continued downstream a brisk wind gradually built up to the point where we were all freezing as we made our way slowly down the valley. I noticed that both Stan and Nico seemed to be getting weaker as they progressed, and I considered the fact that neither of them had been eating properly for several days. They claimed it was because the food—mainly consisting of ham, tinned fish and vegetables, rice, pasta, noodles, dried fruit and nuts—was 'crap'. It certainly wasn't fine dining but it was nutritionally adequate. It seemed clear to me that the main issue was altitude sickness, some of the common side effects of which are deteriorating physical ability, loss of appetite and nausea. With their health rapidly deteriorating I began to accept that, for Stan and Nico, heading back to Zato by river (which, given their slow movements, could have taken up to two weeks) would probably be too risky, so I began considering other options to get them out sooner. Abe seemed to be faring slightly better but his stamina and motivation still seemed to be seeping away with each passing hour.

I still had a slight headache but felt in pretty good shape and throughout the day I regularly had to remind myself not to get too far in front as the guys clearly couldn't keep up with Doujie, Bussr, Jimmy and myself. We camped out that night at the base of a small cliff, which provided limited protection from the winds that had tortured us in the afternoon. By the next morning Stan's condition seemed to have stabilised but he was still far from healthy, while Nico's health had definitely taken a turn for the worse. Abe's strength continued to slip and none of them ate properly the night before or at breakfast, a clear sign to me that they couldn't keep up the physical exertion for much longer.

I felt surprisingly good and ate well, and realised how lucky I was not to be suffering badly from altitude sickness as the guys looked like hell. I decided the best approach would be for the team to take the shortcut back to Huze, where the cars stood by in case of emergency, a journey we estimated would take around two to three days. In the meantime I would continue downstream along the river for a further five to seven days with a nomad and a couple of horses. I knew I would be able to move a lot more efficiently without the guys and I would be relieved not to be heading into an increasingly remote area with people whose health situation could easily deteriorate further to dangerous levels.

After another long day's horse ride we came across one of the first abodes on the Mekong, a small white tent occupied by a family of five astounded locals. The head of the family, old man Rasha, invited us in for some yak butter tea and raw yak meat, which brought some welcome relief from the cold. Rasha would have done Bob Marley proud with his thick dreadlocks, which he had to tie up to prevent from dragging on the ground when he walked, and he always appeared to be completely stoned.

Although Stan seemed to be recovering slightly, Nico was deteriorating and Abe looked completely worn out. It seemed the right time for the guys to head back to the vehicles, from where they could descend to Zato and await my arrival. We arranged for Rasha's eldest son, Changa, to accompany me down the river with three horses, one each for Changa and I and one for supplies, while the rest of the team headed back to the comforts of civilisation. We said our goodbyes and just as the team left, heavy snow began falling. I was concerned for their wellbeing but had confidence in the abilities of Doujie and Bussr to get them back to safety. I must confess, I was also relieved not to have to be around the creeping depression that seemed to have engulfed Nico and Stan along with their bout of altitude sickness. Our energy levels seemed to be at such opposite ends of the spectrum and I felt drained by their presence.

Staying with the nomadic yak-herders of the high plains is a major highlight of travelling in Tibet. These rugged yet hospitable people rarely hesitate to take complete strangers into their homes in a natural display of trust and kindness. The Rasha family's yaks had recently given birth to dozens of calves and before dusk I spent an hour carefully helping Changa and his wife dress all of them in little hand-woven yak-hair jackets. I instinctively kept a sharp eye out for their mum's horns as the gory scenes of cleaning up the face of the herder flashed through my mind.

There was little room in the family tent so I started setting up my own. But the family would have none of it. That night I received a banquet of yak stew and barley bread. Before going to bed I made sure to squeeze up as close to the edge of the tent as possible to make sure there was room for everyone. I fell asleep to the rhythmic recital of tantric meditation verses by Rasha, lying under a thick yak-hair and wool blanket. But at one stage during the night I woke in fright when I felt the blanket move but soon realised I was being tucked into bed under a large wool rug to make sure I didn't catch cold.

Early the next morning I awoke to the same sounds from Rasha as he lay in bed for one hour meditating before getting up. I walked outside and found, to my dismay, Changa and his wife sleeping under a large yak-hair rug in the snow. They had done this to make room for me in the tent. At breakfast I treated the family to my most highly prized culinary possession, Yunnanese six herbs and four fruits tea, to show my gratitude, and guilt. The tea was introduced to us by our driver, Nongboo, and possessed a little bit of everything, including several types of dried fruit that I never did manage to identify, green tea, flowers, seeds and, most importantly, a large solid chunk of raw sugar that made the drink extremely sweet and gave an instant energy kick when we most needed a lift.

An hour after riding out from Rasha's residence Changa and I bumped into the rest of the team at a herder's mud-walled hut further down the valley, where they had spent the night after we split up. I spoke with them briefly and found out that Nico had been sick several times during the night and was in quite a bad way. He had obviously been affected badly by the altitude and had started to angrily abuse the hosts about how he couldn't sleep with all the smoke in the dwelling. It was sad to see him so miserable and struggling to keep going as we were travelling through such an incredible part of the world. I felt a sense of relief that he would soon be back at the vehicles and be able to get to lower elevation quickly.

Changa and I split up from the team for the second time at 9.30 a.m. Our goal was simple: from our current location, approximately thirty-five kilometres downstream from the source, we would follow the river further downstream until there was sufficient water volume to start kayaking (we estimated this would be a further eighty- to one hundred-kilometre trek). At that point I would hightail it by the fastest means possible (probably trekking out of the river valley to a high mountain road where I could hitch a ride) to a designated meeting point on the river near Zato, where I would meet the team before taking a rest day or two in Zato.

The day's ride was long and difficult as Changa and I made our way through fine sleet and snow. We crossed the frozen Mekong several times. Changa's two large mastiff dogs, Bong and Zhah, had joined us. They were keen hunters and didn't mind throwing their weight around when they entered a new herder's camp that was the territory of a different band of dogs. The huge self-assured mutts proved invaluable for spotting herds of deer and chiru at great distances, and also provided some light entertainment by attempting to chase them up incredibly steep mountain ridges.

It would appear that because the area is inhabited only by herders, who have access to an abundance of yak meat, hunting wildlife does not take as high a priority as in other parts of China. Throughout most of China professional hunters are exacting a devastating toll on prized animal species to supply China's insatiable appetite for exotic furs and flesh. Here in the Mekong source area, the wildlife seemed to be only lightly affected by the hunters.

A blizzard loomed on the horizon and engulfed us at about 3 p.m. We attempted to push on but within forty minutes we were both freezing and were forced to set up the tent with five hours of daylight left. It was a long afternoon as strong gusts of wind and snow whipped the side of our sturdy tent—at times it seemed like we would be blown away.

The next morning we woke to eight centimetres of snow. The valley widened but was rimmed by towering mountains over five thousand metres high. A small amount of water began to flow down the valley as the infant Mekong River began returning to life from its icy slumber. Peculiarly, the water forty kilometres downstream from the source was crystal clear, unlike the clay-tinged water at the source.

We passed four herder's camps during the day. Each encounter would inevitably begin with a dog fight as our mastiffs tried to assume the position of top dogs. We would have a brief chat with the herders and occasionally accept an offer to drink yak butter tea. At the fourth camp we decided to spend the night. We were greeted at this camp by the biggest and scariest looking Tibetan mastiff I have ever seen.

In Tibet, large, well-built dogs are highly prized because they are the only creatures capable of keeping the packs of wolves at bay. This dog reminded me of Cujo from the B-grade 1980s horror movie of the same name. Even Bong and Zhah wisely kept a good distance. Fortunately Cujo was chained to a sturdy-looking stake, so I wandered by without too much concern when he viciously barked and yanked at his anchor.

As usual the locals were hospitable and curious, digging through my bags to play with whatever toys they could find. I had repeated offers to swap my mass-produced Chinese machete with the intricately worked Tibetan *grai* knives. Normally this would be an absolute bargain but with the amount of wolves on the prowl and the number of nights I expected to be camped in the wilderness on my own I felt a little more secure with a weapon I was familiar with.

After a good night's sleep, I discreetly snuck out of the family tent to make a nature call. There was really nowhere that was out of sight so I chose a small hill nearby and began to attend to business. I was three-quarters done when I heard a dreadful growl and bark. I looked down the hill to see Cujo bounding up towards me. Someone had obviously taken him off the chain during the night to look after the yak. Mist exploded from his mouth with each bark. He looked mean and was closing in quick. I only had time to either pull up my pants or reach for some rocks. I stood up and pelted a fist-sized rock at Cujo to put him off. Rather than slow him down it seemed to inspire him to a more rapid attack.

I quickly reached for another rock and, with my pants still around my ankles, flung it at him several seconds before he would have been upon me. It hit him solidly on the left shoulder and he let out a semi bark/yelp, hesitated for a moment before closing in to within two metres. I screamed at him as aggressively as I could and faked throwing another rock. He snapped at me, saliva spraying on my hand. This close range stand-off, with me threatening and him snapping, went on for a further two or three seconds that seemed to last for an eternity. Then I heard a yell from down near the tent.

The headman was running up the hill towards me and numerous bodies began emerging from the tent flaps to see what was going on. Cujo looked visibly concerned and backed off a few steps. A couple of seconds later a hail of rocks rained down in the vicinity of Cujo and me as the whole family came to my rescue. Cujo was now in full flight to escape. With him out of my face I reached down to grab some more rocks just in case and it was only then that I realised that my pants were still around my ankles. My modesty took over from my feelings of malice towards Cujo as the family looked on in concern. By the time my pants were back up the entire family had burst out laughing and I kind of wished I could disappear.

I was pleased to finish breakfast and glad that I could not understand the comments, which made the entire family break out in sporadic laughter. I said my goodbyes and knew by the glint in Changa's eye that this would not be the last I would hear about the Cujo adventure.

We proceeded by horse for another two days as the Mekong progressively thawed. Occasional sections of ice with water flowing underneath made the river impossible to navigate. The wide valley narrowed to form a tight gorge and several times I thought it would not even be possible to keep going by horse. Fortunately the locals had carved out a tiny path through the most difficult terrain.

We rounded a bend where a huge pile of mani stones was stacked under several Buddhist stupas. *Om mani padme hum* is the most common tantric verse in Tibetan Buddhism. The devout laypeople and monks alike spend countless hours repeating these words on their path to enlightenment and there is a longstanding tradition of carving the verse into rocks and placing them at sites of spiritual significance. Hundreds of millions of these beautifully carved stones lay scattered across the Tibetan Plateau. I rounded another bend and, to my surprise, encountered Drahiliapough, the first Buddhist monastery on the Mekong River. This came as a complete surprise to me as it is not marked on any maps.

The ancient settlement comprises some forty or so rammed earth and pinewood buildings and it is a true historical gem that, through its remoteness, has escaped the devastation of the Cultural Revolution. During that time it is estimated that ninety-five per cent of all Tibetan monasteries were destroyed. The isolation of this steep-sided valley is no doubt what saved the ornate buildings. I spent the early evening wandering the settlement in the company of monks inspecting some beautifully carved pinewood panelling in the temples, colourful paintings representing the reincarnations of the Buddha and mani stones carved with passages of scripture. I felt lucky to be one of the first outsiders ever to stumble on what can only be described as a cultural treasure chest. My only two regrets were that I didn't have Jimmy around so I could learn more about this fascinating place by asking questions through him and also that the guys had all the cameras with them so I couldn't make a photographic record.

I spent the night in the company of monks who found my experiences with Cujo, told gleefully by Changa, simply hilarious. Of course I played it all down, indicating that I actually had things completely under control. I even managed to distract the monks from what was obviously the funniest story ever told in the monastery by putting on a little concert using a small banjo-style instrument from one of the temples. After some considerable team dramas since leaving Vientiane it felt great not to be sidetracked by the emotional ups and downs of people who didn't seem to be enjoying the experience as much as I was.

The next morning I awoke to the tantric chants of the monks resonating through the buildings, then I roamed around the ancient settlement for a further two hours, inspecting the intricate carvings and finding another huge mound of what I estimated to be about three thousand mani stones. Each one would have taken about twelve to sixteen hours to carve. The monastery was so aged and weathered that it had the mysterious feel of a deserted ghost town, yet it housed possibly forty monks.

Changa and I left the monastery the following day. Five kilometres upstream from where my map showed a road crossing the Mekong, Changa and I came to a narrow gorge where an avalanche had blocked the path, making it impossible for the horses to continue. The Mekong was now flowing freely as the relatively warmer weather had melted the ice and snow. Changa helped me trek back towards the monastery and then out on a horse path that led to a road. I paid him the agreed fee and a tip before bidding my sole trekking partner of the last six days farewell.

I felt euphoric to have completed the land trekking portion of the Mekong's course. The beauty of the Tibetan Plateau had surpassed my expectations and the Tibetan people I had met enchanted me with their kindness and rich culture. It was almost with regret that I had to trekked to the road and hitched a ride into Zato to hook up with the guys who, with the exception of Abe, seemed to be finding their experiences unbearable.

6   The sparks fly

Upon arriving in Zato I was immediately struck by the level of depression that Stan and Nico had settled into and found it difficult to adjust to the massive contrast in our energy levels. While I was still buzzing from a spectacular trek and thoroughly looking forward to starting the next leg, the Frenchmen seemed to have no inspiration at all. They had been in regular communication with James and Lara and it became evident that money, which should have been cleared by now, hadn't been. Yuta had been working to try to track down the promised money and was starting to doubt that it had been cleared as promised by the sponsors.

Another major drama began to unfold. Yuta, the love of my life and the backbone of my support team, had found out that a small lump in her breast might be malignant and she was admitted to hospital for urgent surgery. I tried to maintain a composed presence in front of the team but on the inside my emotions were in turmoil and I offered to fly back to be with her. Yuta was adamant that I continue with the expedition. She knew that if I flew back at this point it would almost certainly cause the cancellation of the project, as it would take many days' travel from Zato before I could even spend time with her. This meant the window for good expedition weather would probably close before I could make it back to Zato to pick up the descent where I would have left it. I was prepared to make that call. Yuta pleaded with me not to give up and said that we would still be together in mind if not body. She repeatedly told me, 'Together we can overcome anything'.

It was an extremely difficult period for me and I can only imagine how hard it was for her. I admired her courage and unflinching belief in what I was trying to achieve. I reluctantly struggled against my natural instincts in order to once again direct my focus on achieving the project goals.

The expedition faced a serious hurdle as the logistics bill for the next section through the Tibet Autonomous Region needed to be paid in advance. I had already put all of my available cash into the project and only had access to periodic instalments, the next of which was not due for another two weeks. To get more money on such short notice meant that I would need to borrow from friends or family, something I had strongly resisted so far. But if I had to swallow my pride and borrow the cash to cover my share of the project, I decided it was worth it.

With the earlier verbal negotiations that took place in Zongjian, Nico, James and Stan were now stakeholders with a combined shareholding of fifty per cent of the project, while Yuta and I retained the other fifty per cent. To my mind it was a simple partnership arrangement whereby in order to share in the benefits, all parties had to share in the risks. I never actually conceived that a partnership could work any other way when I had agreed to allow them to become stakeholders.

However, when it came to the shortfall of funds, it seemed that Nico, James and Stan took a very different view. They thought that everyone should retain full financial benefits from the shareholding if things went well, but if things weren't going so well and more funds were required, it was Yuta and I who should be responsible for covering all project expenses until things got back on track, at which point they would collect their full benefits again. In other words, Yuta and I should take all the financial risks and cover expenses while Nico, Stan and James would keep half of any financial benefits. It was a partnership logic that apparently made perfect sense to them and absolutely none to Yuta and I. The group dynamics became strained and it became increasingly clear that my inspiration and enthusiasm for the project wasn't mirrored by Stan, Nico and James.

It was extremely difficult for me to understand their complacency in a situation where I thought there were remarkable opportunities for everyone. In contrast, Abe seemed to be able to keep himself going with the idea of being involved in an expedition that was breaking new ground and offered experience and credibility for his career in addition to modest financial rewards, which were agreed to by Abe before he arrived in China.

Up until that point I had mainly blamed Lara's disruptions and people reneging on the financial agreements for grinding the team morale down. These were all factors; I was also forced to accept that it was my error in judgment in choosing a team of relative strangers and going against my gut instinct when working with these people. It was frustrating but I now had to deal with the consequences of my mistakes, and accept that my vision and inspiration was not necessarily shared by others.

After two nights in Zato we drove up towards the point where I broke from the river with Changa, about one hundred and ten kilometres from the river's source and thirty-five kilometres upstream from the town of Zato. The snow along the route had been melting quickly as the landscape made a rapid transition from its winter look to spring. About thirty kilometres from Zato, we came across a wolf at close range—a loner, separated from his pack stood just fifteen metres in front of us. Rather than bolt, he gingerly trotted in front of us to the steep embankment of boulders and glacial gravel on our right as he cautiously watched to see if we would react. With instinctive ease he bounded up to the edge of the embankment, some twenty metres high, before stopping to take another look at us. Thin and wiry after a long winter, his coat was in remarkably good condition. We were all astounded by his composure. Stan whipped out his camera and managed to get several shots just before the wolf crested the ridge and disappeared into the expanse of the plateau. It was an awesome encounter.

I went over this experience many times. Maybe it was the loneliness I was feeling as the team disintegrated around me or maybe it was respect for the wolf's composure in the face of a significant threat, but I drew parallels between his situation and mine. The wolf was alone and initially shocked by a potentially disastrous situation, but he quickly regained his composure and didn't lose track of where he was going. His sharp, instinctive reaction was something I would strive to duplicate to help me focus and get on with the project regardless of the unexpected situations that arose around me. That night, after returning to Zato, I started emailing as many potential replacements for the Frenchmen as I could think of.

After more than a year of planning and preparation, my navigation of the Mekong River was about to begin. We drove as far as the road would take us upstream from Zato and I trekked for a further four hours to crest a four thousand seven hundred and fifty-metre mountain to get within sight of the point I had ridden to with Changa. Nico and Stan were too depressed and tired to wait for me to return from this trek in order to capture the first paddle strokes of the descent on film. So just as I had taken the first step down from the true source of the Mekong alone, I also took the first of several million paddle strokes alone, surrounded by nothing more than stark mountains, rolling plains of snow-burnt grass and the occasional yak. It was a great moment.

That first day's paddle was incredibly cold. I paddled thirty-five kilometres in under three and a half hours through sleet and snow, arriving in Zato around 8.30 p.m. The temperature was as low as minus five degrees Celsius. With strong winds and constant splashes of near-freezing water these conditions felt like minus thirty degrees Celsius.

That night, after some discussion with Nico and Stan, we agreed that it would be best for them to edit their work for a few days and think about whether they had the motivation to continue, while I did the navigation south. They decided that they could not work in the conditions at Zato so they would head to the larger town of Garze, some sixteen hours' drive away, back across the border in Sichuan, where they could access a faster internet connection and work in the comfort of a proper hotel with a private bathroom. To me this seemed an unnecessary extra expense at a time when we lacked funds, but Stan and Nico were set on the idea. I let this extravagance slide on the basis that they would be back in five days. As they departed for Garze, I felt particularly sorry for Abe who wanted nothing more than to get on with the job. As Nico and Stan needed the jeep to get to Garze, Abe couldn't accompany me to film the next leg of the descent from several mountainous sections where the road parallelled the river. Rather than sit around in Zato on his own he chose to go with Nico and Stan.

My last words to Stan, who was responsible for managing the daily expenses money, was a request that he keep all expenses down to an absolute minimum as we only had enough money to get to Chamdo, where another guide would meet us with extra funds. Stan told me not to worry, they would be back in a few days. I didn't see Stan, or the project photos he took, for another six months.

Three days after arriving in Garze, Stan and Nico resigned and headed back to Zongjian directly from there, accompanied by Abe, who decided to stay with the car as, after dropping the Frenchmen off, it was supposed to be brought back up to Zato to resume the expedition. In taking the car they also inadvertently took most of my food supplies and expedition equipment, which I had left in the car thinking it would return in four days as promised. On the day

I heard about Stan and Nico quitting, Brian Eustis, a friend I had worked with on another expedition-style documentary in 2003, became available to pick up the game from where the Frenchmen gave up.

To my relief there would only be a short delay while Brian tied up his affairs in the United States. Between Brian and Abe we would still be able to film the expedition and I could take most of the photos along the way. I had already worked with Brian when we were tracking wild tigers along a remote whitewater river in northern Laos, and in testing conditions he proved to be a competent professional with a positive attitude who seemed to thrive on challenging adventures. Brian's solid class V (Expert Level) whitewater kayaking skills meant that he was also able to accompany me on various remote whitewater sections.

The return of Stan and Nico to Vientiane managed to stir up all kinds of rumours and controversy within the small expat community. When friends informed me by email of some particularly nasty accusations that were being circulated I was initially tempted to try to set the record straight via email and phone calls but in the end I decided that I believed in what I was trying to do and not to give a damn about gossip mongers. I figured the best way to silence any critics would be to achieve the project goals and with this in mind I kept my energies firmly focused on the tasks at hand.

Unfortunately the gossip mongers did achieve limited success. Some potential sponsors whom Yuta had been dealing with informed her they had heard through 'the grapevine' that the expedition was facing imminent collapse and therefore they were not completely confident in sponsoring it. This made both Yuta and I even more determined to beat the odds and make the expedition succeed.

I had called Yuta regularly throughout the early stages and on several occasions had shed tears with her over the phone as she went through the pain, uncertainty and loneliness of the operation to remove her tumour, and the agonising wait to hear if it was successful. I wanted to be with her more than anything, yet to do so would have caused the collapse of an expedition that we both believed in. Yuta and I struggled to help each other through an emotional whirlwind characterised by moments of loneliness, doubt, frustration and pain. Yet we supported each other with gestures of reassurance, determination, inspiration and, most of all, love, a deep and undiminished love for each other that helped shed light on our darkest moments. Looking back on that time I believe the project was literally hanging by a thread and that thread was kept intact more than anything else by our belief that we could achieve anything together, we just needed to believe in ourselves and each other.

I paddled out of Zato, heading towards the next destination, Nangqen, two hundred kilometres by river to the south, on the border between Qinghai and the Tibet Autonomous Region. A little south of Zato I paddled through a spectacular section of sheer-sided gorges that, at times, were only twelve metres wide and over two hundred metres deep. The sedimentary rock that the river had eaten through was dry and lifeless, but at one point, as I leant back over the stern of the kayak and looked up at the light blue sky and let the swirls of the river swing my kayak around in arcs, I witnessed the extraordinary beauty of clouds rolling across the rim of the gorge. The entire universe felt like one massive living entity. Despite the emotional ups and downs, the descent was still studded with energising moments of sheer wonder.

Three days later I reached Nangqen, a town similar in size to Zato, yet slightly more developed. When I arrived another issue developed with Lara and James. Apparently we needed to get the TAR permit, for which we had already paid James US$5000, re-issued due to the fact that the Frenchmen had left and their names were still on the existing permit. To my dismay, Lara and James also indicated that they wished to renegotiate to significantly increase their financial benefits from the project if they were to continue working with it. With the Zongjian experience still fresh in my mind, I wanted nothing more than to let them know, as impolitely as possible, that I thought their behaviour was despicable and that they clearly had nothing positive to offer the expedition so the project would have no further association with them. Unfortunately for me, I didn't have the US$5000 permit paper in hand yet and James had the ability to cancel it.

The permit was critical for providing the production team (now Brian and Abe) with access to the Tibet Autonomous Region. Filming that section was considered very important for the documentary and I knew that the odds of obtaining another permit from the extremely complex Chinese bureaucracy in time for the diminishing weather window was about one hundred to one. For the second time in a matter of weeks, the filming permit for the TAR became a powerful negotiation tool and I was reluctantly forced back to the negotiating table with two people who I would definitely have preferred to simply walk away from. A long, slow and frustrating series of negotiations began where James and Lara attempted to dramatically increase their personal benefits, and I tried to negotiate a situation that would allow us to proceed with the project without sending Yuta and I bankrupt.

After ten frustrating days of negotiations, in which we still failed to reach a workable agreement, I managed to contact a frustrated and tired Abe who was languishing in Zongjian, waiting for the go-ahead to continue the expedition. He didn't understand what all the fighting was about and just wanted to come to Zato to film the descent through the Tibet Autonomous Region. I told him there was nothing I wanted more but my hands were tied without the permit. I felt terrible that I could not just head off into Tibet with him and get on with the job, but the possibility of landing him in gaol because we were without the appropriate permit was too high. From dawn to dusk each day I felt I was involved in a bitter wrestling match at every turn.

Eventually I received word through Yuta that Abe had given up and was flying back to Laos. The weather in Zato became warmer as the snow was replaced by rain, which flushed large amounts of sediment into the watercourse. I watched the waters rise by several feet, which in turn increased the flow rate by five hundred per cent on what it had been when we first arrived in Zato.

The prolonged negotiations had literally life-threatening implications for me; as the days and weeks ticked by, the monsoon from South-East Asia gradually made its way north through the regions of Yunnan and onto the steppes of the Tibetan Plateau. The Mekong River outside my guesthouse window in April (when I was originally supposed to cross into Tibet and descend the treacherous gorge sections) possessed an estimated flow rate of around twenty cubic metres per second. When exploring whitewater rivers, high water levels generally translate to an increased level of danger. In order to assess how much additional danger I might face if I allowed the negotiations to delay the descent any further I used a simple hydrological calculation to guesstimate the flow increase over the coming weeks. The results of that calculation could hardly have been more alarming for me.

The weather charts I possessed indicated that rainfall around Zato would increase by around four hundred and fifty per cent between April and July as the monsoon made its arrival felt. I also knew that the widespread snow and glacier melt that occurs between April and July as the weather warms up would add to this water increase considerably. I calculated the summer snow and glacial melt would double the river's original depth. The four hundred and fifty per cent increase in rainfall would also increase the depth by another four and half times over the original depth (people familiar with monsoonal rivers know that a depth increase in this range between dry and wet seasons is nothing unusual). Most people are aware that as rivers rise they don't only get deeper, they also flow a lot faster so I calculated that by the end of July the Mekong would flow around four times faster than it had in April. The bottom line was, that from April to July the amount of water flowing past my guesthouse window per second could reasonably be expected to increase by as much as one hundred and sixty-six times, or 16 600 per cent. Ouch!

Dramatically increasing water flows down a wide valley is one thing, but squeezing massive amounts of additional water into the steeply sloped and constricted gorges adds a whole new meaning to the term 'compounded chaos'. I became desperate to get moving again before the expedition would have to be cancelled due to dangerous water levels. I pleaded the case of compounded chaos repeatedly to James and Lara in an effort to push them to a compromise so that I could get moving. Despite my best efforts, I eventually reached the conclusion that the looming threat to my life was a major concern on my agenda and my agenda only.

As the end of May drew near, with no end to the negotiations in sight, the stress took its toll. I caught a strong dose of the flu, which rapidly drained away my strength, and I hit rock bottom as I shivered under thick blankets in a cockroach-infested guesthouse in Zato. I was devastated as I could see more than a year's worth of full-time work being destroyed.

At the lowest point I considered calling the expedition off as I couldn't see a way out. I emailed Yuta and my mum to discuss the possibility. At this stage Yuta was recovering from a successful operation and was back on her feet. Yuta and my mum were both busy arranging personal money and sponsorship to keep the project moving, and they flatly refused to let me give up based on the actions of Lara and James. I was met with displays of love and support that reinforced my belief in my abilities to make things work and this gave me strength to pull the project back together. Up until those dark days, clouded with fever, I never realised how much I had come to depend on these two remarkable women. They stood beside me and their convictions never wavered.

Emails from friends, family and sponsors also kept coming in to remind me that they were amazed by the achievements so far and could not wait to hear more. I looked back through the list of over twenty sponsors who had pledged money and noted that there were only two who hadn't come through with their money. I came to the realisation that the project was at a standstill only because of the conflict between myself and two individuals who I had absolutely nothing in common with. Enough was enough.

When I looked back at some of my research documents I realised that one of the most common aspects of the major river expeditions I had studied, including descents on the Amazon, Yangtze, Nile and Tsangpo, was team breakdowns, conflict and controversy, and this was even more common than fatalities. The levels of antagonisms rattling my expedition might have seemed exceptional, but falling out with a few people on a project on the scale of the Mekong Descent, and the resulting ill will associated with that, was certainly nothing unusual. The journeys where teams remained best of friends throughout were the rare exceptions to the rules. I finally stopped feeling sorry for myself and started to view Lara and James as I would any other obstacle. That was when I decided to run the restricted area of the Tibet Autonomous Region, without their knowledge and without the permit in hand.

My plan was simple. As Brian was flying over from the States, picking up Yuta in Laos then meeting me in China, I would speed through the Mekong gorges of Tibet, from Qinghai and Yunnan, solo and unsupported, fast enough to avoid the worst of the monsoon floods. If I was questioned about my permit while in the Tibet

Autonomous Region I could legitimately explain and prove, via bank transfers and emails, that I had applied for a permit, that I had paid the US$5000 permit fee to the government via a Yunnan-based travel company, and that the permit had officially been issued for me and my team to pass through the TAR. Unfortunately, I didn't have the actual piece of paper on my person but they could track it down at the tourism office if they wished. To avoid confusion and associated delays I decided it would be best to keep a low profile while I was in the region.

Finally, after being stopped dead for weeks, I was able to focus on challenging the river. My main concern was the rapidly rising waters that would, within weeks or even days, turn the gorges into a suicide run. I had to get through them before that happened. Following the original plan, I would have spent around three weeks and had at least four re-supply points along the way. Due to the permit situation I decided that restocking supplies in bigger towns would be too risky and time consuming. I needed to be self-sufficient. I set my departure date for the leg through Tibet for 1 June 2004. I saw it as being absolutely crucial that I get through the Tibetan gorges region within the first two weeks of June to avoid the worst of the water volume increase.

I estimated that if I was on the river for at least twelve hours per day, I could probably make it from Nangqen to Yunnan, directly south of eastern Tibet, in ten days. I set about getting twelve days' worth of food (two days' extra in case I needed to trek out of the gorges or progressed slower than planned) and equipment. I stocked up on the best supplies I could get, which weren't so great compared to the more substantial food I had procured previously. Noodles, tinned fish with beans, Spam, Chinese sausages, dried fruit and nuts and coffee made up the vast bulk of what I carried. I made special room for a few packs of six herbs and four fruits tea for those moments when I might need a lift.

Getting such a large amount of cold weather gear and food into a whitewater kayak is a major undertaking. I spent the best part of two days packing, repacking, discarding, adjusting, modifying and cutting back on gear. My tent was replaced with a plastic sheet, the first-aid kit reduced by three-quarters and every millimetre of space crammed with food, fuel and clothes. I could only carry one litre of water and would have to refill it from the various streams along the way. The kayak and gear weighed about seventy kilograms even before I hopped into my craft.

At 8.30 p.m. on the evening of 1 June 2004, a Tibetan monk, an old lady and two children helped me carry the kayak down to the river. I then set about getting into my paddle gear.

When tackling extreme whitewater in remote and previously unexplored locations, such as the one I would soon enter, it is important to consider there is a significant possibility that the kayaker can get thrashed out of his boat, which will then be washed out of control down the river, possibly never to be seen again. Therefore the kayaker must have the means on his body to survive for an unpredictable period in the wilderness. Without the right gear in the gorges of the TAR, a kayaker would be lucky to survive a couple of days unless he could find help—and there was no guarantee of that.

First I wore three sets of thermal pants, two thermal tops and a paddle sweater, which all went underneath a waterproof dry top and pants to keep me warm. In the chest pocket of the dry top I placed a silver space blanket—essential for fending off hypothermia in the freezing nights if I was stuck in the wilderness—and several A4 laminated topographic maps of the region, which would be invaluable for finding an escape route by land back to civilisation. Over the dry top went what kayakers call a 'PFD' or personal floatation device (life jacket), which had the world's smallest satellite phone and spare battery housed in a small watertight dry box stuffed into the front zip pocket. Next, I donned a neoprene skullcap and helmet for protection and warmth. I wore two pairs of neoprene socks and a pair of neoprene river booties on my feet. In the shoulder pockets of the dry suit I placed two small waterproof packages that were jammed full of survival gear such as lighters for making a fire, a fishing line and hook to obtain food, a Swiss army knife, super glue for closing lacerations should I get some cuts, duck tape, iodine, waterproof plasters and other such useful knick-knacks. A global positioning system (GPS) was also squeezed into the arm pocket and the final accessory were neoprene 'pogies' (kayaker's paddle mitts), which were all-important for ensuring that some dexterity was retained in my fingers despite the bone-numbing wind-chill factor that takes place when your hands are constantly wet in sub-zero temperatures.

Finally, I was ready to go. By the look on the locals' faces I must have resembled a space man—I probably had nearly as much junk around my body and in my craft! I squeezed into the kayak, clipped on my spray skirt and crab-walked with my hands into the water. In all my years of kayaking I had never seen a kayak sitting so low in the water. I was clearly overloaded, which was an inescapable yet serious concern for me, as a kayak loaded up with gear makes manoeuvring through rapids far more difficult than usual.

I paddled until midnight and it felt wonderful not to be depending on people who, it seemed to me, had such completely different motives for being involved with the project. The nightmare seemed to have ended. The dream was alive but it was far from being reached. I was probably going from the frying pan into the fire. Within days I would enter the most challenging whitewater experience of my life, alone and with rising waters. There was no turning back and no room for mistakes.

7 When all else fails

For tens of millions of years within eastern Tibet, the Mekong River ('Zaqu' to the locals) has carved out one of world's most extreme and desolate environments, the Mekong gorges. In its infancy the river meanders gracefully across the high plains and mountain-fringed valleys of Qinghai province, picking up volume with little turbulence and becoming an 'adolescent' river just north of the Kham capital, Chamdo, located two hundred and forty kilometres downstream from Nangqen.

With sufficient volume and steepness of descent, the erosive abilities of the river reach a critical mass just south of Chamdo. Instead of the river rolling across the plateau, water and sediment start cutting through the bedrock like a serrated knife. The gorges are cut so steeply and the erosion is so severe that long stretches resemble a vertical desert with the most common feature being rock and rubble avalanches. In stark contrast to the high plains of the plateau, the steeper sections of gorges are almost lifeless.

The Mekong drops nearly three kilometres in vertical elevation by the time it reaches northern Yunnan and some sections of gorges have a depth of around three and half kilometres. Even the rugged and resourceful Tibetans, who eke an existence from some of the world's most testing of environments, have not managed to inhabit long sections of the valley.

As I paddled into the TAR I considered the fact that there had only ever been two recorded river expeditions on sections of the Mekong in this region. The first group was a Japanese scientific expedition in 1988. According to Japanese descriptions from this expedition, even the relatively mild sections that exist before the Mekong reaches Chamdo contains rapids up to class VI (whitewater rapids are graded from I to VI; class VI indicates rapids of the most extreme nature possible), but of equal concern to me were the reports that the expedition team had been violently attacked and robbed by bandits shortly after crossing the border into the TAR.

To my way of thinking, if the bandits were bold enough to attack a large group of rafters then chances were they would not hesitate to roll a solo kayaker, and they could also choose do away with any evidence rather than set the victim free to contact the authorities. In the case of the Japanese, who were lucky that the incident occurred near a road, they immediately went to the authorities and this actually led to the arrest of the bandits and the retrieval of stolen goods.

The other first-descent expedition along a portion of the TAR Mekong took place while I was busily trekking to the source in mid April and that was the one that was commenced by the combined international team, some members with whom I was essentially competing for the title of the first person to descend the entire Mekong River. The combined international team of Mekong exploratory veterans from Japan, China, the United States and Australia attempted to navigate the unexplored sections of the Mekong in Tibet located between Chamdo and the Yunnan border, the same section I believed to be the Mekong's most extreme.

From what I could gather, their combined credentials seemed very impressive. The Americans, with an Australian in their midst, were led by Pete Winn and had succeeded in completing two significant Mekong mainstream first descents in central Yunnan in 1995 and 1997 over a combined distance of more than three hundred kilometres, while the Japanese, led by Masayuki Kitamura, the very same man who led the expedition that discovered the source of the Mekong in 1994, had also completed two major first descents from the source to Chamdo in 1999 and a second significant first descent stretch in Yunnan in 2002. The Chinese team, headed up by a Mr Liu Li, included a man called Song Yipin, who was warming up for his own full navigation of the Mekong and was touted to be the white-water hero of China. He had participated in the first descent of the Yangtze River in 1986, which in the annals of whitewater exploration history was at the time referred to by publications such as *Outside* magazine and many others as 'the Mt Everest of rivers'.

With all of these characters' experiences combined into one team I expected to hear that the Mekong's most challenging stretch had been fully explored, or at least mostly explored, by the time I completed my descent from the source to the TAR border. I was surprised to hear that, just one hundred and thirty kilometres into the planned three hundred and sixty-kilometre first descent stretch—and before the international team had even reached the most extreme whitewater sections—they had cancelled the expedition and evacu-ated the gorges on foot. I was slightly relieved in a competitive sense in that the Chinese and Japanese, who both intended to make first descents of the entire Mekong mainstream, were no longer in a position to beat me to it. But the news increased the concerns I already had about the gorges downstream, because I knew that all of these determined characters would not have cancelled their expedition plans without some very good reasons.

I learned from Steve Vanbeek, a friend, documentary-maker and author of several river exploration books, who was with the international team, that due to the challenging whitewater they encountered in the regions south of Chamdo they gradually fell behind schedule. Because the whitewater was impassable for some team members in various places, they were forced to do a number of time-consuming 'portages' (they had to leave the water and carry their equipment on land past the river obstacles). With such slow progress in the early stages the team began to reassess their ability to safely navigate the far steeper gorges that lay downstream before their food ran out. (The gradient drop in the downstream sections where the international team were already making portages was more than two times steeper.) They were also aware of the significant probability that various sections downstream would be impossible to trek out of if they proceeded. As the rapids became more violent and difficult to travel through, the different ability levels of members in this team became more apparent and expedition leaders began to question the viability of proceeding. Eventually the expedition was cancelled for safety and logistical reasons and the entire team trekked out with the help of Tibetan villagers—it took them six days to reach civilisation.

The thing that concerned me as I contemplated heading through the same area was that the international team had undertaken various portages and cancelled their expedition in sections that were less than half as steep as the steeper unexplored sections I planned to enter downstream. Generally speaking, the steeper the river drops the more treacherous it is, so I wondered whether I would be able to handle the conditions. I was acutely aware of the increased water volume of the river, which would make the gorges considerably more treacherous because opportunities for land scouting would be reduced due to the river banks being flooded over. And also the risk of entering gorges that had no banks or places to stop at all due to dramatically increased by that extra volume. But to my advantage I would be moving as a solo kayaker, meaning any portages that I might need to take would be around 90 per cent faster than the international team had taken with their bulky and difficult-to-move rafts. Furthermore, being a solo boater I didn't have the time-consuming responsibility of group safety and different ability levels to consider, which would allow significantly faster progress.

I decided that my advantages over the international team probably balanced out the disadvantages of increased water volume and elected to proceed. After spending weeks slumped over topographical maps of the area, trying to imagine the three-dimensional features of the region and the temperament of the river, I simply needed to find out what was down there for myself.

I set off from Nangqen at night to avoid being pulled up by provincial border guards. After heading downstream for around fifteen kilometres the water slowed to almost a standstill and continued at this pace for many kilometres. The moon was nearly full, but the snow-white provider of light had not cleared the surrounding mountains so, with the lack of direction from the current, I found myself paddling into dead-ends on several occasions, unable to see which way was downstream.

In China, the Mekong does not stay still without reason. I guessed that it must have been backed up by an unmarked dam or a huge avalanche creating a natural dam. Sure enough, as the moon cleared the mountains around 11 p.m., some ten kilometres after the still water had started, I heard a distant roar and eddied out above a massive rapid. The river suddenly dropped on a tight right-hand bend in a sheer-sided canyon.

Fortunately there was a disused horse trail cut into the wall on river right (the right side of the river when you face downstream), which gave me a dry-land vantage point to see what was creating the thunderous roar. There in front of me was a brutal class VI cascade created by an avalanche of immense proportions that extended for about three hundred metres around a sweeping right-hand bend, where the canyon widened into a more open valley. It dropped more than twelve metres in all, from one man-eating hole (a recirculating hydraulic of water that looks like the turbulence at the bottom of a powerful waterfall) to another, before culminating in an almost river-wide ledge keeper hole at the bottom of the river drop (keeper holes are the most deadly form of holes). It was a monster. I was intimidated just looking at it.

The rapid was un-runable at June high water levels and was the first one I portaged on my Mekong first descent. I was slightly disappointed that I wouldn't kayak every inch of the Mekong, but I was relieved there was a convenient path where I could bypass the rapid.

In exploratory whitewater first descents it is not necessary to run every single metre of the river. The idea is to run as much of the river as possible with portages around extremely dangerous runs or waterfalls being permitted without compromising the legitimacy of the exploration. However, if a rapid is portaged by the first descent group but then run at a later date by another group, it is the second group who retain the right to name that rapid.

I had pulled up well above the drop at the base of an avalanche and then spent thirty tiring minutes dragging my kayak, using some webbing, up the edge over some huge boulders to get to the trail that skirted the rapid. I camped above that impressive drop and hoped I would not encounter such a monster in the much larger canyons downstream.

Camping above the rapid probably gave me a little too much time to think about what might lie ahead. In the back of every whitewater kayaker's mind lurks a distant fear of some kind of whitewater disaster. For some it is being recirculated into oblivion by a house-sized hole, for others it is being pinned under water against boulders by the overwhelming force of the water and waiting helplessly to pass out. For me it is cruising down a sheer-sided canyon towards a suicidal class VI rapid with no way of stopping before going over the edge of the falls. In other words, up the creek with absolutely nowhere to paddle but into oblivion. I also considered the consequences of the natural dam created by the avalanche bursting under the strain of rising waters and releasing millions of tonnes of water into the gorges below, which would cause a virtual tidal wave to flush down through the gorges with dire consequences for anything in its path, including me.

Early the next morning I crossed into the TAR and the area where the Japanese team had been attacked. The setting was beautiful—robust stands of pine trees with a backdrop of snow-covered peaks and waterfalls. Terraced fields of barley swayed in the breezes that drifted up the gorges. The local Tibetans would yell out in amazement at seeing a foreigner cruising down the rapids in a weird-looking boat as I passed.

I was officially in the Tibet Autonomous Region headed for Chamdo after nearly two months in China and forty-two days after reaching the source, and it was every bit as beautiful as I imagined it would be. I encountered some of the most idyllic settings I have ever seen on my first day in the TAR. Wildflowers were starting to bloom and there were abundant stands of spruce interspersed with the occasional classic Tibetan dwellings and crystal-clear waterfalls.

I had two encounters with deer. One was with a herd of about twenty, who shot into the forest, leaping over one another to get out of sight. The second was when I spotted a big, brown-eyed buck drinking at the water's edge. He was about sixty metres away from me when I first spied him. I quietly paddled towards him. One of the great things about paddling whitewater is that the wildlife often can't hear your approach because of the sound of the river. I could have sworn the buck was looking at his own reflection and by the time he finally noticed me I was considering back-paddling so I didn't cruise into his hefty antlers. It was the closest I had been to a large wild mammal in my kayak and I was quite chuffed, until he scared the hell out of both of us. When he finally noticed me he literally sprang backwards into the air with such force that I nearly flipped over as I instinctively reacted to defend myself with my paddle. The buck's entire body cleared the ground by over a metre. By the time I got my balance back he was already in the forest. A surge of adrenaline pulsed through my veins and it was fantastic to be thoroughly enjoying this journey.

I had always liked this idea of being able to sneak up on wildlife but I soon came to realise that the experience is not so invigorating when you're the one being snuck up on. Later that day, as I proceeded downstream along a section where the road paralleled the river, I noticed nearly as many police and army vehicles as civilian vehicles on the road. When I heard the vehicles approach I got in the habit of paddling to a spot that was out of sight, behind boulders or to the inner edge of the bends, just in case the authorities became curious and decided to stop me to ask for permits.

The rapids picked up considerably with some nice class III to IV sections (such sections can be dangerous if not run correctly but are quite manageable for experienced whitewater enthusiasts). I was cruising along through some whitewater when, out of the corner of my eye, I saw a police vehicle down low by the river following me at a distance of just sixty metres. It scared the absolute crap out of me and I had no idea how long they had been tailing me. The roads in the region were usually much higher up from the valley floor rather than at river level and I didn't even hear him coming because of the wind blowing upstream and the sounds of the water. I now understood how that deer felt.

My heart was beating in my throat and I began to imagine sirens wailing and me being arrested. One of the policemen waved out of an open window at me. I waved back with a big cheesy smile while whispering between my teeth, 'Shit shit shit'! I proceeded down to a significant rapid that was hemmed in by a sheer-sided cliff to the left and a boulder field downstream on the right. It was the largest rapid I had come across all day and was the first one that needed to be scouted from land as I could not see a safe route from the river. To scout it I would have to stop on river right. With the police just sixty metres from the river's edge all they would have to do was pull up, then stroll down a fifteen-metre gravel hill to come and talk to me. So instead of pulling up at a safe distance above the rapid to scout, I riskily paddled straight into the start of it, spotted a tiny eddy on river right and paddled like hell to catch it before going into a very rough section below. It was a risky move but my reasoning was that from the vantage within the rapid I could probably get out of my kayak, take a quick peek at the risks downstream and get back in before the police could reach me on foot. It was a sketchy spot to get out of the kayak but eventually I managed to gain a secure footing and dragged the kayak up on the rock. I discreetly looked up to see both of the cops walking towards me. 'Fuck fuck fuck!' I uttered through clenched teeth. I climbed up a large boulder to look down the rapid and saw that the run was all bark and no bite. I could run it straight down the middle.

I shot another glance up towards the cops and to my great relief they had come to a standstill at the gravel rill and were just chilling out watching me. I shot the rapid and looked back to see them cheering me on. They continued to follow me for fifteen minutes or so before cruising ahead, tooting their horn and unleashing a haze of dust onto the roiling river. My heart had been thumping for the entire time and I made a mental note to myself to keep my senses honed for all approaching vehicles. If there was a next time I might not be so lucky.

I began to build up a system of covering ground. After breakfast I would paddle for two hours straight, then take a ten-minute floating break to eat some fruit and nuts before paddling another two hours and then stop for lunch and get out of the boat to stretch my legs. I would allow twenty minutes either side of lunch to find a spot where I could shelter from the bitter winds that always seemed to blow straight upstream into my face.

After lunch I would do four or five one-and-a-half-hour paddle bursts, broken up with ten-minute floating breaks. So I could spend more time continuing to paddle, pissing was done from the boat.

I would put a wool sponge, normally used for soaking water out of the kayak, on my thigh, piss straight over the edge of the cockpit and the spillage was soaked up by the sponge, which I then rinsed. I was able to spend between ten and fourteen hours in the kayak, occasionally getting out to scout a rapid or to work out a particularly painful cramp.

My most anticipated moment of the day was always lunch. I was using incredible amounts of energy and would start fantasising about eating at around 10 a.m. But I would snack and hold off having lunch until around 1 p.m., which consisted of three packs of two-minute noodles, a tin of fish, a Chinese sausage (cooked at breakfast time) and some more snacks. This would all be eaten in about ten minutes.

As the day wore on, my arms and shoulders ached from the repetitive strain and my legs cramped up regularly. The pain in my legs in particular was excruciating and I pushed myself through previously unchallenged pain thresholds to stay in the cockpit for so long. I also came to understand what my grandfather meant when he said his back would give him hell. During the night my body would ache and I would spend around half an hour massaging the worst spots with some heat rub.

I pushed my body harder while paddling through the TAR than at any other stage of my life and the river reminded me every single morning why I had to do so. Each night as I left the river I would stab a twig into the sand or leave a marker rock on the river's edge to gauge how much the water level had changed overnight and every morning, without fail, the water was higher—one night it actually rose over fifteen centimetres. I knew that every centimetre increased the risk to my life downstream. Every minute counted, and if I progressed casually (five hours' paddling per day) it would take me an extra twenty days to pass through Tibet, by which time the gorges would almost have reached peak flow levels, the most deadly level for exploration. I again reflected on my pre-expedition research and noted that nearly all first-descent related deaths on the surrounding rivers had occurred during periods of high flow. The fear of death is a supreme motivator.

A snooze at a lunch break nearly brought the descent of the TAR to an early finish. I was nodding off when I noticed something out of the corner of my eye—a red boat in the river. For a brief moment I thought, 'Who could possibly be paddling this stretch?' Then I realised it was my boat. It must have slipped off the rock I had placed it on. I jumped up and bolted along the rocky river bank to catch it. I consider myself a pretty competent rock skipper but I barely managed to gain ground on the boat, which seemed to be taunting me as it raced down on the swift currents. I knew that if I didn't catch up I would probably never see that boat or my gear again. I ran for all I was worth.

After about a kilometre I was getting puffed and had only managed to maintain a distance from it. I couldn't catch it on land. I dived into the water, gasping for breath as a wave of freezing water shocked me. I started swimming after the boat. I was stuffed after about thirty strokes. The run in the thin air had taken its toll, so I floated downstream for a few moments as I caught my breath. I could still see the kayak bobbing up and down, so I swam for it, then rested, swam again and rested, until I reached the boat completely exhausted.

I clung to it and tried to catch my breath but I could hear a rapid up ahead. I grabbed the kayak and scissor-kicked to the water's edge. I was completely spent and almost hypothermic. Fortunately the sun was out and I stripped off my dry suit, left my thermal gear on and lay on the warmish rocks in the sun to get my core temperature up. I had to walk back upstream to retrieve my paddle and the lunch gear. To my surprise I had covered a distance of around three kilometres. I was lucky, as without the boat I would have been stuck in the middle of nowhere with little more than my paddle, lunch scraps and what I had

on my body. It was a foolish mistake and I was pissed off with myself
for causing the loss of two valuable hours while I dried myself out.

At the end of that eventful day I camped on a sandy beach. By the
next morning the river had risen over twenty centimetres. My body
ached from over twelve hours of paddling the previous day but I
knew I had to pick up the pace. As I approached Chamdo, the landscape changed dramatically as did the whitewater. The pine forests
were gradually replaced by de-forested, eroding mountains, and the
rapids, which up until then had been sporadic, picked up several
notches with dozens of closely spaced class III-plus rapids. Along
several stretches of river, teams of hundreds of workers were labour-
ing on major road constructions. Periodically explosions could be
heard as obstructions were blasted from the canyon walls to widen
the tiny horse trails into what would soon become sealed express-
ways. Sometimes the explosions sounded so close that I couldn't tell
which direction they were coming from. The reason for the denuded
mountains became evident when I came across a huge sawmill north
of Chamdo.

As it was still broad daylight I decided it would be best to wait
until dark before paddling through the heart of the town. To pass the
time I wrote in my diary and phoned Mum and Yuta. Yuta was now
faring well after the operation, which had been deemed a success,
and I spent most of my time assuring her that I would be fine on the
next leg to the south of Chamdo. The sun sank slowly behind the
mountains and darkness fell. I paddled downstream past the lumber-
yard, which was still busy. I paddled from shadow to shadow under
the cover of darkness. It made me feel like some ridiculous overgrown kid playing commando, but the risks were very real. When I
paddled along several stretches that were well lit by streetlights I was
understandably nervous.

Chamdo was once an important stopover on a branch of the Silk
Road and had been chosen by the Chinese as the administration

centre in eastern Tibet. In recent years it had become one of the areas that the Han Chinese had been encouraged to migrate to. Up until now the majority of the architecture I had seen along the river had been classic (using traditional building materials such as earth, timber, stone and traditional brick) or contemporary Tibetan in style (modern bricks, tiles, windows and trimmings). As a general rule, the buildings had style. Chamdo was, in stark contrast, glistening with aluminium, white tiles, blue-tinted glass and the cement buildings that characterise so many small towns and cities across China.

It was around 9.30 p.m. and the moon had not yet breached the steep-sided valley the city sat in. I was forced to follow my ears rather than my eyes through several class II to III rapids through the town. As I approached the second bridge spanning the river in Chamdo I plopped into a medium-sized hole and was washing-machined for a few seconds before gaining control and surfing it sideways. It was a tense few moments as I worked myself back and forth in the hole, trying to find where the water was exiting. My stern was caught by the current and I flipped a couple of times before re-establishing the surf position again. I couldn't seem to get out on the edges of the hole, which is usually the best way of escaping. I was getting tired and realised that the situation could get worse if I didn't get out soon.

I decided to try a new technique, surfing as high as I could on the foam and then straightening up to stab the bow of my kayak as deep as possible into the oncoming water to execute a move kayakers call an 'ender'. With an ender the force of the oncoming water pushes the front of the boat and paddler down deep into the water until the kayak is positioned vertically in the water. The buoyancy of the kayak, along with the force of the deep water flowing out under the hole, shoots boat and paddler backwards into the air in a near-vertical launching motion. As my bow went in, the downward force submerged me and the kayak. There was little buoyancy because of the food and equipment I carried and the launching effect was much slower, allowing me to stay in the deeper, out-flowing water long enough to be spat out of the hole. I rolled my kayak upright and paddled for a bridge pylon to rest.

As I passed the third and largest of the four bridges that span the Mekong in Chamdo, large neon lights flashed brightly on both sides of the river, advertising discotheques in new hotels. The capital of eastern Tibet, from the river at least, could hardly have had a more un-Tibetan feel. I continued to cruise through town and was spotted by a few people who seemed quite content to gasp and discuss the sight amongst themselves.

The busy road south of Chamdo followed the river and there were various factories, hydro stations and sawmills along its banks over the next few kilometres. I wanted to get as much space as possible between me and the city before morning but with poor visibility it was quite dodgy navigating the rapids and there were a few more hair-raising moments. I was too exhausted to continue and pulled up to sleep next to the sealed road that followed the Zaqu.

I awoke the next morning to the sound of people murmuring. I looked up the rill to see a crowd of Tibetans looking down at me from the road. I thought I had chosen a spot that was out of sight of the road, but someone had spotted me and every passing vehicle was now stopping to see what was going on. I calmly and quickly packed up my gear, gave the onlookers a wave and set off.

The long days were starting to take their toll. My nose and lips were peeling, my fingertips starting to crack and the pain in my back from sitting in the kayak for between eleven and thirteen hours per day was almost unbearable. I was suffering physically but pushed on, like a man possessed, to cover over one hundred kilometres per day. I was driven by raw survival instinct, literally a fear of death in the gorges if the water levels got too high before I could make it through. In my mind's eye, beating the river rise was the difference between life and death. I was closing in on the gorges and I couldn't afford to become slack. I had to get through before it was too late, just one more day and I would reach the section where the international team pulled off, where the Mekong River started its most rapid and remote descent.

I paddled along two sections with roads along side and on two separate occasions police cars followed my descent. The first one was really curious and I felt a gut-wrenching fear that everything could come to an end if the sirens began to wail. After about ten minutes I entered a mild section of rapids and halfway through I heard something come over the loudspeakers. My heart raced. Suddenly there was a burst of Shanghai rock music shrieking through the valley and one of the cops was cheering me on. Cool cops in one of the most restricted regions on Earth is not what I expected.

The road ended around lunchtime but horse trails continued to follow the river. The difficulty and regularity of the rapids began to increase and the mountains started to close in. By early evening I came to a short and steep class V drop that I identified as the Twin Falls rapid. This rapid was one of the last rapids the international team had navigated. Given that it took the international crew six days to trek out from that general location I estimated that from the far more remote gorges downstream, I would be looking at about two weeks to make it back to civilisation. Given that I had only about six days' food left at that stage, and that there were potentially no trails to follow downstream from where the previous team pulled out, the best bet on a route out of this pristine section would be by river. It was a wild guess as to how dangerous that passage would be.

8   The back of beyond: the Mekong gorges of Tibet

I ran the Twin Falls rapid through a large crashing wave formed in between the two large holes created by the falls. Shortly after heading downstream I noticed that my water bottle was missing. A brief pang of guilt for leaving behind the plastic bottle was soon overridden by the realisation that I had no way to carry water. I considered stopping to treat water with iodine but felt that the loss of time doing this would be more dangerous than drinking untreated water. I decided to take a punt and drink straight from the clear water streams that entered the mainstream.

The first couple of times I got out of the kayak and walked over to a stream to drink from it. Getting out of the kayak was a dreadful experience because of the bitterly cold weather. While my legs were inside the shell of the kayak and the spray skirt was clipped over the cockpit, they were protected from the brisk winds that tortured my face and torso. The moment I snapped off the spray skirt the warmth trapped in the kayak was lost. By the time I was finished drinking I would return to the boat shivering and it would take another fifteen minutes or so of hard paddling to stabilise my body temperature.

The next time I wanted a drink I spotted a waterfall on the river's edge and paddled over to drink, staying in the cockpit. Some rubble at the base of the waterfall, however, prevented me from putting my mouth directly into the flow. I had to try something different. I held my paddle above my head and directed the blade into the waterfall, using it as a type of elbow to redirect the flow. As the water hit the blade it ran down the shaft towards the opposite blade where I was able to drink the essential liquid. I would get covered in water but this method gave me nearly three metres of drinking reach from the cockpit and, because my torso was getting drenched regularly in the rapids anyway, it was preferable to losing body warmth by getting out of the kayak.

About thirty kilometres downstream from the Twin Falls, the gorges started closing in and the rapids became longer, more violent, and the gap between them was decreasing. I had to stay sharp and regular land scouting, to identify safe routes through the rapids before entering them, became essential. I was delighted to see that the horse trails still followed the river for most of the day, offering a lifeline back to civilisation should I need it. The only thing was that the trail ran so high along the ridges that it would take a full day of dangerous climbing up one of the many avalanches to reach the trail, and then up to a week to get to the nearest road.

I kept paddling until last light and then went in search of a farmer's settlement that was low enough in the valley to trek to. The alternative was sleeping under a wet sheet of plastic which had after several days lost its appeal. Around 8.30 p.m. I rounded a bend to see a settlement that was only a one hundred-metre climb above the river. Now that I was a long way from the nearest road I felt confident that there would be no government presence to worry about. What appeared to be a fifteen-minute walk turned into a 90-minute saga as I made my way through a seemingly impenetrable maze of spiky shrubs and bushes. I was surprised to find a complex of about ten multi-storey dwellings completely deserted. I spent another night alone.

I called Mum and Yuta to touch base and give them my GPS coordinates so they could track my progress.

'Is everything all right?' Yuta asked.

'I'm fine, babe, everything is going well. I feel pretty good about the conditions right now,' I said, scratching at the earthen floor on the roof of the deserted farmer's hut.

'That's great, but I've been so scared. I dreamt that you were in trouble,' Yuta said.

'Everything's fine. I'm just a bit worn out, I've been paddling long days.' I tried to reassure her.

'I came back from my mum's house today; we had a *baci* for you.' A *baci* is an ancient ceremony performed in the Issarn province of Thailand and in Laos. It originally evolved as an animist ritual prior to the arrival of Buddhism in the region and has been adopted as a Buddhist ceremony that is still commonly practised today. The ritual is based around the belief that people possess protector spirits, or *kwan*, who watch over them and have the ability to keep them from harm. However, these same spirits also have a will of their own and tend to wander away, leaving the individual even more vulnerable. The *baci* is performed by a Buddhist monk or spiritually adept village elder and is used to call the spirits back to the person as well as asking the *kwan* to watch over that person during the course of a particular activity such as travel. An elaborate mix of food, drink, candles, cotton string, banana leaf decorations and flower arrangements are set up to invite the spirits to the fine meal, and the people attending the ceremony make requests of the spirits to look after their loved ones. It is a beautiful ceremony and I felt honoured that one had been held for me.

'Thanks, babe. I appreciate all the help I can get. There's some pretty tough whitewater up here.' My thoughts swept back to several tense moments from the day.

'When you come back you have to come to the temple and thank the *naga*,' Yuta said.

'Why's that?' I asked, not quite sure what she was getting at.

'Because I have been praying to him to protect you. I have a feeling something is going to go wrong on this stretch. I know you

don't like to pray but just say a little prayer to him, will you!' Her
concern was so genuine and sweet that all I wanted to do was crawl
through the phone and give her a huge hug.

'Okay, honey, I'll say a prayer. Everything will work out fine.'

I felt quite good after the phone call. My map showed that I had
already entered the steepest section and although some of the rapids
were fully testing my skills I didn't feel I was in over my head, and the
outlook for completing the leg before running out of food seemed
good.

The relationship that the people of Thailand and Laos have with
the *naga*, the mythical river dragon, had long been a source of fascination for me. I found that the boatmen and fishermen who worked
around potentially dangerous rapids and cascades on the Mekong
had a special affinity for the creature. I couldn't claim to be a believer
but after Yuta's request I felt that if there was anything or anyone
worth asking for a little help when dealing with the gorges, then the
naga was probably my best bet, so I said a little prayer as I promised
I would.

Occasionally I would see tiny green islands that signalled the
presence of farmers in the otherwise barren and eroding valley walls.
To see the incredibly desolate environments in which these people
can survive makes you appreciate just how resourceful they are.
Entire families live off as little as one acre of relatively flat land
surrounded by precipitous cliffs, steep rills and avalanches.

I navigated three class V and fourteen class IV rapids throughout
the day. The rising waters were eating away the base of scree slopes
that had built up over the winter and it was fairly common to see
glacial gravel and rocks slipping and tumbling into the mainstream.
The seasons were definitely changing—summer was on the
doorstep. It was the most active avalanche area by far and barely a
kilometre went by without my coming across the recent evidence of

avalanches; sometimes in excess of ten thousand tonnes would clog up the mainstream. The warning signs that the river was rising were everywhere and I gave it everything I had to keep moving downstream. Mentally I began to prepare myself to face what I considered to be the worst-case scenario.

Going into an un-scoutable, sheer-sided gorge of whitewater in the heart of Tibet with no knowledge of what lay downstream is the kayaking equivalent of free climbing a major cliff at altitude with no clear idea how high the cliff actually is, no knowledge of whether or not the cliff has a climbable route, and no ropes or safety mechanisms if something goes wrong. It is like a game of Russian roulette and you don't play those types of games if you like living. My plan was that if I came across such a gorge I would find a way to trek or climb around it. If that was not possible, I would trek out of the gorge altogether. I checked my progress on the map and made mental notes of every potential exit route from the valley. I made the firm decision that the descent was not worth dying for and I would not place myself at unnecessary risk if there were other options.

After several days on my own I felt a strong desire to spend some time with people. As the afternoon wore on I was delighted to see the occasional settlement perched on the mountains. Eventually I saw one that looked low enough on the mountainside to walk to for the night. I trekked up to a knoll that housed a classic mud-walled multi-storeyed Tibetan house. As I approached I spotted a young lady locking up the building. I waved and she immediately sprinted away, shocked at seeing a foreigner walking into the village. I heard some yelling, which seemed to announce my arrival.

The village then appeared deserted but smoke was coming from chimneys, which meant that there were people around. For about ten minutes I wandered along earthen paths winding between perhaps twenty dwellings without seeing a soul. I knocked on a couple of doors, without any response. I started yelling out in Kham

Tibetan dialect, 'Chaw de mo,' which means 'hello', but still no response. My hunger got the better of me and I sat down and dug through my bags for some dried fruit. As I sat there eating sultanas, a wiry Kham Tibetan man of about fifty cautiously approached.

'Chaw de mo, neh may la Mick', which means 'Hi, my name is Mick.'

Being the first foreigner in many villages during earlier expeditions had taught me a few tricks to help break down any cultural barriers. I had to make the man smile and relax. My terrible accent was already making him smirk. I started explaining with a mixture of mime, a few words and lots of smiles what I was doing. I energetically recreated paddling through a gorge and hitting a big rapid. Then I started laughing, as did he. Moments after, a whole bunch of people started cautiously approaching from the surrounding houses. I kept the animated mime stories going and before long was getting a few giggles. A pot of yak butter tea and a bowl of *tsampa*, the Tibetan staple of ground barley, appeared. It was all going quite well and I decided that they were ready for the main act: my favourite cultural-barrier-breaking magic trick.

Using the steel bowl they had brought the *tsampa* in, I called everyone in close and using mime explained that I would start a magic trick. Everyone looked baffled but curious. I poured half a cup of water into the bowl, held it up high with both hands as though offering it to the gods, then in an unnaturally deep voice said: 'I offer this to the King of Poooooobaaaaas.' Curiosity was ever so slightly overtaken by concern and everyone stepped back a little, falling completely silent. Balancing the bowl in one hand, I used the other to run my fingers smoothly around the outer rim. Then I started singing the secret mantra.'Uuuummmmmoooooooaaa! Ummmmm-moooooooaaa!'

Children clung to their mothers yak-skin dresses, boys looked at one another ready to run for the hills and elders simply looked petrified. I stopped and lifted one hand up into the air as some kids nearly made a break for it. I pulled one of the hairs from my head and placed it in the bowl, then gestured to Mnob, the man who had first approached me, to do the same, which he did, despite much reservation. A few concerned giggles and whispers broke the silence. I started again. 'Ummmooooooooaaaa! Ummmmmmmooooooooaaaa!'

This time I built up the intensity of the chant and gestured for people to come closer to see the hairs jumping up in the bowl. They cautiously approached, then when twenty people were within four metres of the bowl of water I screamed at the top of my lungs, 'YAAH!', slapping my hand into the water, splashing everyone in the face. People including elders shrieked in fear and started fleeing in all directions. I roared with laughter and within moments so did everyone else. It wasn't a giggle this time, it was a full-scale laughing riot as women, children, grandfathers and cousins realised that this silly-looking foreigner in a strange red suit was just taking the piss and had cheekily scared the absolute crap out of them in the process.

A full two minutes later as the laughing finally began to ease off, I started getting slaps on the back, full-faced smiles, the kids wanted more and everyone saw me as the village clown rather than a scary foreigner with unclear intentions.

I spent a magical evening in the Mnob's residence. Besides the great company I had the best meal I ever had since my long days riding solo. I cooked up my standard gruel of tinned fish and noodles and was able to swap it for berries, yoghurt and yak stew. The berries, which I still have not managed to identify, stained my hands for days, reminding me of the Mnob family experience.

The next morning I took the GPS coordinates of the Mnob's residence at: N 30 07' 54.5" E 097 59' 46.1" altitude two thousand nine hundred and eighty-one metres, not realising at the time just how important those and several other coordinates I took in the area would be. The entire Mnob family, even charming old granny, came down to the riverside to see me off. We reached the river a couple of hundred metres from where the kayak was and the funniest thing happened. Upon arriving at the river's edge Mnob gestured at me to jump in and start swimming. I didn't really know what he was getting at until he mimicked the gestures I went through the night before. In trying to explain that I had paddled down the river, he thought that I had swum down the Mekong and wanted to check out my style. I had to laugh and soon showed him my beaten-up Perception brand of kayak further upriver, which made a big impression on the family. Before long I was paddling down the next stretch and into another extremely challenging set of gorges.

The intensity of the rapids picked up several notches and was soon seriously testing my abilities. Despite my plans to portage around any sheer-sided gorges that could not be scouted, it didn't always work out that way. At several points along the river stretch there were no other possibilities but to enter dodgy-looking sections of gorge. It was impossible to paddle upstream and I was already surrounded by sheer- or near sheer-sided cliffs. All I could see was the water speeding around a bend with nowhere for me to stop on the edges. I begrudgingly paddled around several bends in sheer-sided canyons with my heart racing and adrenaline pumping with no real idea what lay downstream, yet each time it turned out to be relatively safe. Regardless of the outcome, I deeply resented being forced to test my fate based on luck rather than skill. I knew when paddling into such gorges that a fifty-foot waterfall directly onto rocks could be waiting around the bend and no amount of skill or effort would make the slightest difference. For kayakers, knowing the features of a rapid before going into it is about as important as a base jumper knowing how high up he is before leaping off a cliff. When the river forced me to jump with no way of knowing what was below I felt a sense of vulnerability that I had rarely experienced in my kayaking career.

I entered a long section of canyon that I realised would not be traversable if I decided to pull off the river. The rapids here became increasingly violent and at times were almost continuous. Various rapids would test my abilities to the limit and the price I would pay for mistakes at several points would almost certainly be the ultimate. If I made a mistake and bailed from the kayak, just getting myself to the edge on these sections would be a long shot, and rescuing the kayak full of essential supplies highly unlikely. With evening temperatures dropping below freezing, and without supplies, surviving for long enough to get out would be a major achievement.

The level of focus and concentration required in these types of conditions was truly intense. The ravines were so steep that my GPS only worked occasionally. I doubted whether a chopper-assisted rescue would even be possible in such conditions, as unpredictable gale forced gusts of wind occasionally flew up the valley. According to my map this near-continuous section of gorges with similar river conditions went on for another one hundred and fifty kilometres.

Generally speaking it was possible to stop above the most difficult runs and scout a viable route down. However, during the afternoon of day six in Tibet it seemed like my worst kayaking nightmare would come true. I entered what looked like just another canyon, but as I proceeded the canyon walls closed in until there were no avalanches or boulders to stop at. Only eighteen metres wide, the canyon had a steep gradient drop and powerful surges. 'Boils', a powerful whitewater feature with the appearance of bubbling, roiling and boiling water, pushed my kayak around like a cork.

Friction caused by the water rushing along the canyon walls meant that the waterline along the edge was about a foot higher than in the middle of the river where I struggled to maintain control in relentless whirlpools and surges. I was forced downstream around the next bend and I saw the horizon line drop away several metres and bursts of mist shoot up into the air sporadically, a solid indication that there was a dangerous rapid below. I could not see a place to stop and my body surged with adrenaline. When I was within thirty metres of the drop I spotted several boulders on river right of the rapid. Behind one was a small eddy about one-metre square. I paddled for my life. The powerful boils pushed me away from the edge and every one of my muscles was tweaked as I fought against the power of the water. As I neared the lip of the rapid, a massive hole roared as it pumped mist into the air, warning me not to miss the eddy.

Far below I could see that the rapid continued for at least another two hundred metres before rounding a corner. I had no idea what lay beyond, although I could see what appeared to be the start of the next rapid. I strained and groaned, finally managing to pull into the tiny sanctuary behind the rock. It was a close call. A closer inspection of the drop revealed that if I had missed the eddy I would have been done for. Several man-eating holes and a ledge on river right almost certainly would have munched me out of the kayak. Imagining what would have happened next scared the hell out of me. I wasn't through it all yet, though. I clambered onto a small cone-shaped rock, trying not to slip in or to let go of the kayak or paddle. Finally I managed to get secure footing and dragged the boat up, jamming it between the rock and the canyon wall.

I surveyed the class V-plus rapid. A first descent down a class V rapid is a serious undertaking even for an expert kayaker. A mistake can easily land a highly skilled practitioner in hospital or, worse still, an early grave. Yet in most cases, if the kayaker is not injured as a result of the initial screw up, he has a pretty good chance of making a self rescue (making it safely to the edge of the river on his own without third person assistance). But a class V-plus rapid steps up the risks considerably, with the margin of error required before the kayaker is in deep shit being substantially less and the chances of successful self rescue greatly diminished compared to a standard class V. Basically, if a kayaker comes out of his kayak in a class V-plus run with no friends around to help rescue him, he will be thanking his lucky stars if he makes it out alive. For me, I would normally not try full stop to run a class V-plus run in a gorge unless I knew exactly what was around the next bend (which I didn't here); and even after knowing what was located around the next bend I would only try such a rapid on a day when I felt in peak condition and had other expert boaters around to help rescue me if I made the slightest mistake. In this case I had no choice, I had to run the drop or I would be trapped in the gorge indefinitely.

I worked out a route that would require me to drop off the rock into some fast-flowing surges that came off the right wall. I would have to paddle hard to the left to skirt above the roaring holes and use diagonal waves coming off the left wall to thrust me into a less threatening hole, one that looked as though it could be bashed through with sufficient speed. From there a three-metre-tall wave train (a long string of three-metre-high standing waves lined up one after the other) continued to the bend. If I got through that I would just have to see what might happen next.

I looked at the rapid for a long time, trying to build up the courage to run it. Even more than the dangerous rapid I faced, it was the unknown that lay downstream of it that really put the fear in me. As the situation stood, I could theoretically execute the run perfectly (the features of the rapid made even this much a long shot) only to round the bend to face a far more dangerous and completely un-runable section of river with nowhere to stop before entering it. Normally when one successfully completes a class V-plus first descent there should be moments of elation and joy, not intense sensations of apprehension and fear of what inescapable destiny might come next.

Adrenaline surged as I seal-launched off the rock and the river quickly ushered me towards the first hole. I paddled like a man possessed but the stern clipped the outer edge of the hole as I passed, swinging my kayak downstream towards the next one. My momentum was compromised as I made several frantic correcting strokes. Using the power of pure survival instinct I paddled with every ounce of energy my body could muster.

I was convinced that I probably wouldn't make it if I entered the succession of re-circulating hydraulics. I was slammed by the left edge of the hole which caused me to capsize. There was a tense moment as I waited to see if the hole had me within its grip, which meant I would most likely be recirculated repeatedly until thrust out of my kayak. If I was lucky I would be released to swim downstream through the waves and whirlpools that would suck me under for periods of somewhere between five to forty seconds to eventually face the next violent rapid, probably unconscious.

To my great relief the hole released me and I rolled up just long enough to take a breath before being slammed heavily by the large crashing wave that periodically forms a hole as the water surges through it on river left, hitting it sideways. I didn't have enough momentum to bash through so I was recirculated violently. The violence of being recirculated in a large hole is quite a unique experience. The only non-whitewater people I know who can sort of relate to it are surfers. The first few seconds of being dumped by a large ocean wave are similar to being thrashed in a large hole. The major difference is that an ocean wave will inevitably dissipate to nothing. The nastier river holes don't dissipate, they keep tumbling any object within their grasp in a dynamic mixture of somersaults, backflips, cartwheels and general chaos at full power. In theory they can recirculate an object for up to a few months until the seasons change and the hole gets flushed out or subsides with the decrease in water levels. Whether it's five minutes or five days, the outcome for a kayaker will change little. If the hole is strong enough and the kayaker can not regain control by surfing on or out of it, the only chance he has is if the hole decides to release him while he still retains consciousness. When you start getting recirculated in a violent hole there are always a few edgy moments as you wait to see if the hole will toss you out or if you can find a way to surf out of it.

On this particular occasion I was recirculated twice before being spat out into the wave train. I rolled up and tried to take a breath but received a lung full of water instead as a wave smashed over my bow. I knew I had to make it to the edge before the next drop so I paddled as hard as I could to river right to see what lay around the corner before I was in it. I couldn't breathe properly with water in my lungs and I became weaker with every stroke. The next thumping rapid came into view with the mist shooting above the horizon line of a major drop of similar size and scale to the last.

This time the avalanche that had caused the rapid was in clear view and I made for it. Most of the river was moving right to left, forcing me back towards the centre of the river. Before reaching the safety of the avalanche I was sucked into the next rapid. I straightened up to face my fate and spotted what appeared to be a line or a safe pathway through the rapid and committed to a plan instantly. I paddled straight over a huge rooster tail (a type of river feature that spurts water into the air in a shape that resembles a rooster's tail) and skirted a house-sized hole on the other side, more by chance than anything else, before entering a wave train that was followed by huge boils and whirlpools that sucked my entire boat under the water several times. I knew from the overwhelming power of the river, tossing my kayak around like a tiny cork, that I would never survive such a section if I came out of my boat.

I finally managed to catch short breaths of air and re-established control. All this excess exertion made my body feel weak as the boils and swirls carried me toward the next powerful class V-plus rapid. I spotted some rocks I might be able to stop behind and paddled for all I was worth as I knew I didn't have the energy to run another long stretch without resting beforehand. And to my great relief I made it to the sanctuary of the avalanche. I dug deep to rally the strength needed to pull the heavily laden kayak on to the rock, before falling back against the gorge wall exhausted.

The brief period of despair quoted from my diary in the opening scene of this book marks possibly the darkest moment of my life, when I realised that I might not make it out of the gorges alive and that I was forced to rely on a game of Russian roulette around blind bends, as much as skill and experience, to have any hope of escaping the gorges. Looking back on those moments still gives me a very real sense of my own mortality and the precariousness of life.

It was certainly not the first near miss in my time nor was it the last on the Mekong descent. What struck so deep was that I had survived one bend and it was quite possible I could round the next bend and get permanently trapped on a rock much like the one on which I now stood with no way of communicating with the outside world, which meant no escape. I had entered the heart of the Mekong's darkness, literally, as far as daylight meeting the base of the gorge was concerned and, metaphorically, in terms of danger, risk, fear and despair.

Strangely enough, the fear, despair and doubt lasted only as long as I was on safe ground. From the moment my kayak entered the current I was committed to the fight and had a clarity of focus and determination that is hard to define. After leaving the tiny rock sanctuary all sensations of fear and doubt were shoved aside to make room for the concentration needed to duplicate the precise movements I had mapped out in my mind. Below the drop, the narrow and constantly changing path to safety snaked through ferocious and life-threatening violence to the next bend—but this time I managed to stay on track and soon I encountered another large rapid and then another.

After more than three kilometres of near continuous whitewater and several class V-plus rapids, the valleys broadened and eddies sent from heaven began to reappear. I was far from out of the Mekong gorges but I had survived one of their most treacherous sections.

After the best part of two days without seeing a single accessible farmer's settlement or path I finally reached a group of mud-walled huts on day seven in Tibet. I was physically and mentally drained. Despite never seeing foreigners before, the friendly and curious Tibetans gave me five-star treatment. The settlement, consisting of half a dozen stone dwellings, was perched scenically on a ridge high above a solid class IV rapid and was home to an extended family of perhaps sixteen people. After what I had been through it was a godsend to spend the evening in the company of other people, somehow it was soothing to feel the presence of humanity even though communication was mainly limited to smiles, mime and simple gestures.

There were another two full days of extreme kayaking before I reached Yunnan, where riverside roads added convenient escape options to even the most difficult rapids. I now estimate that while I was in the Tibet Autonomous Region I made first descents down some sixty class IV rapids and twenty or so class V to V-plus rapids. I fully portaged two and half drops and made chicken runs, meaning I chose an easier and safer run around the most dangerous section of a rapid, down dozens of the most treacherous sections.

There was only one rapid that I defined as truly un-runable in the Tibet Autonomous Region section of the Mekong. I named it 'The Twisted Sisters' after the three consecutive river-wide keeper holes, each of which was big enough to swallow a house not to mention a kayak or raft. It took two hours to portage around The Twisted Sisters on river left and I camped in a cosy little cave sheltered by oak trees just above the drops.

One of the most amazing sights in Tibet was a short section of extremely narrow, sheer-sided gorge, perhaps three hundred metres deep and about one-and-half kilometres long located upstream from Yanjing, the last significant town on the river before it crossed the border into Yunnan. The swirling waters of the gorge made me enter with caution but the section turned out to be relatively sublime in terms of whitewater. As I rounded the first bend, the shrills and calls from tens of thousands of birds cut through the roiling sounds of the Zaqu.

Above me the sight was staggering. Birds from about eleven different species, including two species of raptor, circled, darted, chased and danced with one another through all levels of the gorge. It seemed to be a significant nursery and I wondered why so many of the birds had chosen that particular section of gorge.

I lay back over the stern, looking up while the current lackadaisically swung my kayak around in semicircles. The silhouettes of the birds circled above me, their black forms contrasting sharply with the backdrop of a bright blue sky. The birds made use of the gorge thermals, making them hover motionless, like particles suspended in a massive cup of ever so slightly stirred green tea. It was one of the most beautiful sights I have ever seen.

As the day wore on the gradient drop began to decrease and my kayaking progress picked up because I didn't need to scout as much. I realised that if I pushed hard I could potentially get out of the TAR before the day's end and reach the town of Foshan, where I could enjoy a restaurant meal and the services of a one-star hotel before catching a ride to Zongjian to meet Yuta and Brian, who were flying up to meet me.

I paddled into the town of Yanjing. Along the banks of the river were hundreds of large wood structures that appeared to be dripping with ice, yet the warmer weather of the area made me think that the dripping was mineral deposits. I later found out that Yanjing is an important salt-mining town.

From Yanjing the river is predominantly trailed by roads and I was nervous each time a vehicle approached and passed. With the grimace of a fugitive headed for the Mexican border I pushed on, concerned that the rule of Murphy's Law would tap me on the shoulder just before I reached the permit-free regions of Yunnan.

9　In the shadows of Kawakarpo

Forty-eight days after taking my first step down from the source, I reached the silver marker at the TAR border checkpoint—a major milestone in the expedition. Technically this is the point where the river's name changes from the Tibetan name of Zaqu to the Chinese name of Lancang Jiang, meaning 'the wild river'. Arriving at the marker signalled a major personal achievement: I had survived the most mysterious and life-threatening section of the river. I felt like I had come through the worst of the ordeal. I knew there was definitely no shortage of extreme whitewater to come, but the next sections were not as remote and had more regular escape routes if things got a bit too hot.

The drama of the previous months coupled with Yuta's health problems made being away from her extremely difficult and I longed to see her again. Even though my body was aching terribly after being on the river for nine straight days, an unshakeable desire to see her drove me to keep pushing on.

At around 4 p.m. the daily headwinds started picking up but this time they arrived with a vengeance. Fifty-knot gales blew up the valley, spraying mist off the river's surface. I remember paddling past a hole that lay over thirty metres downstream to my right, yet the water from its crest was whirled into the air, clearing the expanse before whipping my face. Although the rapids in far northern Yunnan were more manageable than the gorges of the TAR they were still potentially very dangerous. I ran some of the big water class IV to IV-plus runs without scouting and when I did bother to get out of my kayak to take a look, the runs generally turned out to be relatively straightforward sections that I could have negotiated easily without going to the trouble of scouting.

My attempts to get directions from locals led me to believe I was only a few kilometres above the first significant settlement in northern Yunnan, the riverside village of Foshan, so I pushed on into the twilight to reach it. (In reality I was around twenty-five kilometres north of the town.) At around 8 p.m., as darkness slowly descended, I rounded a bend to come across yet another class IV rapid. This one was slightly steeper than most. Without a clear view of what lay below I was tempted to scout it from land but a mixture of fatigue and frustration at scouting so many previous rapids that turned out to be easy made me assume I didn't need to do so, that it was probably going to be another burly but harmless wave train. I peeled out of the eddy, paddling hard to skirt a hole on river left and bashed through a large standing wave in the centre of the river that I expected to be followed by more waves. I was immediately faced with a huge hole about eight metres wide with a two-metre high face. I was headed straight for the middle of it. There was no time to do anything except power into it and hope to bash through. Bam! It felt like I'd hit a brick wall. I rose up and was slammed down again and again and again. I was being recirculated violently by the hole.

In the gorges I had made the firm decision not to bail out of my boat and swim unless there was absolutely no other choice, so I tried to sit it out and hoped that the hole would release me as they often do. It slammed me twice more before I felt a sort of release and saw daylight. Phew! I was relieved for about two split seconds, until I realised that the roaring hole was still behind me. I was making momentary side surf (surfing sideways in the kayak to the face of the wave) on the upstream side of the hole. Before I had time to establish control I was sucked back in and bashed again, over and over.

I was running out of oxygen fast and realised that this beast of a hole was not going to release me as long as I was attached to the buoyancy of the kayak. Holes tend to be quite specific about the densities they hold and release. Generally a hole that will hold onto a relatively aerated object, such as a person in a kayak (where around fifty per cent or more of the total volume is made up of air) won't hold on to a near neutrally buoyant object, such as an individual who is separated from their kayak.

Bailing out gives kayakers a last resort attempt for escaping life-threatening holes when all else fails. But bailing out doesn't necessarily mean you'll survive. The nastier holes can occasionally keep their grip on the swimmer regardless, and being out of the kayak in one of these holes can make it more difficult to catch your breath—you might end up starved of oxygen, which means passing out much faster than normal. If you are fortunate enough to be spat out, you are exposed to a whole new range of threats.

It took a few seconds to get myself out of the kayak because it is a well proven fact that doing backflips, somersaults, cartwheels and erratic acrobatic manoeuvres in the darkness of a hole while not breathing is particularly bad for one's orientation. Once out, I sank into the current and with great relief felt a flush of water push me downstream. I broke the surface and upon seeing daylight tried to take a breath but only managed to fill my lungs with water. I was pissed off, and angrily thought to myself, 'Why the hell did you throw yourself in that after safely paddling hundreds of kilometres of more difficult whitewater?' It's odd what goes through your mind.

I only had a dry top and pants on and could feel the cold water seeping in. I kept trying to take a breath but the water already in my lungs prevented any air from entering. I looked upstream to see my kayak and paddle following me and I made a feeble attempt to swim over and retrieve them. The lack of oxygen in my system gave me the strength of a kitten and I realised that swimming properly wasn't going to be an option.

I looked downstream and saw I was fast approaching another large rapid. I tried to work out a safe route through but because I was in the water all I could see were the tops of waves and foam. In the last moment I spotted a hole and swam left to avoid it. I smiled to myself thinking I'd made it then plopped straight into an even larger hole that tumbled me once and spat me out.

As I struggled to breathe my body responded with a meek cough in an attempt to expel the water from my lungs. My frustration at getting into the situation and not being able to breathe was rapidly replaced by the realisation that I probably didn't have the strength to rescue myself, not to mention my equipment. I looked downstream to see that, again, I was headed for another large rapid.

Kayaks are the whitewater version of rally cars: they allow for an unparalleled level of manoeuvrability in extreme whitewater, providing the skilled kayaker with an almost acrobatic ability to move around, over, through and occasionally under a whole host of potential threats. Kayakers revel in the freedom this manoeuvrability allows. By contrast, the feeling of swimming down rapids with a lung full of liquid, sapped of all strength and unable to see what I was up against was comparable to having one of those nightmares where you are being chased or attacked by someone and you remain terrifyingly unable to respond.

When I realised I might not make it to the edge some twenty metres away, my subconscious mind kept recalling random whitewater statistics. 'In 2003 long swims took more recreational whitewater enthusiasts' lives than blah blah...' I was so tired I thought about just floating into the next rapid without a fight. The experience of being a safety kayaker on commercial whitewater trips for several years made me realise that there was no one waiting downstream with a rescue line or safety kayak. I had to fight my way to shore or I would die.

'I'm not **%@! going out like this!' I mentally yelled to the little demon on my shoulder that was persuading me to just relax and see what would happen next. I dug deep and mentally screamed the same words that I used with frozen-up tourists who, after falling from rafts, needed to be directed to safety. 'Go, Go Go!' Each stroke felt like an extra five-kilogram weight had been added to my arms and I had to stop and float a couple of times to get some air into my lungs again before reaching a boulder on river left, just at the entrance of the next rapid.

The swim took everything, and I mean everything, I had and I don't think I have ever been so beat in my life. I lay there for several minutes in the freezing water, too weak to get out. I finally noticed I was dizzy and shaking and I started to worry that I might pass out in the water. I stood up and staggered over the slippery river rocks to shore.

I looked back for the kayak and paddle. They were nowhere to be seen. Normally I would have been distraught to lose so many thousands of dollars' worth of gear but all I could think about was survival. I could see some Tibetan houses upstream and headed for them. As I walked I could hear my breathing was short and laboured and my lungs felt like they were on fire. I was no longer shaking. I had hypothermia. I was so tired that I actually considered lying down to sleep, which, with darkness closing in, would probably have been fatal. Then I considered crawling into the space blanket I carried, along with the satellite phone and first-aid kit in my dry top and personal flotation device. Sense got the better of me and I pushed on towards the mud-walled houses.

I made my way up to a big old Tibetan house and knocked heavily at the door. No response. I wondered if I had the energy to make it to the next house when a sweet, old Tibetan granny opened the door. She nearly fell over at the sight of a foreigner wearing a neoprene skull cap, helmet, dry clothes, PFD and suffering a considerable bout of hypothermia leaning against her doorframe. In true

Tibetan style she had me warming by a fire and sipping yak butter tea in no time. It was the best cuppa I have ever had and I don't even really like yak butter tea! Dry clothes and blankets appeared and food was heated. I was very lucky to be so close to help.

As I undressed to change into the dry clothes, I remember the look on the granny's face, who insisted I called her 'Amma' (Mother), when I pulled my dry pants off. About three litres of water had seeped into my pants and had been trapped around my ankles by the tight rubber gaskets designed to keep the water out. As the liquid flooded across the cement floor of her living room she looked at me quizzically and I'm sure if she could speak English she would have said, 'No wonder you're so cold, why don't you carry your water in a bottle like us Tibetans?' A little later, while Amma was upstairs tending to something, her husband wandered in—from the look on his face I could tell he didn't quite know what to think when he saw a foreigner dressed in his clothes warming by the stove and I certainly didn't know how to explain. Fortunately Amma rushed down the stairs and set things straight while a bemused looking 'Appa' took it all in with a relaxed smile which seemed to be his constant trademark.

After warming by the fire for two hours and eating a delicious broth of lamb and noodles, I called Yuta and Mum to let them know I had made it out of Tibet, that I'd had a little mishap but everything was all right. Despite being physically exhausted from nine days of extreme physical exertion, not to mention a near-death experience, I hardly managed to sleep. My mind was filled with memories of people, places and faces of my life and the events of the past few days. I felt extremely grateful to be alive. In several intense lessons, the gorges of Tibet had taught more about the fragility of my own existence and the value of being alive than all of my previous adventures combined. Navigating the Mekong gorges of the Kham had been without doubt one of the most challenging, dangerous and rewarding experiences of my life. I have never experienced another environment more hostile or unforgiving nor more ruggedly magnificent. I decided to change my code name of the stretch from the 'Mekong gorges of Tibet' to 'The back of beyond'.

I heard someone walk up to the room I was in, which was situated on the roof of the three-storey dwelling. I pretended to be asleep so as not to worry anyone and felt Amma tucking me into bed, making sure I was fully covered with thick rugs before leaving a single candle in the room and saying a little prayer. It was so sweet. Such an adorable lady, and I felt embarrassed for having barged in on her life so desperately and for spilling water across her living room floor.

I awoke at 9 a.m. to the sound of a passing truck. Being next to a road after losing all my gear was a nice stroke of luck as it made hitching a ride toward Zongjian easy. I was treated to a broth of noodles and some yak butter tea before heading upstairs to pack my gear, which had been left out to dry. Before long a tiny mini-van with go-cart sized wheels and a mixed bunch of Tibetans and Chinese crammed inside pulled up in front of Amma's house. Unfortunately Amma had wandered off to tend her vegetable garden and I didn't get the chance to say goodbye, but I knew I would be back within a few days to pick up the descent where I had left off, as soon as I could locate a kayak to paddle! I left a small tip with her husband as a thank you and hopped in the ride bound for Zongjian.

The chances of finding the kayak and equipment were slim, to say the least. Along the Lancang Jiang there are few natural eddies for floating objects such as a kayak to get stuck in, and with the average flow rate of around six to ten kilometres per hour the kayak could theoretically have been anywhere within one hundred kilometres by the time I hopped into the van. I managed to convince one of the passengers to let me sit at the right window for a clear view of the river, even though much of it wouldn't be visible from the road, and later moved to the left side as the road crossed a bridge.

Throughout the road trip I anxiously scanned the river at every opportunity while trying not to get my hopes up.

I had a replacement set of all the gear ready for such a situation but what could not be replaced were the hundreds of photos and dozens of GPS readings I had jotted down throughout the TAR Mekong. Because I was the first person to travel through the gorges I knew it was necessary to prove the descent, through more than just words. I had taken over two hundred photos and recorded the GPS locations of dozens of notable features, such as suspension bridges, the villages I had stayed at, distinct rapids and so on. Along with the names of locals I met and hung out with in the previously unexplored section of the TAR, these records were important for providing clear physical proof of the descent. Without the physical proof I would need to wait until the next person went down the gorges to verify my descriptions. With other people keen to be first down the Mekong I feared they might request verifiable proof that I had descended the area, and that physical proof I no longer had.

As we drove along the bumpy dirt road the chances of finding the boat seemed to diminish with each passing kilometre. More than forty kilometres downstream from where I took that eventful swim I spotted a tiny red dot on some rocks above a set of rapids about one kilometre downstream and some two hundred metres below us in the base of the valley. I asked the driver to stop the van and to my utter delight found the boat. I could hardly believe my luck.

Through sign language and my thirty-word Kham vocabulary I managed to convince a red sash-wearing Kham gentleman to accompany me down to the river and help to retrieve the boat. His superior trekking skills on the dangerously steep scree slope became apparent as he took off, reaching the kayak a couple of minutes ahead of me.

I had been mentally preparing myself to discover that a significant portion of the gear had been ripped out during the kayak's tumultuous journey through dozens of rapids, but to my surprise found that everything, except my wool sponge and the wayward paddle, was still tied in. Closer inspection revealed that everything was completely waterlogged, including my cameras and notes, so I had to wait and see what could be salvaged. An exhausting ninety-minute struggle up the slope with the kayak, with my Tibetan helper lugging most of the bags, took us back to the road.

I tipped the gold-toothed porter for his efforts and tried unsuccessfully to persuade the driver to tie the kayak onto the roof of the van. I was left stranded by the roadside to wait for more suitable transport. I pulled all the gear out of the bags and spread it out on the rocks to catch some sun while I waited. A large bus dustily came into view from the direction of Tibet and drove me the rest of the way to the county capital of Deqen, the prefecture capital of 'Shangri-la' located high on a mountain overlooking the Lancang Jiang, just south of the TAR/Yunnan border. I hired a small car in Deqen for the seven-hour drive to Zongjian and arrived at midnight. Yuta and Brian had been delayed by a day and a half because of difficult travel connections. All my rushing had been in vain.

Both cameras were ruined but I took great care in trying to dry out the rolls of film in the darkness of my hotel room cupboard. I thoroughly enjoyed a long, loooong shower, my first in two weeks in the comfort of the hotel room, and slept like a baby on the first soft bed I had been in for months. After two American breakfasts at a little place called the Tibetan Café it was time to go and face my demons in the form of Lara and James. They still had several thousand dollars' worth of project equipment that had come back to Zongjian with the Frenchmen and I needed some of it to continue the expedition with Brian.

I had contacted them by an email, informing them that I would be passing through Zongjian to pick up the gear while waiting for the

Chengdu authorities to finalise the TAR permit. To keep up the pretence of making them believe that I hadn't travelled through the 'restricted' part of Tibet without the permit in hand, I had to get rid of the evidence of a gruelling nine days spent in the gorges. I spent half an hour in the bathroom pulling away the peeling skin from my nose, lips and fingers, the signs of prolonged exposure to the elements that would not match up with the bus rides and permit meetings they would assume I'd been involved with.

They presented me with a new list of demands, feeling that they were owed significant amounts of money due to the huge contributions they had made to the project. From my perspective their contributions had been overwhelmingly detrimental to the project's goals in both financial and practical terms, and it seemed quite absurd that they felt the project owed them anything. When I asked where the project equipment that had been left in their care was, I was told that a lot of it was being kept 'somewhere safe' until the financial issues were resolved.

It wasn't long into the discussions before things blew up and Lara stormed out. Brian and I still needed some of that equipment and the spare kayak actually belonged to a friend of mine so I continued to discuss things with James to see if we could come to some kind of resolution. James and I drafted a basic agreement whereby they would return all project equipment, photos, articles and contacts gathered during their paid employment for a further fixed amount of cash.

When it was almost time to sign the agreement Lara, who had returned by now, again changed the nature of her demands. I quite happily walked away from these negotiations. James was somewhat more cooperative and I continued to discuss terms with him but as time wore on I came to the conclusion that walking away and cutting the project's losses was going to be the wisest decision. Brian and I just had to make do with the equipment we had and I needed to buy my friend a new kayak as soon as I could scrape the cash together.

Meeting Yuta and Brian at the airport was a huge relief. After driving around Zongjian for nearly two hours and making ten hotel stops we had found only one available room. By this time Yuta and I were genuinely struggling to control our overwhelming need for some intimacy. Before the tension between Yuta and me got any worse, we found another room that happened to be in a brothel. A perturbed looking Brian was promptly dropped off at reception with a couple of giggling Chinese girls who appeared most willing to provide him with a personal tour of the residence. My profuse apologies and declaration that it would only be for a night offered little comfort as Brian cringed, trying to explain to the girls that he was only there for a bed. I jogged back to the car and to the girl I had waited for, what felt like, an eternity to see.

The next day Yuta and I put my now dried rolls of film into the shop. Out of the five rolls and sixty digital photos I shot, only one roll of film and fifteen digital photos were not destroyed by being water-logged. Fortunately, images of key landmarks and people I stayed with in the heart of the gorges, which could verify me paddling through the virgin sections of the river, had survived. Along with the GPS coordinates, this meant I had the evidence to prove I had made the descent as planned. However, it was still hard not to be disappointed after losing so many photos of such a dramatic region of the TAR. I reasoned that the Mekong wanted to keep some of its most amazing sights in her most turbulent inner sanctums a secret from the outside world for a little while longer yet.

I had dropped around four kilograms of weight on the trek to the source and about seven hundred grams a day slogging through the gorges. By the time I made it to Zongjian I had shed around thirteen per cent of my total body weight since starting the expedition. During the three days' R and R in Zongjian I worked hard to put some of it back on at the local barbecue houses. Besides eating and catching up with Yuta I met an enthusiastic local lad called Young, who agreed to be our translator through northern Yunnan, and a Tibetan man, known as Mr Hands because he sported an immaculate pair of white gloves every time he got behind the wheel, who became our driver. Mr Hands was a cool character who rarely found anything not worthy of a laugh and his favourite pastime was having a chat. It was a passion he pursued vigorously in Chinese with Brian and me, even though we usually had no idea what he was talking about.

Yuta, Brian, Young, Mr Hands and I squeezed into the Toyota four-wheel drive and began the journey back towards the Tibet Autonomous Region border, towards Amma's house where my descent had come to an abrupt halt just days earlier. The drive from Zongjian to the Mekong near Deqen is magnificent. After crossing the Yangtze Valley we steadily gained altitude through thick stands of old growth pine in the Three Parallel Rivers protected area. This World Heritage-listed site is located in the mountainous area in northwest Yunnan province and features sections of the upper reaches of three great rivers of Asia—the Yangtze, the Mekong and the Salween. These rivers run parallel with one another, north to south, through steep gorges which in places are three thousand metres deep and are bordered by glaciated peaks more than six thousand metres high. We then drove above the tree line and over a four thousand two hundred-metre pass into the Mekong Valley. The snow-capped Tibetan spiritual mountain of Kawakarpo, with a height of over six thousand seven hundred and forty metres, could be seen through the clouds on the opposite side of the immense valley. Below us the Mekong raged through canyons as deep as three thousand metres.

We spent the evening in the town of Deqen. Early next morning we headed off to the same place I had taken a life-threatening swim only a week before. The first priority, before challenging that rapid again, was to pop in and give a special thanks to the lovely old couple who had taken me in during my hour of need.

Amma was delighted to see me safe and sound, and I greeted her with a gift of chocolate bars, something she had never tried before. We had a long chat, translated via Young, over a pot of yak butter tea, and we eventually invited the couple to come and watch me re-challenge the rapid. As we approached the drop I noticed that the river had risen several feet over the week and the hole that had almost thrashed me into oblivion was now semi-flushed out—now it was a huge crashing wave and could be run right down the middle.

When I tackled the rapid, Amma had obviously never seen someone put themselves in such great and seemingly pointless danger. She was convinced I was going to die. I had no idea that she would be so distraught. As I paddled down towards the rapid completely unaware of her concern Brian filmed her reaction from the river ride. Amma was frantically praying for my salvation and crying when the wave violently slammed down on me, tearing off my helmet and flipping me before I casually rolled up. It was really no big deal down on the water and I quite enjoyed the experience of bashing through such a large crashing wave. I spotted her seventy-two-year-old husband, Appa, running along the bank in an attempt to rescue me. I eddied out and tried to explain through sign language that I was fine and actually having a good time so there was nothing to worry about. It wasn't until the end of the day's paddling that Brian showed me the footage and I realised how distraught the old couple had been.

Brian and I paddled downstream through a succession of class III and IV rapids. It felt good to have a paddle buddy after tackling so many dangerous rapids solo. We encountered one particularly chunky class V that managed to flip both of us at exactly the same place. We called it 'double-take'. The next day, leaving us with the ground support of Mr Hands and Young, Yuta headed back to Vientiane to get on with coordinating project matters.

We had now descended into the heart of the huge one million seven hundred-hectare, three-parallel rivers World Heritage site. This incredible area is also one of the most diverse bio-realms on the planet. The site is believed to be the world's most biologically diverse temperate zone, making it one of the world's most important areas in terms of conservation.

We pulled up for the day in a small village above a gorge containing a ferocious class V rapid. As we scouted the run from above, the landslide to river right began periodically slipping into the rapid as the rising current ate away at its base. Although it looked a bit sketchy we decided that a challenging 'line' (safe path through the rapid) that skirted below the avalanche would be runable, as long as the avalanche did not slip into the river on top of us as we passed underneath it. We decided to take advantage of the clear weather, which provided nice light for filming—the run would have to wait until after our detour to the glaciers of Kawakarpo mountain.

Kawakarpo lies in the heart of the Hengduan mountain range which contains dozens of peaks over six thousand metres. The mountains are a dominant feature of a protected area containing the greatest biodiversity of all the protected areas of China. Huge glaciers feed steep creeks in the area, which in turn carve out steep-sided valleys and the occasional piece of flat land inhabited by Tibetan and Naxi villagers. We decided to head out on foot to inspect Minyong, one of the southernmost glaciers in the northern hemisphere, located on the slopes of Kawakarpo.

When we approached Minyong Glacier the next day we were surprised to see just how fast it was melting. Like a block of ice in the desert, the glacier dripped and dribbled from every corner as shards of ice could be heard snapping off and falling into the many crevasses below. As we looked on, two avalanches took place only a couple of hundred metres from where we stood. The effects of global warming in the Himalaya are very real. Most glaciers are retreating dramatically and it seems only a matter of time before many disappear. After three days of exploring the forests, glaciers and temples of Kawakarpo we returned to the Mekong to set off from the gorge rapid.

It became apparent that the rising waters and eroding avalanche had combined to make the rapid even more treacherous. A long class IV bend of powerful boils and whirlpools made staying on the right line extremely difficult. Heavy erosion of the avalanche had compromised the previous line we had chosen to navigate, and there was only one viable route left—to bash through an enormous hole that took up over half of the river. From our vantage point on the gorge wall some fifty metres above the rapid, we guessed that the hole would probably flush a kayaker through. But we both knew that accurately assessing the vertical height and backwash of the hole, that is its ability to stop and recirculate a kayaker, from that far above was about the equivalent of gauging a person's height and body shape looking down at them from the top of a ten-storey building.

After analysing it for a long time, and taking into account the long swim I took near Amma's house, Brian and I decided not to run the drop. We skirted around the rapid for over a kilometre to the nearest put-in point on the river. This portage was the largest one we did in China. We arranged to meet Mr Hands and Young at a village called Latsaa Jiang, around forty kilometres downstream. We told them that we expected to arrive that afternoon but not to get worried if we didn't arrive on time as progress was always difficult to predict. If we didn't arrive in the afternoon they would simply need to hang around until the next day.

Brian and I continued down through lots of fun but manageable sections until we came to one of the most violent rapids in Yunnan at times of high water, a drop we called 'full stop'. As with many of the other more difficult drops, full stop was located in a sheer-sided gorge, which was caused by an avalanche and could not be scouted properly.

Full stop had several unusual features. Just downstream of the main drop the gorge was so constricted that an immense bottleneck occurred, backing up the water and causing a unique level of chaos. Massive amounts of flow were thrust into relatively stationary sections of water creating huge holes, whirlpools and 'eddy lines' (points where two currents of different speeds converge with one another; the friction from the two currents is what typically causes whirlpools and strong downward water circulations) that would appear then disappear at random along a two hundred-metre length. With the rapid constantly changing it was impossible to pick a line. Attempting to paddle through it looked extremely risky and neither of us wanted to do it. Along both sides of the main channel were extremely powerful eddies and the one on the left was so large and powerful that it behaved more like an oversized whirlpool. If I could use the relatively calm current along the eddy's right edge to sweep downstream for sixty metres past the worst of the bottleneck, then I hoped to use the whirlpool's momentum to bash back into the mainstream, effectively bypassing the most dangerous section.

Negotiating the main drop before the whirlpool consisted of a risky class V move from right to left above the most violent section. If this particular move wasn't executed perfectly, the line would inevitably place me in the dire straits of the main channel. This was a serious undertaking. Brian filmed from the base of an avalanche as I cut across the top section of the rapid with a narrow safety margin, before plopping into the whirlpool leg as planned. But what I initially thought was a surging sanctuary turned into a dangerous trap.

From higher ground, where we had initially scouted the rapid, it looked as though the solution to getting through would be to use the downstream momentum of the whirlpool. Within the whirlpool, however, things looked quite different. The downstream end of the whirlpool was backed up due to the bottleneck to create a level of 'compression' (too much water squashed into a confined space with nowhere to go), the likes of which I had never seen. The result was that the downstream end of the eddy sat one and a half metres higher than the upstream end, making it look impossible to break out of as planned.

I looked back to where Brian was filming and getting back to that point didn't seem viable either. It occurred to me that I could be stuck in the immense whirlpool. Downstream looked like the best bet. I gave it five bursts to try to force my way out of the whirlpool downstream, but each time I was thrust back by large waves that were erratically flowing into and across the prison of water.

After two attempts to get out on the upstream side of the eddy I just made it to land and realised that luck had been on my side. The last resort would have been to launch myself into the violence of the mainstream, which was dangerous to say the least and I was feeling tired from battling the whirlpool already. This option would have had a very uncertain outcome.

Eventually Brian took to the river in his kayak and tried for several minutes to break out of the whirlpool eddy on the down-stream end but was eventually forced to concede it couldn't be done. We agreed it was too dangerous to run down the middle so the only option left was to portage it.

For three hours we searched for climbing routes out of the near sheer-sided section of canyon and for a while it looked like we were trapped. Eventually we spotted an avalanche about six hundred metres upstream and by pure chance there was a succession of eddies on river left that would possibly allow us to paddle and portage upstream over sharp rocks and boulders until we could ferry across to the escape avalanche. It worked and was a very lucky break. As far as we could see there were no other ways out of the gorge with our kayaks. If the avalanche plan failed we would have been forced to leave our kayaks there and make a dangerous near vertical climb over a four thousand-metre pass, which would have taken several days. The lucky outcome still included a gruelling two-hour climb up the avalanche as we hauled the kayaks up one by one with our rescue throw rope.

We checked out the maps while we caught our breath and noted that we were about ten kilometres south of the county capital of Deqen and were about to enter another significant roadless stretch of gorges that were even more difficult to escape than the ones we were in already. Brian decided it was all getting a bit too sketchy due to the risk of encountering an unportagable class VI rapid in a similar type of gorge. He decided to bypass the next section of river by car, leaving me to go on alone. After around an hour of waiting by the roadside with Brian I flagged down the first vehicle that passed by, a small van. I tried to convince the driver to take Brian to Latsaa Jiang, where Young and Mr Hands were waiting with the support vehicle, but with the use of our maps, a lot of miming and creative communications we eventually came to understand that the only way to drive to that town was to backtrack upstream about two hours on bad roads, cross a bridge spanning the river then drive for two hours up to Deqen before driving over several large mountain passes and finally descending down to Latsaa Jiang, a seven-hour drive in all, and this driver wouldn't be the one to take us. If I didn't already know that there were very few roads along the next stretch of river I probably wouldn't have believed it could take seven hours to go just eighteen kilometres, but looking at our maps it actually made sense.

While Brian stayed with the kayaks I hitched a ride to a village about two kilometres downstream, where I spotted a car parked outside one of the stone-walled houses. Within two hours Brian was on his way by car to Latsaa Jiang and I was putting back on the river about eight hundred metres below the whirlpool rapid.

We agreed to rendezvous the next day at the Latsaa Jiang bridge where Mr Hands and Young would already be waiting. I arrived at the bridge late that afternoon after an uneventful run through several gorges that did not contain large rapids. Mr Hands, Young and Brian were nowhere to be seen and the village, which on our map should have been down by the river, was actually high up on a ridge. I checked and rechecked my location using the global positioning system, which showed my location on the map as already being at the town of Latsaa Jiang. It became clear that the map was wrong. Assuming they would be waiting in the village, which I could see up on the hill, I started climbing the steep-sided valley towards the village at around 6.30 p.m. Avalanches blocked my path several times and what started out as a well-trodden track eventually disintegrated into goat trails interspersed with avalanches. By 8.30 p.m. I had already backtracked twice to find alternative routes, acutely aware that darkness was closing in.

At one point I spotted a goat trail that looked like a shortcut up to a path and began climbing. The trail got steeper and steeper until I could hardly believe goats could climb such a track. Eventually it simply petered out—even the mountain goats must have realised it was dangerous. Night was descending and because I expected to be in the village before dark I had not brought any rain protection to camp out in. Heading back down the trail would have left me wandering around the precipitous paths at night. Above me to the left was an avalanche that blocked my progress but thirty metres beyond it I saw what appeared to be a path built for humans that would get me to the village within half an hour or so.

I decided to cross the avalanche. I used my paddle to check out the stability of the footing and in the process dislodged a bunch of scree that scuttled and rolled down the rill for fifty metres before tumbling over a cliff towards the bottom of the valley. Not a nice spot to take a stroll. I started to do some landscaping, shovelling scree with my paddle to create a somewhat stable platform. As I stepped onto it my heart raced and I prepared to launch myself back onto the rocks if it all started to slip. There was the rustle of some scree sliding down and a few fist-sized rocks tumbling towards the valley floor, but it held.

I started on the next foothold and the next, and some twenty minutes later I was about two-thirds across the avalanche. As I started to transfer my weight onto a new footing the earth around me started to slowly slide towards the cliff. I knew that without proper purchase on the ground below me, springing towards the edge would be fruitless and would most likely increase the speed of my fall. I dug in my heels and concentrated on going feet-first over the edge of the cliff in the hope of making a semi controlled ski down the rest of the slope, about two hundred metres towards the valley floor.

Because the rill was mainly made up of scree, without many large boulders, I thought I could probably survive skiing and tumbling down its face. The problem was the cliff. On the way up I wasn't planning on skiing before sunset so I didn't take note of the cliff's height—was it five or forty metres? It was a slow and surreal moment and after sliding around seventy centimetres over the space of four seconds I stopped as the dislodged rocks and rubble continued tumbling down towards and over the cliff. I could hear the larger rocks tumbling for a further ten seconds or so after the cliff but I still couldn't gauge the size of the freefall.

It was a truly terrifying moment and I sat there for about thirty seconds trying not to breathe before pulling myself back together. I slowly stood and gingerly shovelled the scree for my next step. Every cell of my being was focused on shovelling the dirt in front of me while not changing the pressure of my feet on the slope. Silently I cursed myself for choosing to cross the avalanche. The intensity of the next step, as I slowly moved the weight from my right foot and moved it over to my left towards the next footing, was something else. I was acutely aware of the movement of every piece of gravel and dirt that was dislodged as I slowly transferred my weight. It was another twenty minutes of shovelling and stepping before I was finally on firm ground.

I reached the village in complete darkness an hour later and scared the hell out of a few Tibetans by asking them if there were any foreigners in the village. My badly constructed Kham sentences were only partially understood because the Kham dialect I had been practising and the Zongjian dialect spoken in the village were quite different. Eventually my limited vocabulary convinced an old man that I was not a yeti coming in from the cold and that my attempts at communicating would provide some light entertainment for the family. He invited me into a large pinewood and mud-walled home. The guys weren't in the village and as it turned out the map was completely wrong, indicating that a road came to the village when no such road existed. I was exhausted and after eating some stew that appeared on the table with some yak butter tea I fell asleep on the family couch watching the kids of the house reading stories to one another from a small comic book. By ten the next morning, still unable to phone Brian, I decided to push on alone.

I came to a section referred to as 'moon gorge'. The steep-sided valleys in the area were home to a surprising quantity of prickly pear cacti that seemed to be the only plant capable of surviving the desert-like environment. I was familiar with the plant from Australia and checked some of them for the red edible fruits that I had enjoyed as a kid, but they weren't in season. It seemed surreal to have cacti growing in such a cold place. As soon as I entered moon gorge I immediately had flashbacks to the hellacious sections I faced in the TAR. It was a run that Alan and I had identified on our first survey to China nearly a year earlier as being potentially one of the most risky rapids in Yunnan, due to the fact that it was not possible to scout it fully before entering the gorge.

Before I entered the gorge I climbed to a village and managed to hitch a ride on rough dirt roads to the downstream side of the gorge to check the viability of the final rapid of the run, which had even looked challenging at lower water levels on the earlier 2003 scout. After a long walk along mountain trails I was able to ascertain that the final rapid would be challenging yet runable. I returned to the upstream side of the canyon.

As I entered the sheer-sided section, a distinct shiver ran down my spine. I was entering another point of no return, not knowing exactly what might lie around the next corner. The only consolation was that the section continued only for a couple of kilometres instead of days. I proceeded as cautiously as possible down a succession of class III to IV rapids until I could see the water building up at the corner of the gorge. I spotted an eddy on river right and made for it to inspect what was to come.

I dragged my kayak up on a jagged boulder and took a look down the river. 'Nothing too difficult,' I thought to myself. I heard two 'plops' in the river and then a rock the size of a yo-yo bounced heavily off a boulder and into the river just seven metres from where I stood. They were falling from far above me, perhaps four hundred metres. The gorge was so steep and sheer-sided that I could not tell which side they fell from. It didn't matter. It was time to get out of there.

Fearing an avalanche I quickly climbed into my kayak and seal-launched, half sideways, into the river. As I paddled my legs were getting wet. My first thought was that my spray skirt was not clipped on properly but a quick check revealed that it was. With each stroke through the next class III rapid the boat was becoming heavier with water and I made my way to the nearest eddy. I inspected the boat to find a gash some twelve centimetres long had been torn into the hull of the kayak by the jagged boulder I had launched off. I looked up and down the gorge for a way to trek out. No chance!

I had to mend the kayak as best I could. Using duct tape and a dry bag I managed to plug the hole enough to continue, although some water still seeped in. The gorge had a nasty class V rapid right at the end and the sight of the mist shooting up from above was intimidating, but it turned out to be all bark and no bite. It was a gruelling three and a half hour hike up to the road with my kayak. Two full days had passed since I had been in contact with Brian and the guys so I decided to track them down before going any further. I arrived in a small village by nightfall. On the third day since I had set out on my own I managed to get hold of the guys by phone and they came to pick me up.

They had been waiting at a village twenty kilometres downstream from where we originally agreed to meet. Without a GPS to get a fixed position they had used only the village name, which left them waiting at the village of Lancang Jiang while I nearly took an unplanned ski ride to oblivion to get to the original meeting village of Latsaa Jiang. Both village names sound almost identical when spoken with a Chinese accent but Brian and I still managed to squarely blame each other for the mistake. Back in Lancang Jiang we set about patching the hole in the kayak, using sixteen tubes of epoxy resin, thirty-six screws bought at a local shop plus a length of truck inner tube and a piece of scrap metal found on the roadside. The resin and inner tube were placed over the slit, followed by the screwing down of the scrap metal over the top to make a permanent seal. When we filled the kayak with water to test the seal to our surprise nothing leaked. With only six hundred kilometres of whitewater left in Yunnan I decided to put my handyman skills to the test and paddle the ailing kayak through the rest of China.

The one hundred and twenty-kilometre stretch below Latsaa Jiang was one of the major sections that had still not been navigated and unknown to us it contained one of the biggest rapids we encountered in all of Yunnan, a ginormous class V through a tight gorge. Brian went down it first with a plan to paddle to the edge near the middle of the rapid so that he could get out of his kayak to film me making the run from a good angle. Halfway through the rapid I watched him paddle hard for the edge as planned but the incredibly powerful surges launched him and his kayak around the eddy like a tiny cork. One moment he would be surging ten metres from right to left, the next he would get sucked violently towards the middle of the river then just as suddenly a huge wave would rear up and crash him towards the shore. It was complete chaos. He quickly reached the conclusion that the best thing to do was get the hell out of there. He paddled frantically to get back into the downstream current and as that current caught his hull he quickly disappeared over the top of a string of waves exceeding five metres in height.

I waited to give Brian time to get out of his kayak at the base of the rapid and set up the camera before paddling into the gorge. I decided to take a more central run than Brian to get some good footage for the documentary and proceeded down the middle into the roughest section of the rapid . . . and got the shit kicked out of me. From the time I entered the mid section of the rapid, I was bashed by a series of massive waves that rained down on me from all directions to such a degree that for a few seconds I had no idea which way was up or down, yet somehow I stayed upright and found I had been surged to the left of the run.

Brian flagged me down so I paddled over to chat with him. 'Shit man, I missed the first part of that, I wasn't ready for ya. That looked awesome, man. Carry your boat back up there and do it again, I'll get a closer angle.' My response, as the adrenaline continued to surge through my body and my pride recovered from a thorough thrashing, was pretty concise.

'There's no fucking way I'm doing that god damn !!#@!!#% rapid again.' With that settled we were soon on our way.

With each passing day the waters of the Mekong rose significantly. We paddled past the snow-capped mountains south of Kawakarpo for another three days and as suddenly as a window can be opened we entered a new climatic realm. One moment a brisk temperate breeze off the high Himalaya chilled our faces and hands, the next a humid and significantly heavier type of warm air engulfed us. The temperature rose by ten degrees Celsius and from that day on we wore shorts, T-shirts and splash tops instead of thermal underwear, dry suits and layers.

That same afternoon, for the first time in many weeks, I saw a significant horizon line come into view instead of another high string of mountain peaks. I yelled out to Brian, 'Say goodbye to the Himalaya!' The eroded and steep-sided valleys that characterised so much of the Tibetan region were replaced by lush green hills and rice terraces. As the terrain changed so did the architecture and cultural demography. From predominantly Tibetan, Naxi and Lisu ethnic groups we passed into the realm of Bai, Yi and Han rice terrace farmers.

In the southernmost reaches of the Tibetan realm we stopped to visit a peculiar historical site, a Catholic church built in the late 1800s in the Mekong riverside village of Cizhong. Set slightly back from the river on a gently rising hill, Cizhong stands in a glorious valley of bright green fields of barley, corn and vineyards used to create China's most famous wines. The church is sur-rounded by a traditional Tibetan village that, with the exception of some satellite dishes and powerlines, could be straight out of the eighteenth century. Nearly one hundred and fifty years ago priests from the foreign missions of Paris made their way onto the Tibetan uplands, eager to spread their gospel to what they considered a benighted land. They soon found the local people difficult to convert and there was strong resistance from within the Buddhist establishment.

In 1905 the church was destroyed and two priests murdered in an insurrection. Nevertheless, the church was rebuilt but the hostility towards what it represented persisted for decades. The final blow came in 1952 when the advancing communists evicted the last foreigners. Today many villagers from the area are still said to visit the church for mass on Sundays. What I found most interesting while wandering the grounds were the ceiling tiles and walls that were decorated with brightly painted yin-and-yang symbols of Taoism, the crosses of Christianity and the lotus blossoms found in Buddhist iconography. It was the first time I had seen the iconography of the two major philosophies of the east so openly juxtaposed with the iconography of Christianity. I had visited many churches in Indian areas of central America, and some within Indochina, where the locals were forced to incorporate their traditional iconography in far more discreet ways to avoid reprisals from the right-wing religious establishment. So it was slightly refreshing to see that it was not always like that in the nineteenth century.

Brian and I also noticed some recently created posters that we could only assume were created by foreign churches as gifts to their Tibetan brethren. They depicted priests and angels helping to pluck people out of the fires of hell and elevate them to a heavenly paradise. A nice enough gesture but they possessed a rather disturbing characteristic; all of the angels and priests were Caucasian and all of the people being helped out of, or burning in, hell were Asian. Going by the condescending paraphernalia it left us with little doubt as to why conversion to Christianity was scarce in the area.

The next two days of paddling south from Cizhong took us into some peculiar landscapes, where pine trees grew amongst banana palms and bamboo, before we finally arrived at the Yongping bridge, the approximate halfway point of our descent through the province of Yunnan. I had descended approximately one thousand three hundred kilometres from the source and approximately seven hundred kilometres of river lay between us and the first of the Mekong's downstream nations, Burma. From the bridge, Mr Hands and Young needed to head back to the cooler climates of Zongjian. Brian and I decided to join them in order to film Zongjian's annual horse racing festival for the documentary. As we drove north, Mr Hands crashed his car for the second time in a week. The first time he crashed into a large rock while practising his mandatory twenty-three point U-turn on a mountain pass and the other was with a sedan. His reaction on both counts was the same. He would inevitably blame the other party before laughing about the incident.

We arrived in Dali, a city set on the banks of the beautiful Lake Erhai, a major catchment of the upper Mekong. The site marked the furthest point reached by the longest recorded manpowered journey along the Mekong River prior to 2004.

In the nineteenth century, amid speculation that the Mekong might provide a lucrative trade route into southern China, Commander Doudart de Lagrée was asked by French colonial authorities in Saigon to explore the river to the furthest extent possible, with the primary goals of locating the river's source and assessing the commercial opportunities that existed along its course. The explorers departed Saigon in 1866. Two years and twenty-four days later the expedition team, by that time led by Francis Garnier, returned to Vietnam from their epic journey carrying Lagrée's mortal remains to be laid to rest in Saigon. Lagrée had succumbed to severe fevers, dysentery and stomach abscesses.

Lagrée's team had collected thousands of pages of meticulous research and mapping data that would forever change the face of what is currently referred to as South-East Asia. The team was the first to travel via the river through the five nations of the lower basin. Although largely forgotten in the twenty-first century, in its day the French Mekong expedition was celebrated as one of the greatest exploratory journeys of the nineteenth century and Francis Garnier, who was promoted to expedition leader after Lagrée's death, received the Royal Geographic Society's Patrons Medal in London.

As testimony to the importance of the expedition at the time, the following year Garnier was one of two people to be presented with another special award at a geographical congress in Antwerp —the other recipient was Sir David Livingstone, the explorer of Africa. The expedition team succeeded in exploring the Mekong River mainstream from the sea to the southern Yunnan town of Jinghong, a river distance of over two thousand seven hundred kilo-metres, slightly more than half of its total length. They trekked to Dali, planning to return to the river one last time towards the end of their quest in 1888. Yet upon getting an audience with the local Mandarin they were informed that they had best skip town before his hospitality ran out and he lopped their heads off. I wondered if the Frenchmen ever thought it would be one hundred and thirty-six years before another person would see more of the river's length by manpower than they did.

10 Yunnan and the king of fat bastards

After spending five days visiting Zongjian we returned by bus to Dali, where we recruited the owner of a guesthouse to provide logistical support by car for the duration of our remaining seven hundred kilometres in China. Brian almost immediately nicknamed the spectacle-wearing Bai (a minority ethnic group centred around the town of Dali in Yunnan) gentleman 'Goldfinger', due presumably to the slightly devious cackle he produced instead of a laugh.

Goldfinger drove us to the Yong Ping bridge and yet again, in our absence, the Mekong had risen several feet. It was now just one and a half metres below the river's natural highwater mark at the Lincang Bridge and it had become a big river by any standards. For a change, we had some idea of what we were in for over the next two hundred and eighty kilometres, due to some accounts left by Earth Science Expeditions, the team led by Pete Winn who made two well-documented first descents on the stretch, half in 1995 and the rest in 1997. In these accounts there were long and detailed descriptions of a rapid called Dragon's Teeth. This particular rapid was formed by a major landslide that occurred in 1988 as a result of two earthquakes, just thirteen minutes apart, both registering over seven on the Richter scale. They caused the northern face of a mountain to collapse into the Lancang Jiang and about fifty thousand tonnes of rock and rubble were flushed downstream, obstructing the entrance to a canyon.

Previous boaters had graded the run as almost off the scale and at lower water levels it had flipped a large percentage of the rafts that dared to attempt it. We worried that with much more water now flushing through the rapid, the section may have turned into a suicide run.

We put back on the river at the same point we had pulled off and soon paddled past the remnants of the old Jihong Bridge that had played an important role with the southern Silk Road and dated from 105 BC. It was China's oldest bridge, probably the world's, until an earthquake destroyed it in 1986.

After encountering various rapids of moderate difficulty throughout the day, I noted a large avalanche scar on river right around the general area we expected to find Dragon's Teeth; as anticipated it was the avalanche scar left by the 1988 earthquake. At the base of the avalanche-scarred mountain, there seemed to be a disproportionately small amount of debris, and it was clear that a lot of it had been flushed downstream.

Over a kilometre before reaching the rapid a roar could be heard and as we rounded a left-hand bend we could see where a lot of the boulders from the avalanche upstream had come to a stop, right at the entrance of a sheer-sided gorge. The horizon line suddenly dropped away and mist rose up from the violence ahead. We eddied out on river right just above the drop to inspect the rapid and to our relief it looked as if it was a challenging yet still viable run. With the light fading fast we decided it was best left until the next day.

Camp was set in the scenic gorge and we settled in for a night under the stars. It was one of the first times that Brian and I really had some time to chill out and catch up. I cooked up a tuna and cheese casserole and over coffee we talked about life at home, the women in our lives and our ambitions for the coming years.

Brian was keen to use the Mekong First Descent to further his budding film career and had just bought a house in Portland, Oregon, after shifting there from Maine with 'a very special lady'. He had such a good time working on the tiger tracking survey/documentary we had both participated in that coming back to South-East Asia was high on his work agenda. My call to him had come at the right time.

Getting along with Brian came easy; his well-timed, dry sense of humour always seemed to hit the spot and neither of us was interested in playing a game of one-upmanship on the river. We took it in turns to go first down the whitewater sections or based the decision of who went first on where the best camera angles were. We were open to each other's suggestions and both of us knew how to roll with the punches if things didn't go to plan. I felt I was working with someone who was right for the type of expedition we were undertaking.

The next morning it was decided that I would go first into Dragon's Teeth. The steep drop of the rapid made it hard to see the preferred line we had chosen, which skirted around some monstrous keeper holes and ledges from upstream, and by the time I crested the lip of the drop I was already five metres off course. Some urgent corrections sent me into the eddy downstream without so much as getting my face splashed by the rough sections. Brian, on the other hand, nailed our planned lead-in perfectly but was suddenly surged several metres to the left, where he was slammed by a large breaking wave and swept rapidly towards a dangerous ledge. Some dramatic paddling ensued and he made it safely to the river right sanctuary. This scene highlighted the level of chaos the river had as it approached peak water levels. Sometimes even when everything was done right you could end up headed for disaster.

The monsoon season was now in full swing and the rainfall mixed with the melting snow and glaciers from Tibet forced ever more water into the valley, which made for some incredibly chaotic conditions. Even when we followed each other, separated by just ten metres on the exact same route through massive rapids with waves over four and a half metres high, we could never predict whose turn it was to get hammered by the waves. We came to realise it was as much up to the river's discretion as our kayaking abilities.

The massive crashing wave trains were a common feature that really made this section a lot of fun. Crashing waves are a phenomenon created by various circumstances but their universal feature is that they rear up considerable volumes of water into the air before reaching a critical mass, where the base of the wave can no longer support its height and volume. Then it all comes crashing down with energetic force.

Essentially these waves look like an ocean wave but have less predictable timing. These river waves build up and crash repeatedly in the same spot hundreds of times per hour. At times, long strings of crashing waves would chaotically roar up in front of us like angry sumo wrestlers daring us to confront them. It was a challenge Brian and I rarely avoided, even if there was an alternative, because their bark is generally worse than their bite.

We called these massive crashing waves 'fat bastards' in honour of the aptly named character from the Austin Powers films. Brian and I would cruise, single file, into the foray of belly-flopping fat bastards and paddle hard up the face of each one to test the wave's timing. With skill and a little luck it was usually possible to avoid the worst of the belly flops. As each fat bastard dropped his guts there was the opportunity to zoom up his chest and catch air off his nose before landing on the back of the wave to face the next threatening bastard. The problem was that every fat bastard had his own timing or, as I prefer to see it, coordination.

Perfect runs through entire strings of fat bastards were not uncommon—neither was encountering those waves that had impeccable coordination. You always knew when a particularly talented fat bastard was about to land one on you. The last thing you see is a wall of water several metres high looming overhead; the world goes quiet for a split second and you can almost hear the fat bastard's degrading chuckle, 'Heh Heh'—BAM! At that precise moment you come to understand the forces involved in having several tonnes of water dumped on your head from a significant height. We called getting slammed, 'spanked'.

The main advantage a kayaker has over the efforts of fat bastards is forward momentum. Yet getting slammed generally strips you of speed so that even the most uncoordinated fat bastards suddenly have a fairly good chance of spanking the unfortunate boater. On a couple of occasions, after being heavily spanked, I would emerge on the arse of the assailant somewhat disorientated yet aggressively paddling towards the next growling bastard, in the knowledge that building up sufficient speed to get over him was my only chance. With my momentum compromised on the upslope, just before reaching the bastard's nose, the kayak would start slipping backwards against the current, down to the bastard's feet where he would take great pride in delivering a crushing belly flop, flushing me, semi-delirious, into the next bastard's path.

Trains of fat bastards were usually followed by extremely powerful sections of whirlpools and boils that often continued for the best part of a kilometre. These posed the most serious risk. The fat bastards had no ability to hold a kayaker or swimmer for long periods and even most of the humongous holes we came across on this section would eventually flush out anyone unfortunate enough to wander into them. The rapid aftermaths had the capacity to hold a swimmer under the surface for up to a minute at a time. Brian and I both agreed that if we came out of our kayaks it would be unlikely that we would emerge from the whirlpool and boil sections in a conscious state. We reassured each other that we would not bail out of our kayaks, but would try to stick reasonably close together through the bigger rapids to make it easier for rescue.

The big water sections of southern Yunnan were not without their risks, but mixing it up with those fat bastards provided Brian and me with more fun than words can explain.

We came to a particularly 'gorgey' section and some of the most challenging rapids on the journey so far. Usually Brian and I didn't even stop to inspect large rapids, being content to just enter in our kayaks together and take the necessary actions on the river. On the more difficult rapids we would pull up for a minute or two and one of us would volunteer to go first. On this day, however, we paddled into a gorge, which had a particularly nasty stretch that was so violent and unpredictable we both stared at it for a long time without really talking. I suspect we were both waiting for the other to volunteer to lead the way.

The problem with the section was that there was literally no reliable paddle route through it because the extreme constriction of the gorge caused the only slightly safe pathway to intermittently merge with a neighbouring section of extreme turmoil. To make matters worse, we couldn't see what lay around the next bend but the speed of the water going around that bend indicated that whatever was there was significant and possibly dangerous. It was a hardcore rapid.

We decided not to film the run so that we could paddle down it simultaneously in readiness to help rescue the other person if he made a mistake. We geared up to take on the gorge—it was one of those runs where all my attention was focused on doing it right.

Under situations of truly extreme stress people have been proven to harness incredible reserves of physical strength that are seemingly beyond that of mere mortals. In the fight for survival mothers have been known to heave cars off their toddlers and men to strangle hungry leopards. For kayakers there is generally less residual evidence of the amazing physical feats that are achieved as they cheat looming death, so some of us have devised a unique system of classifying the energy output during such moments to help people understand just what is involved. Although it is not yet officially recognised in most whitewater manuals, this system is known as the 'sphincter factor' and it operates on a scale of one to ten. A factor of one is where the sphincter is in a normal relaxed state; a factor of five is what a healthy individual might experience while lifting their absolute maximum weight in the clean and jerk. A factor of ten marks the point where mothers reef up cars and where your sphincter is clenched so tight due the near superhuman efforts being exerted that its cells temporarily fuse together. Theoretically, the only known way to remedy a factor ten sphincter situation is to survive the experience and have your friends calmly say 'wow!' to you when you tell them the story. Then those same friends change the subject as you try to portray the profound life-altering experience of cheating death.

Well, I clocked a factor six just paddling towards the start of that rapid. I paddled like hell to keep up momentum and, as I prepared myself to feel the wrath of the most violent section, the waves and surging holes in front of me seemed to part as though it was the biblical Red Sea being held back. It was weird. I went through what was supposed to be a section of extreme violence and barely got splashed.

Brian was forty metres behind me and must have been hoping for the same conditions. As I rounded the bend an absolutely massive rapid came into view with tufts of mist being shot into the air by what could only have been a bunch of truly ginormous holes. I was headed straight for them, the sphincter factor shot to an 8.5 as I spotted the only tiny eddy on river left and paddled for my life. When I reached it I looked downstream and, with a mixture of awe and shock, whispered, 'Jesus Christ!' It was by far the biggest fat bastard I had ever seen.

The steaming king of fat bastards had a face of water approximately nine metres high and was topped with a relatively modest crashing section at its peak of around one and a half metres. I assumed that the boulder creating this beast would also create a house-sized hole on the other side but I couldn't quite see it. I barely had time to say to myself, 'screw that', when out of the corner of my eye Brian came flying around the bend looking a little worse for wear. I could see he wouldn't make the eddy I sat in, yet for a brief moment he fixed on me and paddled several strokes before realising it was hopeless. He was in the middle of the eighty metre-wide river with nowhere to go except into the violence below.

I was terrified as I watched Brian being swept rapidly towards the heaving mess. I could see no safe line from where I sat. 'Oh no,' I whispered, looking on helplessly while trying not to get swept out of my tiny eddy towards the same fate.

Brian knew what he had to do: his only chance was to go in fighting. The vision of what happened next is still as clear for me today. With a straightening stroke he sat high in his cockpit for a moment, to assess the best route, then screamed out, more determined than scared, 'F***!' He leant forward, focused his energies, and dug his paddle in, pulling himself straight towards the king of fat bastards.

I was crapping myself. As Brian closed in I wondered if it were even possible to maintain momentum up a wave that big and deeply feared what might be waiting for him on the other side. From the trough some nine metres below me, Brian went up and up and up its face until he hit the peak slightly right of centre, then he disappeared over the other side. The rapid continued its munching roar.

'Shit!' I yelled while frantically scanning the scene downstream. There was no sign of Brian and I tried to decide whether or not to follow him into the abyss. One of the basic rules of whitewater rescue is that two people dying is much worse than one, so rescuers should not place themselves in imminent danger if there is a high probability of getting into the same circumstance as the victim. I couldn't even tell if there was a victim down there or a very relieved Brian thanking his guardian angel for a lucky break. I looked to my left and saw a cliff that couldn't realistically be scaled without proper climbing equipment. To my right was a section of rapid that looked at least as bad or even worse than the king of fat bastards. I had no choice. I peeled out of the eddy some six seconds after Brian had scalped the fat bastard.

With a sphincter factor approaching nine I paddled down into the trough, aiming for the left side of the fat bastard because I could see a little of what lay downstream. I paddled hard and from the trough at the fat bastard's base it took nine frenzied strokes to climb the belly and bash through the icing on top as I prepared for the worst. To my sphincter's great relief there was nothing life threatening downstream and I could see Brian paddling into a calmer section. We were both still pretty buzzed out when I caught up to him.

'Did you see that shit, man?' Brian's eyes were huge and the residual adrenaline in his system was evident in the quiver of his lip.

'Holy shit! We were lucky, dude,' I said, shaking my head, realising that fate had been kind to us. The energy was electrifying.

Brian adjusted the chinstrap on his helmet. 'That first section gave me the worst spanking. I was upright the whole time but didn't see daylight once.' Using his hands, Brian re-enacted the constant blows of water that rained down on his head. I could fully relate to what he was talking about but I knew that the scalping of the king of fat bastards was a moment we would carry with us for many years to come.

Late that same afternoon the upstream gales returned, bringing back memories of those terrifying moments in Tibet. As we paddled, the afternoon headwinds began to blow up the valley. Before too long they reached an incredible intensity and began launching vast amounts of mist from the river's surface into the air. We had to wear our sunglasses to reduce the sting from the spray on our faces.

We tried to push on but on approaching a large rapid we were awestruck by the sight in front of us. The entire river seemed to turn into one huge hole around seventy metres wide and two hundred metres long. The winds lifted incredible amounts of spray off the tops of waves, and there were so many holes and riffles it was impossible to tell where these features started or finished because everything was white. We paddled like hell for the edge and nearly dropped straight into several powerful holes because of the almost nonexistent level of visibility. It was quite a phenomenal experience.

Now I'm convinced that at least one person I know fully appreciates the phenomena of the Mekong gales.

It took us just two days from the Yong Ping bridge to complete the one hundred and fifty-kilometre stretch that the team led by Pete Winn completed over a ten-day period in 1995. We were probably putting in longer days on the river than the former expedition but our swift progress mainly highlighted the fact that the river was flowing near its natural peak levels. The unbridled mother of water powered us along at an average of around ten kilometres per hour without paddling—she was alive, well and brimming with the energy of an untamed river.

11 Shaky ground and the tidal waves of change

After many days of some of the best whitewater Brian and I had ever encountered, the Mekong suddenly stopped dead and we soon became all too aware why. We were approaching the construction site of the world's soon to be tallest dam, the Xiowan. The Chinese are in the process of planning and constructing a cascade of eight immense dams across the Mekong mainstream in Yunnan, two of which have been completed with another four, including the Xiowan, currently under construction. The Mekong Cascade of Dams constitutes one of the largest engineering feats ever undertaken. To give an impression of the scale, an incredible six hundred and fifty kilometres, or more than thirteen per cent of the Mekong's entire length, will be flooded by these dams by 2017 to create a veritable inland sea above the regions of South-East Asia. The scheme is designed primarily to provide cheap energy for China's booming economy.

By their very nature, these mega dams are controversial. They permanently change the vitality of the river systems upon which they are built, impacting on the extremely complex and delicate natural environments. The Mekong cascade is second only to China's infamous Three Gorges dam project (the world's biggest dam and the world's biggest contemporary construction project) in overall scale.

Brian and I had paddled our way into the biggest man-made monstrosity I have ever seen. As we rounded the bend into the main construction zone we came across an absolutely enormous class VI rapid, created by hundreds of thousands of tonnes of rock and rubble that had been blasted, pushed, shoved and collapsed into the Mekong. It became clear that this direct dumping of boulders into the mainstream was the reason the river was backed up for several kilometres. Both sides of a huge canyon were cemented up to a height of five hundred metres. Thousands of construction workers toiled throughout the site.

We spent a few nervous minutes discussing which side we should try to go down, as getting around the restricted access construction site looked risky on both sides. We both decided on river right after noticing there was an active truck haulage road that offered a portage route if the river became too dangerous. In the distance a siren could be heard, followed by an explosion as a powerful blast of dynamite exploded hundreds of tonnes of rocks into the water on river left. We knew that we had chosen the 'right' side.

About five hundred metres up the gorge wall on river left a large excavator nudged boulders the size of twelve-metre shipping containers into the river. They tumbled, half rolling, half airborne, down the near vertical cliff, crashing into the river below and sending water dozens of metres into the air. It was an awesome sight. As we passed, groups of workers downed their tools to watch a couple of crazy kayakers sneak along the riverbank above the long class VI rapid. We hurried through, concerned that falling rocks or dynamite blasts might put a swift end to the expedition.

The sheer size of the construction site was something that will remain etched in my mind for years to come. In the distance dozens of huge earth-moving vehicles went slowly about their business, looking like miniaturised, two-centimetre high children's toys on the edge of a ten metre-high pile of sand. Hundreds of thousands, possibly millions of tonnes of cement in the form of shot crete (cement mixed with steel shavings for added reinforcement which is then shot through cannons onto unstable ground in an attempt to firm it up) and ground support columns coated the mountain sides in a bold attempt to resist nature's obvious intent to collapse the steep-sided valley in on itself. We had been warned by several Chinese not to take photographs of the site otherwise we might be arrested, so we couldn't get our cameras out. Once we had paddled as far as possible before entering the class VI rapid, we got out of our boats and climbed up piles of boulders to the road, where huge yellow haulage trucks were carting their loads. We shouldered our kayaks and trekked downstream, until a Toyota Landcruiser equipped with yellow flashing lights and roll bars pulled up beside us.

A concerned looking Chinese gentleman jumped out and using sign language asked us to stay put while he pulled out his radio and started informing someone of our position. It seemed almost certain he was calling security so we promptly re-shouldered our kayaks and continued on. When he gestured again that we should stay put until someone arrived I gestured back saying, 'We're full already. We'll eat lunch downstream, but thanks anyway!' With a smile and sense of urgency Brian and I moved on. For once the inability of the locals to communicate in English worked in our favour.

We trekked downstream along the rapid until we could trek no further and asked a diamond drilling team to help us launch into the base of the class VI rapid. I wanted to stay and chat with the workers, as I had done a short stint of exploratory diamond drilling in Australia's outback so I was curious about their work, but I thought better of it as our concerned follower still looked on from above, talking into his walkie-talkie. The friendly and fascinated drillers held my kayak on a rock as I clipped my spray skirt on, then on my signal let go with a group cheer as I slid off the rock, launching three metres into the powerful flow. We paddled down and I caught a large eddy where it was possible to sit and view the construction site for a while. The huge earth-moving machines now looked like ants on the distant side of the immense valley and I thought I could make out the final height markers of the dam that were some three hundred and ten-plus metres above me.

The enormous rapid upstream was in clear view. It was holding back millions of cubic metres of water yet it was created by the hodge-podge dropping and blasting of rocks into a powerful rapid. Theoretically it could burst at any time and, looking at the force of the water flowing down the face of the rapid while physically feeling the boulders bouncing and grinding over each other under the surface, I gave it a fair chance of happening. The nine-metre wall of water that the rubble dam was holding back would pale into insignificance next to the three hundred-metre high, one hundred and seventy-kilometre long wall of water that the Xiowan Dam would soon hold above the valley, or the six hundred and fifty kilometres of inundated area held back by the entire cascade. The thought sent a distinct shiver down my spine.

China has the unwelcomed record of having more dam-related disasters than any other nation on Earth. The meticulously com-piled research and informed work of Patrick McCully in his book, *Silenced Rivers*, points out that since 1950 official figures indicate China has had over three thousand two hundred dam failures, or approximately four per cent of the eighty thousand classified dams in the country. Not surprisingly, the world's most devastating dam bursts took place in China. In 1975 a calamitous series of dam bursts in Henan province claimed approximately two hundred and thirty thousand lives and devastated the lives of millions, although the event was covered up by the authorities until quite recently.

The dubious dam engineering record in China is one ingredient but when you add the extremely unstable seismic conditions of western China into the mix, the wisdom of building the Mekong Cascade of Dams is put into an entirely new light.

Due to the incredibly high incidence of powerful earthquakes, western Yunnan has been designated as an international earthquake prediction experimental test site. North America, including the San Andreas Fault system, is seismically extremely quiet compared to western China, where there have been over one hundred major earthquakes measuring more than seven on the Richter scale in the last century alone.

According to China's State Seismology Bureau, during the last century five hundred and fifty-three thousand people, or around fifty-three per cent of all the world's total earthquake victims, have died in China, which shows just how intense and devastating the earthquakes in the region are. China has around twenty per cent of the world's population and just seven per cent of the planet's land area; the fact that over half of all recorded earthquake-related deaths have occurred in such a tiny portion of our planet's land surface provides a disturbing insight into the risks being taken.

The storage capacity of the Mekong Cascade of Dams project will amount to tens of billions of cubic metres of water. Imagine, if you can, a tidal wave created from a Mekong Cascade collapse. Six hundred and fifty kilometres of reservoir would suddenly flush through a constricted valley, the low-lying flood plains of which are inhabited by over thirty million people below China. A flash flood with a frontal wave hundreds of metres high would wreak a level of devastation, the likes of which humankind has never seen, right through the sovereign nations of South-East Asia to the sea, wiping out the capital cities of Laos and Cambodia (with a combined population of about three million) in a manner even more complete than that witnessed in Aceh, Indonesia, during the Asian tsunami of 2004. A dozen other cities with populations of around one hundred thousand would cease to exist, and the remains of several thousand low lying villages would next be seen in the South China Sea. It is easy to imagine the greatest non-war related man-made disaster in recorded history.

On a personal level I was deeply saddened to see such a great and powerful river subdued into a flat and lifeless lake. It was my great privilege to become the first person to experience the entire upper section of the Mekong. I had been able to study the mother of water's temperament—from its playful folly across the Tibetan Plateau to the violent mood swings in the gorges of southern Tibet and northern Yunnan. I had gaped in awe at kilometre after kilometre of gigantic gorges and tried to calculate how many billions of tonnes of rock and land the river had eroded away along a single one hundred-kilometre stretch.

This motionless body of water that Brian and I faced lacked all of the river's personality I had come to know. From the base of Xiowan the river gradually began springing back to life, yet just as it got to its knees we hit another lifeless section, the seventy kilometre-long Manwan reservoir, a dead still body of water created by the first mega dam ever constructed across the Mekong's mainstream.

While checking my email just before starting the section above the Xiowan and Manwan dams, we read that downstream nations were experiencing a severe drought, with some of the lowest Mekong water levels on record. This was affecting millions of local farmers and fishermen. Yet where we were, just a few hundred kilometres north of Thailand, Laos and Burma, the river was almost at peak flow levels. The unfortunate fact was that despite the drought downstream, a great deal of the available water was being withheld in China to fill the two operational hydro-power dams and to assist Chinese river trade.

After discussing this man-made disaster, Brian and I decided not to paddle the man-made Mekong reservoirs of Yunnan as a sign of protest against the devastating effects the construction of dams across the Mekong mainstream was having on the local people living downstream. Shortly after arriving at the Manwan reservoir we flagged down a passing cargo boat and convinced the driver to ferry us across the reservoir for a fee.

As Brian and I sunbaked on the cargo boat as it cruised across the length of the Manwan I was surprised to see large islands of mud breaking the surface in the middle of the lake, some forty kilometres downstream from where the water initially came to a standstill. Theoretically the reservoir should have been dozens of metres deep at that point. The Manwan's sedimentation rate is clearly phenomenal and the folly of constructing such dams in China's southwest was obvious.

At the base of Manwan Dam the rapids returned. The dam had just started to overflow so the water levels at its base were about the same as above. The whitewater was awesome. Four metre-plus wave trains were followed by enormous whirlpools and boils that would surely render a kayaker unconscious should he bail from his kayak.

One of the most fascinating aspects of paddling through China prior to encountering the dams was the near complete lack of interaction the people had with the river. During the first one thousand eight hundred kilometres on the Chinese leg of the Mekong, I had perhaps seen only about twelve groups of people fishing; none of them were using traditional methods or appeared to be local villagers. Brian and I watched a group of people use a backpack-mounted fertiliser spray gun to squirt cyanide into rock gardens, while another group was throwing sticks of dynamite into the shallows, waiting with a net on the end of a pole to scoop up perhaps five per cent of the dead and dying fish that were not swept away with the strong current. The rest were people who seemed to be from the city, fishing with modern rods. There were no riverside gardens, virtually no boats, only ferries to get people across the river, hardly anyone doing their washing in the river. In most of China people seemed to avoid the Mekong almost completely.

Only in the four hundred kilometres or so before the river leaves China did we start to see locals interacting with the waterway on a daily basis. These people are culturally more closely related to Thai and Lao people than the Han Chinese, China's dominant ethnic group, who tend to call the shots when it comes to mega projects.

It seemed the ultimate injustice that the destructive decisions that have the most widespread implications for the Mekong River, its peoples and the environments it supports, should be made by the bureaucrats from the one Mekong nation that in terms of survival depends on it the least.

12 The Mekong flute master and a new rhythm of life

The cargo boat dropped us at Manwan Dam face, where Goldfinger was waiting for us. He drove us around the dam to a put-in near its base. There we continued our quest but yet again it didn't take long before the river's natural flow was killed by another man-made monolith, the Dashaoshan Dam, the second dam to be completed across the river's mainstream and the second dam to be completed as part of the cascade. By the time we reached it our visas for China were close to expiring, so we were forced to make a long drive to the large town of Baoshan for extensions. It wasn't until I needed some cash after arriving there that I noticed US$600 had been stolen from my bag while we had paddled the previous leg. The missing money threw a real spanner in the works as we didn't have enough money to get us to the major centre of Jinghong in southern Yunnan.

Although we had no physical proof of who stole the money, as it had been stuffed deep into my bag which was then stored in the car while we were running the river to Manwan we had to assume it was someone who had easy access to the bag and the car in our absence. Suddenly our driver's nickname, Goldfinger, took on devious new connotations.

Brian would now be forced to make a long and frustrating multi-day drive to withdraw more funds while I continued paddling solo from the base of the Dashaoshan Dam towards the last substantial Chinese city we would encounter, Jinghong, before leaving the country. Things soon soured as Goldfinger started to feel the heat. We looked around for a new driver yet were unable to get one.

We found ourselves in an uncomfortable situation where we were forced to continue working with a driver whom we were reasonably sure was a thief.

At the base of the Dashaoshan Dam, the Mekong suddenly became an unrecognisable, medium to large volume river instead of the extra large volumes of water we had previously paddled. We estimated that water flow rate below the dam was approximately fifty to seventy per cent less than we had encountered before. At a time when the drought in the lower Mekong was making global headlines we were tempted to contact the media with what we had found out, as access to China's dam sites is strictly controlled so that few, if any, outsiders had information on the flow rates into and out of the dams. Brian and I knew that to do so would be to risk being thrown out of China and the cancellation of the expedition. We decided it was better to wait for a more constructive time.

I paddled off alone from the base of Dashaoshan while Brian drove with Goldfinger. That afternoon I passed under the Lincang bridge, where the 1997 expedition had finished. Below the bridge lay the last previously unnavigated section of the Mekong River in China. The one hundred and twenty-kilometre stretch included two challenging class V rapids and numerous class IV's before the gradient drop gradually started to decrease.

As I continued alone over the next two days I began encountering more and more folk who interacted with the river on a daily basis rather than saw it as an obstacle to be avoided. I was in the process of crossing into the Tai ethnic area of southern Yunnan. The Tai are the ancestors of modern-day Thais and Laos and are as at home on the river in a hardwood *sampan*, a traditional hardwood paddleboat, as they are on dry land. In the mild sections between rapids, children swam and played along the banks while their fathers fished and women came down to the river's edge to wash clothes. I felt at home being back in the realm of river people.

I continued paddling into the late afternoon through terraced valleys of rice that shimmered in the fading light and broad expanses of wild bamboo forest that chimed to the rhythm-less wisps of wind. I chose a wide sandy beach below fields of corn as a suitable camp for the night. Just as I started setting up my tent a man in his mid-forties and two sons from a nearby homestead appeared to inspect the rather odd phenomenon of a foreigner setting up camp in their secluded section of valley. After a few smiles and some basic communication with sign language they invited me to join them in their stone house further up the hill. With thunder and dark clouds threatening to turn my beach into a mud pit I was pleased to accept the offer.

As we trekked away from the river's edge, where the Mekong's swirling waters ensured only the liveliest of birdcalls were audible, I noticed a distant melody that came and went with the breeze. It was so faint and peaceful that I initially thought it was my imagination, but as we gained ground through stands of corn, the flurry of notes became clearer and I realised I was hearing music from some type of flute.

The beautiful nature of the tune, with its perfectly honed notes rising and falling with fluid grace, struck me as being in absolute harmony with the picturesque valley we walked through. I became increasingly curious to see who was playing the magical tune. As I approached the sturdy rock-walled dwelling from where the music was coming I was set upon by a large dog. As my host and I yelled and threatened the mutt, trying to keep him away, the music stopped and the family came out to see what was causing the commotion.

A young boy of about twelve appeared on the landing of the house with a flute in his hand, gasping in surprise at seeing a foreigner fending off his large mongrel. I moved forward in the fading light to meet the maker of the most beautiful music I had heard in all of China.

As soon as the dog was shooed away I smiled to everyone and gave the obligatory *nihou*, hello, with a slight bow, before pointing to the boy's flute and giving a round of applause in honour of his obvious talent. When I saw that the child suffered from the most severe facial deformities I have ever seen I might have subconsciously flinched. Despite the extreme nature of his affliction, which I soon discovered left him unable to form words properly, I could still make out a smile and a blush.

Before long I was inside my host's house and changed into dry clothes. I gave the lady of the house some of my supplies as a contribution towards the dinner she was preparing before heading out to the balcony where the boy was hanging out. I knew he was curious about my things from the way he eyed them when I sorted out my bags. I brought out a map and compass and invited him to take a look. I started naming the large towns on the map of China, many of which he instantly recognised, and the Lancang Jiang, his river. He was genuinely excited about the map and was soon pointing out his own towns to hear me recite the Romanised names. As he leaned over the map I could see he had enormous humps on his back. His demeanour and interactions with me left me in no doubt that he was mentally as sharp as a tack.

With our inability to communicate through language, I soon moved on to a couple of my poorly performed magic tricks, which actually managed to get the desired response. After fifteen minutes or so of general hanging out I asked that he play some tunes on his flute. Before long his melodies swept me into a state of peaceful self-lessness. I've always maintained that a musician's melodies provide a glimpse into their soul. If the boy's music is anything to go by his soul is swimming in an ocean of nirvana. I would quite happily have stayed there the whole night if pangs of hunger were not awakened when his mother came out to let us know dinner was ready.

As we settled into a dinner of homegrown corn, vegetable soup and rice (they wisely decided not to use my tinned fish and noodles), the family chatted amongst themselves, seemingly about their daily lives. Although they spoke in a dialect I was not familiar with, their body language indicated this was a close and loving group of people. I'm no romantic when it comes to the realities of subsistence living in remote areas as I have witnessed significant suffering in years of poor harvest or drought, yet spending a night with this family I couldn't help but make me feel there was probably nowhere better on Earth for them to be. They seemed happy and at peace.

Early the following morning I tipped the family and bade them farewell before heading downstream with plans to paddle to the last significant stop in China, Jinghong. I encountered a few more rapids before the whitewater relaxed. For the first time on the Mekong I came across commercial cargo boats just north of Simao. I took the opportunity to surf their bow waves but the captains were not always as fond of the experience as I was. One of them ran out of the wheelhouse waving his fist and blurting obscenities at me. Later that afternoon I came across what appeared to be the foundations of several large bridges but they were so close together that I knew they had to be for another purpose. Then slightly north of Jinghong I paddled through another huge dam construction site. I realised it would only be a few years before the family who took me in so naturally upstream would be flooded out of their home, and they would probably be inadequately relocated to a distant large town. I wondered whether the boy's music could survive in such a dog-eat-dog environment of uprooted people, all struggling to survive in a very different world. Would the special needs of that family be taken into account?

There is so little public information available from China's dam builders that I doubt I'll ever find out. I knew the family's special status as Chinese citizens meant the dam builders would at least acknowledge that the family would suffer immense losses, unlike the unfortunate souls south of the Chinese border, yet the spirit and peace in that boy's heart, expressed so vividly through his music, left no doubt in my mind that he was where he was supposed to be in this world. The reality of the Mekong Cascade project would hit hard.

I pulled up in Jinghong, where I met Brian and Goldfinger and we made plans to undertake the final leg out of China before entering the region referred to as the Golden Triangle, which marks the tri-partite border area of Burma, Laos and Thailand, the river's midway point. Brian and Goldfinger would drive directly to the Lao border where they would be met by our Lao ground support team from Green Discovery Travel. I would meet up with him in about a week's time in Luang Namtha, a province in the northern part of Laos.

I was stamped out of China at the port of Mengla. As I went through the final formalities I was made aware that another bunch of foreigners had just paddled through the previous day. It was the team of New Zealanders who had also been doing a first descent of the Mekong Valley by mountain bike, foot and kayak. As far as I know their expedition and my own are the only two attempts to explore the entire Mekong Valley since the attempt made by the French Mekong Expedition in 1866.

Shortly after leaving Mengla, the landscape changed from magnificent terraced fields of rice to extensive expanses of wild bamboo forest. I was surprised to find long sections of the river deserted. By late afternoon I crossed into the area where the Mekong forms the border between China and Burma and a new section of the journey began, the middle Mekong. The Lao border was still an overnight paddle trip away so I would be in no man's land for the next twenty-four hours.

There was something peculiarly appealing about spending a day as a citizen of the world, not registered in any nation on Earth. The

Our four-wheel-drive, piled high with the kayaks, driving past Tibetan prayer flags en route to the Mekong source. *[Photograph: Stanislas Fradelizi]*

Left: Mick passes the Mekong just below its source, at an altitude of 5190 metres. *[Photograph: Stanislas Fradelizi]*
Right: Mick defrosts his fingers over 'Mani' stones on the Tibetan Plateau. *[Photograph: Stanislas Fradelizi]*

The team, Stan (at front), Mick (back left), Nico (middle) and Abe.
[Photograph: Stanislas Fradelizi]

Pushing on through a snowstorm near the Mekong source.
[Photograph: Stanislas Fradelizi]

A Tibetan nomad woman in traditional dress.
[Photograph: Stanislas Fradelizi]

Mick navigates the whitewater in southern Yunnan. *[Photograph: Brian Eustis]*

The Daschaoshan dam site in Southern Yunnan. *[Photograph: Mick O'Shea]*

Mick takes on Mekong whitewater at Liphi Falls in southern Laos.
[Photograph: Hutch Brown]

Hutch and Mick interview local fisherman at Tonle Sap Lake in Cambodia.
[Photograph: Brian Eustis]

Left: Mick runs the Leuk Falls near Vientiane in Laos. *[Photograph: Stanislas Fradelizi]*
Right: Mick meeting monks in Pakse in southern Laos. *[Photograph: Hutch Brown]*

A Lanten lady and her family in the Nam Ha area of north-western Laos.
[Photograph: Mick O'Shea]

Left: A Thai monk blesses the kayak in north-eastern Thailand.
[Photograph: Hutch Brown]
Right: Staff of the UXO in Lao dig up a 'live' two hundred-pound bomb in the Champassack province. *[Photograph: Phillipe Andries]*

Mick is dwarfed by the Khone Falls in the Lao/Cambodian frontier area.
[Photograph: Inthy Deuansavan]

The boys, Hutch (left), Mick (centre) and Brian, at the Lao/Thai river border area.
[Photograph: Rattaproom Youprom ('Thong')]

Left: The paddy fields and floodplain in the Mekong delta. *[Photograph: Hutch Brown]*
Right: Mick makes his final approach to the sea past the mangrove palms in the Mekong delta region. *[Photograph: Hutch Brown]*

Made it! Mick arrives triumphantly at the South China Sea. *[Photograph: Hutch Brown]*

novelty of this status amused me and I relished the sense of freedom as I paddled late into the afternoon and darkness descended. Paddling silently through the swirling waters of the Mekong at night had an exciting yet slightly disconcerting feel to it, not least because the region I was entering is considered one of the wildest in South-East Asia.

Since the first time I visited a Burmese refugee camp in Mae Sot, Thailand, during the 1995 refugee crisis, I was touched by the desperate plight of the fleeing Burmese students and ethnic minority people, all of whom had experienced the unrestrained brutality of the State Law and Order Restoration Council (SLORC), as the Burmese military junta preferred to be called at the time. While at the camp, shells could be heard bombarding the last stronghold of the Karen national union military base belonging to the repressed minority Karen people, located just sixteen kilometres across the border where some four hundred Karen fighters were surrounded by several thousand SLORC troops. The looks on the faces of newly arrived Karen women and children, whose husbands and fathers were trapped on that mountain, said it all.

I have since read as much as possible about the situation in the border regions of Burma. When Burma's first multi-party elections in thirty years took place in 1990, Nobel Peace Prize laureate, Aung San Suu Kyi, won a landslide victory. Even after rigging the vote, the military junta still only managed to capture a small number of parliamentary seats yet this was not enough to convince them to hand over the reins of power. On the contrary, their definitive loss sparked a crackdown on all pro-democracy activists and supporters, which resulted in the deaths of thousands.

Declarations of autonomy from various minority peoples in the border regions led to the emergence of several powerful rebel armies, funded primarily from the trade in gems, timber and narcotics. The most powerful of these groups is the United Wa State

Army. The Wa are the biggest producers of opium and ampheta-
mines in the Golden Triangle, and have a private army in excess of
twenty thousand men.

As I paddled past their lands in the darkness that night, in the
back of my mind was a gruesome story told to me by my paddle
buddies Rubin Ghan and Carl Traehol who, to the best of my
knowledge, were the first foreigners to paddle kayaks along the
entire Burmese Mekong in 2001. On the same stretch they encountered two floating corpses, one of which had his hands tied behind
his back.

The real tragedy in Burma is that 'the golden land' has a natural
and cultural heritage that remains unsurpassed in the region.
Located at the cultural crossroads of India, China and South-East
Asia, the predominantly Buddhist nation is a treasure trove of diversity and natural wealth. From snow-capped Himalayan mountains in
the north to the exceptional coral reefs and tropical islands of the
Andaman Sea on the country's southern fringes, it is a region that has
a great deal to offer.

As the world's largest exporter of teak and one of the world's
greatest producers of high quality gemstones, Burma also has significant reserves of fossil fuels. According to many international
observers, it is the lucrative revenue streams from trade in these
resources, both legal and illegal, that motivates the military junta to
maintain the debilitating political and business status quo.

That night I slept on a sandy beach on the Chinese side of the river
and was woken up several times by a pack of monkeys perched in
trees on the opposite bank. I lay there basking in the moonlight and
realised that this would be my last night in China and I couldn't help
but wonder how things might evolve within the People's Republic
and beyond over the coming decades.

13 Hope and harsh realities: the Lower Basin

The first culture shock when crossing from China into Laos on the Mekong route occurs at the immigration checkpoint. At the last stop in China, Mengla, a major customs and immigration facility is under construction. At the site every document is scrutinised closely, details are fed into and cross-checked on a computer and a guard actually follows departing foreigners down to the river to ensure they board the designated craft leaving the country.

From the water I almost couldn't identify the wood and tin shacks nestled among bamboo thickets as being an official Lao immigration checkpoint. It was only when I spotted a river depth gauge on the riverside and a small Lao flag fluttering in the distance that I realised I was paddling by an 'official' settlement. I was alarmed to note that the water level was so low it did not even register on the gauge despite, only three hundred and fifty kilometres further north in China, above the Dashaoshan Dam, the Mekong was at almost peak levels. I took a snap of the gauge for the record. I then had to seek out and interrupt the customs guards, who were either napping or playing cards in a ramshackle teak wood hut.

They continued to play out their hand before finally acknowledging my presence. A discussion then broke out about whose turn it was to stamp in the traveller. The brief debate was settled when one of the card players leaned across and tugged at the hammock of another officer, waking him from a deep sleep. Slowly, he rose bare-chested, stretched noisily, slipped into his flip-flops and dragged his feet to a nearby desk where he proceeded to slip on an immigration officer's shirt, doing up the top button only. Taking my passport in one hand, he opened a large notebook and started taking down some details with the other. I noted that in the arrivals book there had been only perhaps twenty international arrivals in the past month and four of them had been the New Zealanders from the other expedition. He stamped my passport and handed it back before saying 'goodbye' in English, a wide smile animating his face.

I looked at the visa and noted that he had failed to stamp in the arrival date. When I pointed this out, he agreed it was in fact his job to do five steps when checking someone into his country and not just four. He completed step five by stamping in the entry date and handed the passport back saying *sok dee*, 'good luck', and dragged his flip-flops across the floor to the hammock before slumping into it, seemingly exhausted. It must have been a stressful day at the office!

Back in my kayak I paddled down long sections of swirls and boils until I noticed what seemed to be a stick spinning in the current. In fact, it was a king cobra attempting to swim across the Mekong. Not one to miss a photo opportunity I paddled as close as I safely could and began pulling out my camera. I knew that cobras were good swimmers as I had seen a couple cross creeks in the past, even one swimming across a lake, but this guy was exceptional. I watched as he was dragged into a succession of large whirlpools. He appeared completely unfazed as each whirlpool swirled him around until he reached the vortex and got sucked under, then, with a few quick whips of his tail he would fight his way free before slowly getting dragged into the next whirlpool.

While getting my camera out I took my eye off the ball for a couple of moments and before I knew it I was inadvertently sucked into a whirlpool with the snake. He disappeared under the boat and there was a tense couple of seconds while I waited to see where he would pop up. I saw his tail flick to the right of my kayak and then he was gone as the whirlpool spun me around. To be bitten by a king cobra in remote country such as the Lao/Burma border area would be fatal so I kept my elbows up high and my paddle at the ready to fend off the snake should he attack.

To my relief he popped up three metres in front of me and as the whirlpool dissipated he decided to play dead. A perfect chance to get the shot. I started snapping. As I lined up for the second shot, the cobra turned and started swimming straight for my kayak. I clicked again just before his head went up over the bow. I quickly clenched the camera strap with my teeth and reached for my paddle. By now he had his head up over the bow and was closing in fast. With instinctive speed I flicked him back into the water with my paddle blade and he disappeared again. This would rate as a sphincter factor of six—he didn't actually hiss at me. Another tense couple of seconds passed as I waited, paddle at the ready, imagining the cobra launching up out of the water for my throat. Fortunately when I next saw him he was heading for shore so I took another couple of snaps of him in flight. It was a pretty wild experience. I estimated that he swam over two kilometres, crossing the river in conditions that would drown a person not wearing a life vest.

I camped in a small rural Lao village that night and swapped stories by candlelight with the bemused crowd of locals, who could hardly believe that I had paddled down from Tibet over two thousand kilometres away or that I could speak Lao. Speaking Lao makes it all the more difficult to say no to the endless shots of rice whisky, known locally as Lao Lao, that inevitably break out around dinnertime. I was in the home of Mr Tee, a thirty-something fisherman who shared his home with his wife, four children and ageing mother-in-law. However, another twenty villagers of all ages were also constantly in the house as the whole village seemed to rotate in and out, one by one, to check out the *falang* (Lao for 'foreigner'). We sat on the teak wood floor around two hand-woven oval-shaped bamboo tables, warmed by a soft light that exuded from two miniature Red Bull bottles that had been converted into miniature kerosene lamps. The tables were overflowing with the remnants of a long-waited-for Lao dinner comprising sticky rice, barbecued Mekong fish, small cucumbers dipped in salt and *jeow*, a spicy chilli paste and fish sauce concoction. After over two months of not drinking more than a beer or two it wasn't long before I went from tipsy to bullet-proof and finally to a state I can't quite recall. It felt great to be able to communicate directly with the locals using my imperfect but comfortably conversational Lao language skills. Lao people possess a great sense of humour and it wasn't long before we were all in fits of laughter as the Lao Lao shot glass made its rounds. I can only assume that the boat race was arranged somewhere between the bullet-proof and passing-out stages of the evening, but the 5 a.m. chorus of pigs and chickens under the thatched-roofed stilt house was soon followed by the murmurings of a crowd of locals gathering outside, patiently waiting for the big event to start.

I opened my eyes to the sight of about fifteen people who had been sitting and watching me sleep for god knows how long. With a throbbing headache, I crawled out of bed and was immediately reminded that I had unwisely agreed to race some Lao lads along the Mekong. After a light breakfast of bamboo soup and sticky rice, there was no getting out of it. I had to race three strapping young fishermen in a long, sleek wooden pirogue. Made essentially from three long planks of teak wood that are slightly wider in the centre than at the ends, one for the hull and one each for the right and left gunwales (sides), the traditional Lao fishing craft are initially nailed together and then sealed with a resin extracted from several types of hardwood tree that must be tapped using fire to burn the trunk, causing the resin to seep out. A degree of sturdiness is provided to the narrow design by the addition of tiny strip-wood seats that are nailed between the gunwales. Made for speed and efficiency rather than stability, they are amazingly easy to flip, however you would never guess it while watching these highly skilled locals casting throw nets from the tip of the bow as though the craft was securely fastened to the river's surface.

There's nothing Lao people love more than a good boat race and all the people from the village, about one hundred and twenty of them, came down to watch their boys whoop the *falang*—they couldn't believe I had agreed to such a challenge. My boat was designed to be slow and easy to turn for whitewater purposes, whereas the villagers' pirogue was designed for efficient travel on the relatively flat surface of the lower Mekong. Over the three hundred-metre course the boys pulled away by about twenty metres. By the end of it I dry-retched violently as my body threatened to hurl my sticky rice breakfast into the river. The delighted crowd cheered their boys home as I recovered, promising myself to never again race with a septic stomach full of Lao Lao.

Later that morning I bumped into the New Zealanders. They were a nice bunch of people and we spent hours swapping experiences from the upper Mekong as we floated through various sets of whirlpools and small rapids. Like my trip, their expedition had been plagued by unforeseen problems and they had also struggled financially to keep things on track. To their distress they were forced to leave the Mekong Valley through a portion of the Tibetan section, entering the Salween Valley, because the roads that permit brokers had told them were 'bike-able' did not exist.

It was a major letdown for them but it was a stroke of luck for me as it meant I did not need to race them to the South China Sea to claim the title of the first descent of the entire Mekong Valley, but the sports rivalry between Australia and New Zealand would no doubt have ensured some excellent media coverage. Although the Kiwi team had trekked and biked on roads around many of the more treacherous gorges, if they had not been forced to leave the Mekong

Valley, they could still have claimed to be first to travel by manpower along the full length of the Mekong Valley. Not having to race the New Zealanders meant that I could spend time exploring some interesting areas for the documentary Brian and I were putting together.

Another blow for the Kiwis came when they were forced to spend three full weeks in Jinghong waiting to get their imported kayaks out of customs, followed by sorting out the permits to cross by kayak into Laos. Customs officials were determined to charge them full import tax rates, which amounted to thousands of dollars for their equipment even though they planned to only paddle the kayaks from Jinghong to the Lao border, about two to three days, and then leave China.

Unable to persuade the customs authorities, even with letters of recommendation from various Chinese ministries and the government of New Zealand, the group were forced to leave their sponsored kayaks in customs and buy an inner tube-style Chinese raft. This slowed their progress down by approximately fifty per cent. It was comforting to know that having an expeditionary dream held to ransom by individuals who seemed completely unmoved by the hardship they caused was not limited to my own experience. We bade each other farewell. Even with my slow moving whitewater kayak I soon sped ahead of the New Zealand team, who patiently oared their oversized inner tube at an agonisingly slow pace downstream.

I was paddling along what seemed to be a deserted stretch of river when a wooden sampan manned by two buff fishermen appeared from nowhere. The fishermen signalled that they wanted a race. Keen to redeem myself from the previous abysmal effort, and comforted by the fact that there was no one around to watch me get thrashed, I raised my paddle and leaned forward into a racing position, indicating that I was ready to give them a run for their money. They immediately edged up towards me, aligning our bows at the starting line. The scene was set for another Mekong challenge showdown.

Suddenly loud whoops and yells rang out from the river's edge and I saw several other pirogues nestled amongst thick shrubbery, with the local ladies sitting on their haunches excitedly stirring their boys on. Further up on the embankment, naked children ran down towards the river's edge and a chant broke out. 'Aye, aye, aye!'

In perfect unison the motley bunch of spectators started hooting a chorus that echoes back through the centuries in Laos and most of the lower Mekong. The percussion of paddles on boat gunwales and clapping hands joined the rhythmic chant of the boat race, and I'm sure I could hear some Burmese join in on the other bank as people began appearing all over the place. It was as though word of the previous day's thrashing had travelled ahead of me. An entire village of locals had set an ambush for the sorry-looking foreigner who got so upset about losing a race that he would start dry-retching and convulsing in his boat.

It was too late to bail out now. With a mutual look of challenge between me and one of my competitors, we were off. This time I gave it a real burst, straining every muscle to run them down and for the first forty metres or so I actually nudged in front by half a length. But once the superior efficiency of their craft (that's my theory) came into play they soon closed the gap and edged past me. After another one hundred metres or so they were nearly a full boat length in front. I had to face the fact of defeat.

The crowd went wild when I gave up but this time I refrained from the much anticipated encore performance. I gave the fishermen the thumbs up followed by the ultimate blessing that any strapping Lao boat racer could hope to receive from their competitor: *kheng heng*. The loose translation is, 'You have the power'. The fishermen blushed, chuckled to one another and, in an attempt at diplomacy, tried to make me feel better by saying, *Heua ni baw die laew, pen saa phort*—'your boat's a piece of crap, it's too slow'. I was pleased that they acknowledged my handicap, waved them on with a smile, and paddled ahead as they veered towards the bank as heroes.

I decided that for the protection of my dignity as a paddler I would ban myself from racing until I was in a faster, sleeker flat-water boat. An hour later I pulled into the Mekong riverside town of Xieng Kok, a ramshackle collection of houses and huts nestled on the eastern bank of the Mekong. This 'town', really a small village, represents the northernmost settlement on the Lao Mekong and has a port servicing large Chinese steel-hulled barges that ply the route between Mengla in China and Chiang Saen in Thailand. From here I had to catch a ride east to the provincial capital of Luang Namtha, where I was meeting Brian who would have driven for five gruelling days to meet me there.

Luang Namtha is a remarkable province of Laos and it shares the border with the southern portions of Yunnan. This province has the largest number of ethnic groups of any province in Laos. The presence of the sprawling Nam Ha National Biodiversity and Con-servation Area also adds to the uniqueness of the area. This protected two hundred and seventy-six thousand-hectare area is home to tigers, elephants, leopards and gibbons along with an impressive array of other threatened critters. I boarded a muddy pick-up known as a *song thaew* (or 'two rows'), a reference to the two rows of seats in the back of the vehicle), along with a mixture of people from several ethnic groups. The most notable were three Akha ladies who wore their elaborate traditional dress with its complicated and colourful embroidery and multi-coloured beading, forest-seed bracelets, intri-cately worked silver jewellery and a prominent headdress of bamboo and antique French piastres. The women were carrying sacks of cardamom, a type of pod collected from the forest and highly prized in traditional Chinese medicine.

I tried to spark up a conversation with the Akha ladies but their Lao language was nearly nonexistent and my Akha vocabulary of twelve words ran out in about one minute. A bemused Khmu couple, Aon and Noy, and their child, who were sitting next to me, were quite surprised that I could speak Lao, so we started chatting.

Khmu people are descended from the Mon Khmer people who have inhabited the area for thousands of years and are widely considered to be the original inhabitants of Laos. The Khmu's extensive knowledge of the forest and medicinal plants is second to none, and Noy chewed on a local forest drug called betel nut, which causes a mild state of sedation and stains the teeth and lips with a grimy red tinge. The couple spoke Lao with a thick northern Khmu accent and they told me they had come to Xieng Kok to sell bamboo shoots and the fleshy heart of rattan cane so that they could buy fish, rice and cooking oil to supplement their diet.

They lived three hours' walk from the nearest drivable road and their village was almost out of rice for the rest of the growing season. I knew that it would be another two to three months before the first hill rice crops the Khmu generally grow would be ready for harvest. Serious rice shortages are not uncommon in the area. The couple had had nine children, two of whom had died as toddlers. From the condition of their worn-out bodies and tattered clothes I could see that these people were doing it hard.

Aon took advantage of being able to chat with a foreigner for the first time in his life and barraged me with questions about my own country and lifestyle. 'How many people in your family? What are you doing here? Do foreigners eat rice? How cold is it in the foreign countries?' As we talked, Aon's wife Noy pulled out some sticky rice and fish from her bag and without a thought offered it to me as well as her husband and child. I thanked her but declined. The natural generosity of rural Lao people, so many of whom live well below the poverty line, is something I find amazing.

Barely a day goes by in the Lao countryside when one is not invited to eat and drink with complete strangers who expect nothing

more in return than some friendly interaction. These simple uneducated farmers of Bokeo province were qualified professors when it
came to the virtues of generosity and goodwill.

Before long the family got off and the *song thaew* continued
through various villages on red, muddy roads as the car slushed its
way into the dense tropical forests of the Nam Ha area. We eventually
approached Nam Pha River, where less than a year before I had
worked with Brian on a tiger tracking survey—we were trying to
record the presence of the rapidly disappearing Asian tiger with
camera traps. It was an amazing journey and it included thumping
whitewater and the discovery of a remote tribal Akha village that even
the provincial authorities did not know existed. We didn't actually see a
tiger but we did find evidence including footprints, fur balls and state-
ments from interviews with local tribal peoples. Brian and I rated that
expedition as one of our favourites. To see the roiling waters brought
back the memory of some truly remarkable moments from that trip.

It began raining heavily for the rest of the journey. At 7 p.m.
I pulled up at the Saikhonglongsak guesthouse in Luang Namtha,
located on one of four paved streets in the town, where I bumped
into Brian, who was enjoying a meal and a cold Beer Lao, the local
brew. We shared a beer and discussed the events of the previous five
days since we had split up. Across from the restaurant, a band of
short, stout Lao ladies went about their business of setting up *khai
looke* and beer stands—*khai looke* is an all-time Lao favourite delicacy
comprised of steamed, fertilised chicken eggs that are eaten with a
tangy salt, pepper and chilli powder. The steamed eggs typically
come in three main stages of development. Stage one is a just
fertilised egg with no distinguishable chicken features, stage two is a
featherless and soft-boned foetus that is still attached to a yolk sack,
and stage three is a fully feathered and ready to walk but not yet
hatched chick, complete with crunchy bones and beak. I decided to
settle for some chicken kebabs instead.

Luang Namtha's electricity, which is provided by a single diesel-powered generator, had still not been turned on and as the darkness closed in it was hard to believe we were in one of the biggest centres in northern Laos. With a population of around two thousand five hundred people and unsealed roads leading in and out of it in all directions, Luang Namtha would not even register as a town on a map of China. Yet in the remote regions of northwestern Laos it plays the important role of a fully fledged provincial capital. The plan was to spend a couple of days visiting some of the minority villages in the national park, but the heavy rain and the weather outlook for the next couple of days made us sceptical about the filming possibilities. By the following afternoon the rain was still bucketing down so we decided to head back to the Mekong and continue south. We drove back through the Nam Ha. The road was in a terrible condition and there was some exciting driving as our two-wheel-drive vehicle sloshed and jostled its way from one tyre-reamed trench to another.

The Nam Ha River, around which the sprawling protected area is based, is not particularly different to all the other hundreds of small rivers that act as veins providing life-giving water throughout the forested mountains of Laos, but it was a tributary of the Mekong that I had come to know well. In close cooperation with the UNESCO Nam Ha eco-tourism project between 2001 and 2003 it was my job to train local people from several ethnic minority groups to guide tourists through the protected area on kayaking and rafting excursions. The activities were designed to provide the local people with alternative income sources to their usual hunting and land clearing for crops within the protected area. I helped train over twenty river guides, most of whom are still working in the area as guides almost four years later.

The opportunity to spend significant amounts of time in the company of minority peoples in the upland Mekong tributaries played a big part in capturing my imagination while working within the Mekong Basin. Experiences with the Lanten people of the Nam Ha River is a typical example. The Lanten are referred to by the ethnic Laos (lowland paddy farmers) as *Lao hoey*, or 'stream Lao', due to their habit of settling on small upland streams. The Lanten culture originates from the steppes of Tibet and differs greatly from the Buddhist Lao majority. As a people they made an incredible migration across China several centuries ago to escape war and persecution. Starting from the Tibetan steppes the journey took them across the full breadth of the Celestial Empire to the South China Sea, where they built ships and sailed to the island of Henan in search of a peaceful place to settle down.

Still not content, they made another extensive journey, this time heading west via the Red River Valley (the principal river basin of northern Vietnam), where many of them chose to cross over into the Mekong Basin to settle in the regions of northern Laos. Today, several thousands of Lantens live a subsistence lifestyle in the area. The stream Lao practise a unique mixture of animism, ancestor worship and shamanism, and a council of elders often makes the decisions on important village matters. The Lantens' cultural heritage and connection to nature remains strong and it is a heritage I have had many moments of wonder experiencing.

The Lanten women are really distinctive. Their lack of eyebrows, completely plucked from puberty, gives them a unique appearance, and their hair is always parted in the middle and pulled back tight across the brow before being styled into a loop behind the head and fixed with an intricately crafted silver hair comb. The indigo-coloured dress and short trousers worn by all of the women are offset by a bright purple sash and several distinctive pieces of silver jewellery. These days, the men are starting to replace their indigo-dyed traditional clothes with T-shirts and shorts and the young children tend to wear a mixture of traditional and modern clothing.

Spending time with the Lanten people of the Nam Ha is a fascinating introduction to the trials and tribulations of subsistence living. Survival is the primary objective and it is the women who play the key roles in placing food on the table of most families.

The Lanten ladies collect a remarkable variety of river foods from the waterways around the village. Crabs, shrimp, dozens of species of fish, watercress, snails, frogs, snakes, eels, edible river weeds and various invertebrates are harvested and these provide more than half of the village protein needs throughout several months of the year. Hill rice and paddy rice are often grown simultaneously while the production of opium, the traditional pain-killer and recreational drug of the elderly, is generally limited to supplying village demand.

While the more active men are off hunting, the women work on the sides of the streams, watering organic vegetable patches using bamboo buckets and dyeing their fabrics in wooden vats using the indigo roots collected from the surrounding forest. Several varieties of ingeniously woven bamboo fish traps keep the protein supply coming in during the rainy months. The Nam Ha area suspension bridges are fashioned from forest vines and bamboo, and provide access to the other side of the river, ideal for overcoming the seasonal surges in river currents.

One of my favourite sights in the Lanten villages is the hydraulic rice pounder simply made from a machete, wood and some old-fashioned ingenuity. A two- to three-metre-long piece of timber is carved into the shape of an oversized spoon. A hammer-like wedge is fixed into the handle end of this and then it is balanced on a central pivot, with the wedge end being slightly heavier than the spoon. The spoon end of the implement is positioned under a stream of water where it rapidly fills with several litres of water, which gradually makes the spoon end heavier than the wedge end. The pounder seesaws the wedge end up and the spoon end down towards the earth until it reaches an angle where the water flows out of the spoon onto the ground. The spoon end see-saws the other way, slamming the wedge-end back towards the earth. A large wooden pestle is placed under the wedge end and unhusked rice is poured into the hollow of the pestle. The rice is pounded until the husk is loosened enough for it to be sifted through later.

No amount of ingenuity, however, can make the survival game in the remote forests of Laos an easy affair. The Lanten people, along with the remote villages from dozens of ethnic groups across the nation, live precariously between periods of abundance and scarcity. During years when rice yields were significantly less than normal I would paddle down the Nam Ha to see emaciated children with bloated stomachs, a sign of chronic malnutrition, and near-desperate parents struggling to get their families through to the next rice harvest. With so many people balanced on that knife edge of survival, it became clear to me that even the most marginal shifts that can affect the bounty in the natural environment can hugely affect the viability of entire communities.

The quaint Nam Ha River forms a tiny thread of the expansive Mekong River system and its ecology and vitality is closely linked to the health of the mainstream. As Brian and I passed over the beautiful tributary shrouded in forest on our way to the Mekong, it was bizarre to consider that the energy decisions made in Beijing, a booming, highly polluted concrete and stained-glass city located over five thousand kilometres to the northeast, would impact on the resources of the people living on the banks of Nam Ha.

I wondered whether the implications of damming the Mekong might be enough to eventually force people out of the valley for good. If the dams do tip the balance against the Lanten and they are forced to leave their valley, then the balance will likely be tipped in hundreds of other small tributaries and thousands of villages throughout the Mekong system. Where would all these people go?

Because international standard research on the potential effects of the dams on people who, like the Lanten, live on the connected waterways of the Mekong, was never undertaken by the Chinese I guess only time will really tell. For now at least the Lanten, like the vast majority of the basin's most vulnerable people, remain completely unaware of the processes that will probably change the course of their lives forever.

Brian and I returned to the Mekong at Xieng Kok. We continued downstream between Laos and Burma, the river forming the border between these two countries. We tried to chat with Burmese fishermen at several points but without a translator present our communications were limited to smiles and waves. There was a noticeable lack of villages along the Mekong River in Burma.

The forced relocation of minority peoples from their traditional lands and into those firmly controlled by Yangon's (formerly Rangoon) military had been occurring for years and I wondered whether Burma's Mekong regions were part of the merciless mass clearance program or whether they had been deserted by chance. We pulled into a small port town which was not marked on our maps, where we tried to get some directions from the locals. Gruff-looking porters were offloading stores from a large Chinese trading vessel onto nearby trucks. Most of them had serious expressions that were probably a mixed reflection of the hard manual labour and the repressive conditions they lived in. It is not uncommon for the military to subject local people to forced manual labour without reward. On the other side of the river in Laos the people were all smiles. Brian and I desperately wanted to talk to some of the workers but with armed officials looking on and without filming permits we thought better of it.

We walked into the village of Ban Thaat, where Brian and I had spent an evening a year earlier as part of the tiger tracking expedition on the Nam Pha River. Our previous visit had coincided with the annual village festival and had also been the last night of the expedition. Everyone had been in the mood to celebrate our success, and it had definitely been a night to remember. The locals embraced us like old friends. Because of their determination in forcing Lao Lao down our throats I can only remember a select few scenes from the night. Some memories include Brian playing bongo drums with a bunch of adolescent monks in tow chanting, 'Bring the noise, bring the noise', then there are slightly disconcerting flashbacks to participating in a drunken group pile-up on top of the village headman, who eventually crawled out from underneath all us looking as though he had been hit by a truck.

We immediately met up with familiar characters from our last trip. They knew exactly who we were and wasted no time in opening a bottle of Beer Lao and inviting us in for a chat. Fortunately for everyone involved it was a significantly toned down version of previous events and there were no injuries. We were pleased to hear that the headman made a full recovery from the pile-up and the monks returned to playing traditional temple rhythms instead of Brian's rap melodies.

We made good ground as we approached our first significant stop on the Burma side of the river. We were being sponsored by the Paradise Casino resort overlooking the Mekong in the Golden Triangle and were able to stay there for as long as we liked. Brian and I said little and paddled like champions, covering around ninety kilometres a day in whitewater kayaks specifically designed to turn and resurface fast rather than move efficiently through the water. Unfortunately we had to reach Thailand before we could upgrade to faster touring kayaks. After arriving at the resort, we quickly took our first showers in several days before hitting the buffet dinner like wild dogs. After more than three months of eating almost nothing but local village food and food from packets, our culinary fantasies were out of control. We must have been quite a sight in our trashy river clothes, which had not been washed in two weeks, and our appetites verged on the insane. Six servings later, things started to slow up and we eventually retired to our rooms which, compared to our usual accommodation, were palaces. I talked with Yuta by phone and she had made a full recovery from her surgery and was looking forward to my arrival in the Lao capital around nine hundred kilometres downstream.

That night as I tried to sleep I was regularly awoken by my hands going to sleep, followed by that dreadful pins and needles feeling that only disappears if you sit up in bed and shake your hands around. The constant tension on my wrists resulting from forcing the paddle repeatedly through the water for up to ten hours per day was starting to take its toll in the form of repetitive strain injury, which restricted the blood flow in my arms. The Paradise Casino resort in Burma was located approximately two thousand four hundred kilometres downstream from the river's source, basically the halfway mark of the descent. I knew it would be a long run if my body started to break down at this point so I spent a lot of time massaging my wrists in an attempt to regulate the blood flow.

When I went to the breakfast buffet on our second day at the resort there was Brian, slumped over his chair with three empty plates on the table. He looked the most content I had seen him in weeks. That day I had three meals with Brian and throughout the day I passed by the buffet room a few times to snack on delicious king prawns, Thai curries and sushi. Every time, Brian would sit in the same spot with a new array of empty plates and a look of complete bliss. That night when I went to have supper I asked Brian what he had done for the day and he replied, 'Jesus Christ, Micko, I haven't left the room all day.' He saw the bemused look on my face and defensively said, 'It's not my fault, man, I arrived for breakfast, then you came along and I had to eat with you, then Todd came for a chat, followed by Ton. I had to be polite and eat with each of you. Next thing it's lunchtime and everyone's back again. When they brought the sushi out for dinner I couldn't leave, so I was kind of stuck here.' It was an astounding gastronomic achievement and I realised that maybe the two-minute noodles and canned fish we were living off was not quite hitting the spot for poor old Brian.

Our sponsorship agents, Todd Leong and Chris Bohren from Admotiv Media, arranged for sponsored touring kayaks from Feelfree Kayaks and had managed to get support for most of our ground costs in Thailand. Todd introduced us to Ton, the charismatic owner of the resort, who is one of the most superstitious and entertaining characters I have ever come across. Ton entertained us over the next couple of days with colourful tales of doing business and politics in Burma and Thailand, all washed down with fine Australian wine and lashings of delicious food. If nothing else the Mekong descent was becoming a journey of extreme contrasts.

Ton had hoped to arrange special permission for us to undertake a journey into the countryside with an escort from the provincial military governor, but recent rebel activity nearby meant that this permission was refused at the last minute. The resort was protected by a military garrison but outside of the immediate vicinity our safety could not be guaranteed. It was a shame but we knew that while we were escorted by the military our chances of catching candid interviews on tape with locals would be next to none.

From the buffet room where Brian and I had been spending an inordinate amount of our time, we could see the Mekong rising at an incredible rate. A glance at prevailing weather conditions proved that the rise did not seem to be the result of an immense monsoonal downpour upstream—it was clear to us that the Chinese had decided to release some of the water they had been backing up in the

Manwan and Dashaoshan dams. In the space of four days while we were at the resort the Mekong rose almost two metres.

After almost a week of rest, relaxation and feasting we bade farewell to our host and the nation of Burma on 17 July. It had been one hundred and one days since I had arrived in China to start the expedition. Now we were heading south into a new section of the Mekong, where it forms a large part of the border between the nations of Laos and Thailand, with Thailand forming one bank of the river and Laos the other.

14 Lands of contrast: the Lao and Thai Mekong

After forming the border between Burma and Laos for around two hundred kilometres the Mekong continues south, separating the nations of Laos and Thailand where it is known to the Thais as *Mae Nam Khong* or 'Khong, mother of water'. To the Laos it is *Nam Khong* or 'Kong River'. As the similar names suggest, the nations of Thailand and Laos are linguistically as well as culturally similar. The majority of their populations are descendants of the Tai people of China (not to be confused with Thai people, who are actually descendants of the Tai people), whose presence in Yunnan was chronicled by the Chinese as far back as the sixth century BC. Despite this, these nations have distinctly different political, social and economic characteristics as a result of the influence of foreign powers on the regions of South-East Asia, along with their inherent cultural qualities and national achievements.

Thailand has had the good fortune to remain the only nation in South-East Asia never to be colonised by western powers, due to its strategic geographical location between what in the eighteenth century were the rapidly expanding French and English colonial empires. With the English colonies expanding towards Thailand from Malaysia and Burma and the French from Cambodia and Laos, Thailand was seen as a convenient buffer state separating the all too often hostile foes. With a tendency towards openness and cooperation with the outside world, due in part to its relevant lack of foreign domination during the last century, Thailand strategically allied itself with the United States during the second Indochina war, also known as the Vietnam War, and has consistently held its doors open to the outside world in recent decades, resulting in its emergence as one of the world's fastest growing 'tiger' economies.

Laos, on the other hand, has consistently been forced to bow to the demands of more powerful foreign influences since the nation's powerful founding kingdom of Lanexang went into rapid decline during the late seventeenth century. The Burmese, Thai, Vietnamese, Khmer, Black Flag Chinese and French have all exerted varying amounts of control over the struggling state of Laos in recent centuries. The level of decline is evident when one considers that currently there are around five times more linguistical Lao people living outside of the existing Lao borders (mostly in Thailand) than within.

In relatively recent times the nation was once again reluctantly drawn into the vicious cycle of war when the United States and Vietnam both deliberately broke the terms of the 1962 Geneva Peace Accord, which declared Laos to be a neutral nation, and prohibited any external nations from basing troops or undertaking military operations there. The end result of this breach of international law is that Laos remains one of the poorest nations in Asia.

Paddling between the two countries on the Mekong provides a fascinating insight into the effects of these historical circumstances on the region as we enter the twenty-first century. The contrast is particularly stark when one considers that up until the early 1960s both sides of the Mekong had comparable levels of economic, political, infrastructure and educational development and all of the major Lao settlements along the Mekong were in fact more developed than their opposing Thai sister cities or villages.

Today on the Thai side of the river, one finds 7-Eleven convenience stores, transport infrastructure that rivals that of most western nations and an increasingly transparent political system that makes it one of the most advanced democracies in the region.

Glancing to the eastern bank, to Laos—a communist country—one finds predominantly subsistence farming locals, thatched roof hut villages, dirt roads, low levels of literacy, a significantly lower life expectancy and a one-party political system that is almost completely intolerant of domestic criticism of its actions or policies. It's a stark contrast and highlights the effects that the foreign policy of powerful nations can have when they decide to fight their wars in weaker countries.

At the town of Chiang Khong in far northern Thailand we teamed up with Hutch Brown, a laidback friend of Brian's, who would fulfil the role of assistant cameraman for the rest of the expedition. It was Hutch's first time in Asia and I initially had some reservations when Brian recommended him for the job of assistant cameraman. But Brian, who had worked with Hutch for years on North America's rivers, assured me that with his extensive river running and filming experience he was the right guy for the job and, most importantly, that he knew how to deal with the ups and downs of expeditionary travel. Brian's judgement had not let me down yet so I agreed to take Hutch on board. Hutch has an easygoing temperament, which seems to be a legacy of his freelance lifestyle as a river guide in several states of the United States, and within minutes I felt at ease with our newest addition to the team. We were also joined by Jan, a Lao friend and former guide who had worked for my company for around a year and now acted as a freelance guide. Jan followed us in a Zodiac rubber dinghy, sponsored by Green Discovery Travel, to help us with filming.

Jan was the first Lao friend I ever had and he actually nursed me back to health from an acute blood infection caused by a machete cut on my leg in 1998. Besides patiently bringing me food, water and comforts for nearly a week before I could walk properly, Jan also helped the nurses hold my leg still while a doctor used a surgical scouring brush, which looked identical to a pot scrubber, to thoroughly scrub the badly infected cut without anaesthetic for over a minute to clean it. I wasn't immediately grateful for his efforts while yelling in pain but I have been ever since.

The delivery of three of our four sponsored kayaks was delayed so I took to the Mekong in a fast, sleek Perception Contour touring kayak while Hutch and Brian were forced to mix paddling in their slow whitewater kayaks with riding along with Jan in the Zodiac to catch up. Before we left Chiang Khong a local monk came down to the Mekong to bless the new vessels for safe passage. It was a beautiful little ceremony that was set off by the early morning light over the Mekong. Of particular concern to the Thais and Laos that we spoke to was the fact that we planned to run the infamous Khone Falls in the south of Laos. The Khone Falls are arguably the largest volume cascade on Earth and contain by far the largest volume of any waterfall in South-East Asia. In the rainy season the falls have around eight times more water than Niagara. Water levels would be peaking towards the end of June, making it a major challenge to kayak.

Fifty kilometres to the south of where we stood, the Mekong veered away from Thailand before heading in an easterly direction through the heartlands of northern Laos en route to the former royal capital of the nation, Luang Prabang. We estimated the three hundred and eighty-kilometre stretch would take us four days to complete. At this stage of the journey we had a full team again and with the monk's blessing I felt a little better about things staying on track. We followed the Mekong downstream for three long days, covering over one hundred kilometres a day before pulling up in an isolated village where we spent the night and found that we were the first foreigners to stay overnight with the community. It's always a pleasure to be the first to stay in a Mekong village. The kids are the best fun. A large pack of them gathered around us, cautiously watching every move we made, whispering and daring one another to get close enough to touch the foreigners.

There was a little show-off trying to imitate our voices as we spoke to one another so I initiated a surprise game of chase to fire up the situation a little. I would charge the pack for a few steps, causing screams of terror to break out as the kids dispersed in every direction. They soon started laughing and regrouped once I returned to what I was doing, realising that I didn't really want to murder them. Experience has taught me to never catch one of the kids because, even though they will laugh, getting caught by a strange-looking foreigner is terrifying for village kids. I have seen a teenager start bawling from fear when caught.

As we waited for our hosts to prepare dinner I helped Hutch pick up some basic Lao language. Hutch is a quick learner and he rapidly picked up some basic vocabulary. His main problem, as with most foreigners, was coming to terms with the five different intonations used in Lao language. A slightly different intonation can make the meaning of a word completely different from the original. For example, in Lao the word 'I' and the word 'penis' sound almost identical to the untrained ear. Shortly after the lesson I spotted Hutch going around to the locals trying to say, 'Hello, my name is Hutch.' What he was actually saying, to everyone's amusement, was 'Hello, penis name is Hutch.' I waited until the next lesson before training him to be more accurately aware of the different tones. His efforts provided such great entertainment value for the village I didn't want to ruin it.

Jan helped by scouring the village for some fresh vegetables or fish to purchase for dinner but despite his efforts returned almost empty handed and decided to see if our hosts could come up with something while he went off to tinker with the Zodiac's engine. Eventually dinner emerged in the form of a strange tasting gruel with boiled eggplant, morning glory stalks and a type of meat that I could not readily identify. As I ate the gruel I noticed bits of fur getting caught in my teeth. Hutch indicated that he had a crunchy piece in his mouth. Upon sucking the gravy off, closer inspection revealed it was the head of a bat that he had been chewing on.

In three days Brian and I had gone from Australian wines, king prawns and satellite TV to bat giblets, boiled Mekong water and bamboo mat beds on the floor to sleep on. After being in Asia for just four days Hutch seemed completely at home and happily continued nibbling on the bat's nose as he leaned back on a teak wood chair. Brian and I watched him sucking the juices out of the bat's nostrils; we looked at one another and Brian just couldn't take it any more.

'Jesus, Hutch, you're all fucked up man, don't suck its snot.' Hutch didn't see what the concern was about.

'What? Ya gotta try something new man, shit it's only a bat, and it tastes good,' he replied. In a peculiar kind of way I admired his fearless curiosity but as I pulled another piece of fur from between my teeth I decided there had been enough culinary adventurism for me for one evening. I decided to put my tastebuds out of their misery with a customary shot of after-dinner rice whisky.

The friendly smiles and welcoming nature of the locals we stayed with made the stretch all the more memorable. Most of the people we met were fishermen and farmers, eking a subsistence way of life from the Mekong's banks and mainstream. We talked with as many people as we could while paddling down the river and visited the villages to get a clearer understanding of their relationship with the environment.

For most, fish caught in the Mekong made up the bulk of their family's protein intake. A universal statement by the locals was that fish were becoming increasingly more difficult to catch each year. When we asked why that was, we received varying answers but on one stretch between Laos and Burma a lot of the fishermen seemed quite clear as to why their catches had rapidly decreased. Kham, a fifty-three-year-old father of seven, became quite agitated when he told us that he could barely catch enough fish to feed his family.

'They came through here and blew up all the rocks and the fish with them. The government tells us that we are not allowed to use explosives to catch fish but then they come through and blow everything up anyway. All the fish were wasted.'

What Kham was upset about was the Chinese government-sponsored blasting of various sets of rocky outcrops along the course of the river between Laos, Burma, China and Thailand. To be able to increase the size of cargo boats that can ply their trade down the Mekong between the ports of Mengla in China and Chiang Saen in Thailand, the Chinese have been systematically blasting away the many rocky reefs that were a prime habitat for fish populations.

Most of the Lao fishermen we spoke with knew that the high water levels of the monsoon were arriving much later in the year than they once did. But didn't know, as we did, that this was directly attributable to the filling of dams in Yunnan, which bottled up water that would normally flow into Laos in the early months of the monsoon. Another thing the fishermen did not know is that soon the Mekong in their area will probably never become as full as it has been for thousands of millennia, further altering the ecology and fisheries of their river.

Once the mega reservoirs, like the one hundred and seventy-kilometre-long Xiowan inundated area, become operational the water flow released downstream of China will be fully regulated year round, meaning that the water levels will always be around medium. The annual flood cycle, the primary factor affecting the ecology of the river, will be permanently altered and the annual replenishment of the fertile riverbank sediment on which local people grow their vegetables will be greatly reduced.

The lack of knowledge amongst the fishermen about what was happening on their river and what was in store for their communities highlighted how isolated and uneducated the majority of the small rural Lao Mekong communities are. In all of the villages we visited, books, newspapers and radios were almost nonexistent. People were spending all their time and energy on getting enough food and resources to keep their families fed.

As the fisheries rapidly decline and the riverbank areas lose their fertility we can only assume that the people will take urgent measures to make sure they get any resources they can to help them survive. If the people are unable to catch enough fish, they will turn to the nearby forest for other sources of hunted protein. This will place unprecedented pressure on the many threatened wildlife species in the basin. With tens of millions of people in the lower basin eating Mekong fish daily, doing the sums on how many land-based mammals would need to be slaughtered each year to replace this vital protein source highlights what the catastrophic effects of a fisheries decline could be. Not only will there be fewer fish, but the wildlife in the region will become a finite supply of food.

Another environmental consequence will come from people trying to continue growing vegetables in areas that were once replenished annually by nutrient-rich silt. Farmers will be forced to use chemical fertilisers to get the same yields that nature provided in the past. The chemical run-off into the river will have a significant effect downstream. Vietnam's most productive agricultural region, the Mekong delta, is already experiencing the effects of acid soils and algae blooms in certain areas and if people in the regions of Thailand, Laos and Cambodia are forced to increase fertiliser use to replace the sediment loss resulting from the dams, these currently limited algae blooms could become extensive.

After forming the border between Laos and Thailand for around fifty kilometres, the Mekong veers eastward and here we paddled our way past thickly forested mountain ranges of emerald green. We arrived at Luang Prabang two days after the bat head meal. With its rich history and unique blend of royal Lao/French colonial architecture, the town has been awarded World Heritage status and remains one of the best kept secrets of the region. Gilded temples abound as do fine restaurants, boutique hotels and a thriving night bazaar where ethnic minorities bring their wonderful handicrafts for sale. Despite becoming a relatively busy tourist destination, Luang Prabang has managed to maintain the feel of a country town with a touch of royal elegance.

We spent three days visiting waterfalls, temples and other historic sights around Luang Prabang. One beautiful location was the famous Buddhist pilgrimage site of the Pak Ou caves, located on the confluence of the Mekong and Nam Ou rivers. Originally thought to have been a sight for animist ceremonies, the Pak Ou caves consist of two large cave chambers that are jammed with thousands of old and disused images of the Buddha that have been deposited there over the course of several centuries. Every year the residents of Luang Prabang and, in pre-communist times, the king would make a pilgrimage to the caves as part of the Buddhist Lent rains retreat, known as *Phansa*. Buddhist Lent starts on the first day of the waning moon of the eighth lunar month and is a time devoted to study and meditation. The magnificent views across the Mekong to limestone cliffs on the other bank give the caves a special ambiance around dusk, when an orange glow descends over the river and the silhouettes of local fishermen can be seen casting their throw nets in the fading light.

From Luang Prabang we set off for the Lao capital of Vientiane, some four hundred kilometres by river from the former royal capital. From Luang Prabang the Mekong heads in a south-southeasterly direction back towards Thailand. Brian and Hutch were still paddling the slower whitewater kayaks while periodically catching up to me in my sleek touring kayak using the Zodiac, which was captained by Jan. On the third day, however, I paddled ahead and didn't see them for the remainder of the day.

At one point I spotted what appeared to be a dead cow in the water but upon closer inspection it turned out to be a bloated corpse floating face down. Dressed only in his underwear I assumed the unfortunate fellow was a fisherman who had fallen from his pirogue into a rapid or fast current. I considered towing him to a village just in case people upstream were looking for him but when I caught a whiff of him from downstream I decided to paddle ahead and alert the next village. An hour or so later I approached some fishermen in front of a village and told them about the corpse. They were curious but not particularly perturbed. I asked them if they had seen many corpses in the river before and they replied that every year their village pulled out a couple. A fisherman called Ti said, 'Usually they are the victims of speedboat accidents.'

Rickety plywood speedboats with V6 engines often travel along much of the middle Mekong. Cruising at speeds in excess of sixty kilometres an hour they are particularly vulnerable to accidents around the sections of the river with frequent rapids. In these areas, semi submerged trees and logs act like icebergs as they are sucked under by the swirls and currents in the rapids before resurfacing somewhere downstream. If they emerge from the depths at precisely the wrong time they can cause a hurtling speedboat to launch into the air with devastating consequences. I felt glad to be cruising with paddle power.

As darkness closed in I assumed the guys must have had engine troubles and pulled up at the Lao riverside port town of Pak Lai. I informed the port authorities that a corpse would soon be floating by and checked into a simple cement riverside guesthouse for the night. I waited around for Brian, Hutch and Jan until 9 a.m. the next morning but decided to push on. If they had broken down they could float to Pak Lai for repairs or to catch a motorboat if repairs weren't possible. Me waiting around for them would only have slowed overall progress at a time when we were scraping the bottom of the barrel in terms of finances. I was also enthusiastically looking forward to catching up with Yuta and couldn't bare the thought of spending an extra night away. I paddled from Pak Lai to just north of Vientiane in a day and spent some quality time with my girl.

Two days later, Hutch, Brian and Jan finally reappeared at a pier in Vientiane. Looking tired and sunburnt, the boys seemed to be getting frustrated with the blistering speed I was travelling down the river. They had lost filming opportunities in having to keep up with me. I was acutely aware of their concerns yet I tried to explain to them that unless they knew where we could get some additional cash for the descent, we either had to keep things moving or we wouldn't be able to feed ourselves for the last thousand kilometres or so. It turned out that the Zodiac engine had seized up so we were forced to bid farewell to Jan, who returned to his home town of Luang Prabang. From Vientiane onwards we would be without a motorised support vehicle for the duration of the descent through Laos.

More of an oversized town than a city, Vientiane provided a base where we could rest up and arranged various interviews and meetings for the documentary, including representatives from the Mekong River Commission and environmental experts from various agencies, before crossing back into Thailand for a press conference attended by several print media representatives and a couple of TV news crews.

We were fortunate to arrive just in time to witness the candle festival in Nongkhai, Thailand. The festival is an old tradition to mark the start of Lent in northeastern Thailand with a candle parade. Over the generations simple processions with candles have grown and evolved to incorporate elaborate and overwhelmingly beautiful works of art. Trucks are loaded with floats made almost entirely of beeswax. On some of the floats we saw there were children dressed to represent characters from the Thai version of the Ramayana, an epic saga that explores the mythical struggle of religious and moral law against evil and anarchy. Other floats were based around a central theme of the *naga*, travelling with and protecting the Buddha as he made his way across the region passing his wisdom to laypeople. Yuta was our guide, leading us around her childhood hometown set on the banks of the Mekong. At the city's most famous Buddhist temple of Wat Luang Prophrasai we were blessed for good luck by an elderly monk in a short but charming traditional ceremony that involved chanting and using a Mayom branch (a type of branch from the gooseberry tree that is popularly used in religious ceremonies) to splash us with blessed temple water.

It's always an amazing experience to be in Thailand during festival times. Families take to the streets, food vendors, street hawkers, fundraising monks and dancing troops all seem to come out of the woodwork to celebrate and make merry in a manner which is half religious, half carnival. It becomes obvious at these times that the favourite Thai national pastime is eating. There is an endless array of delicacies from fried scorpions, crickets and centipedes to every type of sweet and spicy food you can imagine.

The same evening we attended a small press conference where we met Thailand's most famous and intrepid paddler, Mr Rattapoom Youprom, or Thong as he preferred to be called. Thong had just weeks before finished his own amazing three thousand-kilometre solo journey around the entire coastline of Thailand by sea kayak. Thong walked up to shake my hand at the media reception saying, 'Mick, when I heard about your trip on the Mekong, I had to come and meet you.' A warm-hearted and goateed Thong had a relaxed charm and peaceful nature. He was an easy character to get along with and we made an instant connection. Before the night was out I had spoken with Hutch and Brian and we all agreed that it would be a pleasure to have Thong join us for as much of the rest of expedition as he could.

The following morning a flotilla of eight kayakers, comprising

Thong and a group of seven members of Bangkok's Feelfree Kayak Club took to the river. Hutch and Brian were relieved to finally have our touring kayaks delivered, which enabled us to stay together for this part of the expedition. The group dug deep and we covered over seventy kilometres that day to the village of Ban Khen. That night we bade farewell to all of the extra kayakers, except Thong.

As we continued down the river from Ban Khen, we started to hear stories of a bizarre phenomenon that the locals called *bung fai payanaak*, the *naga* fireballs. Every year around the full moon of Buddhist Lent, large luminous balls of light are known to rise up out of the murky depths of the Mekong and float into the atmosphere. The occurrence has been recorded on temple walls and village journals for many generations and occurs along a stretch of the Mekong located between forty and one hundred and twenty kilometres downstream of Vientiane.

Earlier generations decided that the balls of light were released by the equally feared and revered *naga*, who is said to dwell in the area. Less superstitious people tend to propose that a mixture of fermenting gasses in the murky depths of the river are triggered for release by the forces of the lunar cycle. One thing is for certain: there is no shortage of people claiming to have witnessed the fireballs.

'They are one hundred per cent real, I have seen the fireballs every year since I was a child, all along there,' said forty-five-year-old Boonmee, one of several villagers we spoke to along the Thai stretch of the river south of Nongkhai. With unflinching certainty he pointed a finger towards the Mekong from the balcony of his house. 'Everyone here knows they are real. People come from all around just to see them.'

'It does not matter if people don't believe in them because they are as real as I am,' said Som, a thirty-year-old fisherman in a teak pirogue slightly downstream from Boonmee's village. When I suggested that maybe it was a ploy by the locals to attract tourists to the area, Som responded confidently.

'Tourism? I'm a fisherman, I don't get anything from the tourists. I tell you I see them because I have seen them many times. It's just the way it is.'

I was initially more than a little sceptical about the fireball phenomenon and simply put it down to folklore. I became more and more intrigued after talking with a number of people like Boonmee and Som about their experiences.

There would be only one way to put the matter to rest and that would be to visit the site of the fireballs next year in August to check it out for myself.

Our days were split between long stretches of paddling, stopping to chat with locals, discussing our lives amongst ourselves and making sure we were eating enough to keep up with our high levels of physical exercise. I talked with Thong about his own expedition around the entire coastline of Thailand.

'I did it for my mum,' he said with sincerity as he looked across the vast brown expanse of the Mekong while we drifted towards the sea. 'She loved the ocean but never had the chance to live there before she was killed.' Calmly he went on to explain one of the most tragic stories I have ever heard.

'I phoned my mum many times that day and was worried when she didn't answer the phone. When I went to her house I found her lying on the floor in a huge pool of blood. She had been shot. Next I found my young nephew. They had both been murdered. I went crazy and wanted to find and kill whoever had hurt them.'

Thong's relatives were the innocent victims of a hitman taking out the wrong targets. In a cruel twist, the killer turned out to be a former childhood friend of Thong's who had taken to a life of drugs and crime. Thong's expedition was inspired by a great need to find peace within himself after his world had been shattered. At the time, Thong was consumed with hate, pain and a desire for revenge and he knew these emotions would eat him up or lead to a life behind bars if he carried out the bitter plans that were brewing in his mind.

He decided to take to the ocean in a bid to save his sanity and his soul. For seven months he paddled along the Thai coastline, living like a sea gypsy. In true Buddhist tradition he lived off the generosity of local people who believe they gain merit for the next life through helping others on their quest for inner peace. 'I still miss her so much but I learnt to get rid of the anger and hate. Otherwise I would become like the man who killed her.'

As the days passed, Brian, Hutch and I came to really respect Thong. He never seemed to get the slightest bit flustered or worked up in any situation. After an experience that is almost beyond imagination I was inspired to note that Thong had dealt with his demons and he is the epitome of a man at peace with himself and the world.

Thong is in the process of creating a water foundation in Thailand to dedicate resources to the conservation of the nation's precious resources. Thong epitomises a new breed of Thais who are stepping up to the challenge of protecting what remains of their nation's natural heritage against mismanagement. Unlike Laos, Burma, Vietnam and China, the people of Thailand to a large degree see it as their political right to actively protest against the construction of projects that destroy their livelihoods. It is no coincidence then that the only Mekong nation that no longer allows the construction of major hydro-power dams within its borders is the same nation in which people are allowed to publicly fight for their rights against powerful institutions. I hope that some day the resource rights of the Mekong people from the other five nations can be voiced and heard without the threat of reprisals, because once the Mekong people are provided with a political voice, it seems almost certain that they will make the same decisions about contemporary mega dam projects as the rest of the free world. They will ostracise them and only in the rarest of circumstances accept that they are viable. Unfortunately, for most Mekong nations, that day is still sometime off and until it arrives the only human rights protection that many of the Mekong subsistence people are likely to receive will come through the efforts of people like Thong and the concerned international community. I felt privileged to have Thong on the Mekong descent team, even if it was only for a short time.

We skipped our way down between Laos and Thailand, staying in rural villages and towns on both sides of the river. As we proceeded we passed the confluence of various tributaries I had been privileged enough to explore by kayak and raft over the years. There was the Nam Ngum where I had pioneered the first fully authorised multi-day whitewater rafting trips in Laos, the Nam Leuk emerging from the dense forests of the Buffalo Horn Mountain National Park and the wild Nam Theun/Nam Kading River, which provides ten days of wilderness whitewater as it descends from the Nakhai plateau.

Four long days' paddle south of Vientiane brought into view a spectacular range of karst mountains on the Mekong's eastern flank, the Annamite chain. This ruggedly beautiful string of mountains, which forms much of Laos' eastern border with Vietnam, is perhaps best known internationally due to the strategic role it played in one of the last century's bloodiest conflicts. As the war in Vietnam intensified in the early 1960s it became increasingly important for the northern communist forces to adequately supply their comrades in the south. With the nation effectively cut in half at the heavily fortified seventeenth parallel the most convenient way to do this was to illegally cross men and equipment into Laos from northern Vietnam and transport them southward using the geology of the Annamites as both physical protection and camouflage, before infiltrating south Vietnam either from southern Laos or further south in Cambodia.

This method allowed the effective movement of men and equipment around the heavily fortified 'demilitarised zone'.

Despite the fact that the 1962 Geneva Peace Accord recognised the neutrality of Laos and Cambodia and forbade the presence of all foreign military personnel, both Vietnam and the United States openly violated this accord causing the Vietnam War to spill over into Laos and Cambodia.

What started as a hodge podge of random walk trails and overgrown dirt tracks soon grew into one of the most complex and successful military supply routes in history, which ran through Cambodia, Vietnam and Laos. In the west it came to be known as the Ho Chi Minh Trail. The United States recognised the trail as the communists' greatest strategic weapon and decided to destroy it by using saturation bombing. At a time when the United States' involvement in Vietnam was facing increasing opposition at home, the powers that be risked getting offside with the electorate if they publicly acknowledged their plan. They decided that the US public did not really need to know that their nation would be expanding the war into a couple of extra countries in South-East Asia, so in classic US military tradition they went on the offensive covertly.

Under the auspices of the CIA, the largest and most expensive paramilitary operation in world history commenced in the Lao People's Democratic Republic with catastrophic consequences for rural people along its eastern flank. Between 1968 and 1972 the United States dropped more bombs on the neutral nation of Laos than it did in both theatres of World War II (Pacific and European). The United States dropped around one million nine hundred thousand tonnes of ordnance on Laos, or the equivalent of half a tonne per person in the nation, making Laos the most bombed country per capita in the history of warfare. Over the course of the bombing raids this is the equivalent to a planeload of bombs every eight minutes, twenty-four hours a day for nine years. By the early

1970s the trail consisted of a complex network of roads, trails, bomb shelters, clinics, supply depots, fuel pipelines, armouries and bases that seemed virtually indestructible despite the incredibly intensive campaign.

We arrived at the town of Nakhorn Phanom where Thong was forced to leave us for Bangkok to attend the funeral of a relative. Hutch, Brian and I were all sad to see this colourful character leave us and we wished him all the best with his plans. We enjoyed some beers on the Thai side of the river where Ho Chi Minh had lived for around five years of his life in the 1920s, trying to avoid French colonial administrators and planning the revolution. At dusk we gazed across the Mekong to the mountains, enjoying the fiery eastern Thai cuisine and I wondered whether Ho Chi Minh could have predicted that the mountain range he must have gazed at from the same stretch of river in the 1920s would one day be synonymous with his name.

It's fascinating to compare the Thai town of Nakhorn Phanom to the Lao provincial capital of Tha Khaek on the other side of the river. At the start of the Vietnam War Tha Khaek was a bustling provincial centre on the land route between Thailand and Vietnam. Today several streets of dilapidated French colonial villas and shopfronts stand as testimony to the relative prosperity the Lao town experienced just a few decades ago. During the same period Nakhorn Phanom was a small dirt-pathed village without any regional significance or prosperity to speak of; its only real claim to fame was the historical site of the Wat Phra That Phanom stupa, twenty kilometres to the south of town. The sleepy village of Nakhorn Phanom suddenly changed when the operational headquarters for the US 7th Air Force set up shop with a major airstrip just outside of town. From this base and others the air force undertook devastating bombing raids in the Annamite mountains that forever changed the destiny of Laos.

As the number of Lao civilian dead from these bombing raids increased from tens of thousands to hundreds of thousands, resentment for the Americans and the Lao monarchy, whom the rural people felt had sold out to the United States, grew. The resulting backlash was that a large proportion of the rural populace backed the communists, who in turn gave them the opportunity to fight back against those who, in direct violation of international law, carpet bombed their villages. The end result was that seven hundred years of monarchy in Laos was brought down via a 'communist revolution' partly inspired by communist ideals and predominantly inspired by a will to fight back against illegal acts of sheer brutality. The economic infrastructure that had made Tha Khaek prosperous compared with its Thai sister city was destroyed by war and the archaic policies of the early Lao communist movement.

In a textbook example of communist philosophy's failure to deliver economically, the nation of Laos has progressed very slowly since those dark days of revolution. However, recent free market reforms are starting to increase the pace of development. Although winning autonomy from foreign domination is a historical achievement, something most Lao people are extremely proud of, the sad fact remains that as a result of the conflict between the United States and Vietnam that played out on Lao soil, the nation remains one of the most impoverished and politically insular in the world.

The day after seeing Thong off in Nakhorn Phanom we paddled past the Fai River, which enters the Mekong from the Lao bank and is one of the most impressive rivers I have ever paddled. Passing from the Vietnam border regions to the Mekong flood plain via dramatic karst mountains and sheer-sided gorges, the slow and meandering Fai River shares characteristics with many Mekong tributaries in the area. But it has one particular characteristic that takes it into a world of its own. This medium-sized river actually passes under a mountain range, in one side and out the other some six kilo-metres away. I initially heard about the existence of the cave via Lao friends and then some friends, Nat Stone and Marcus Rhinelander, passed through the cave while making a documentary on the Ho Chi Minh Trail and they talked me into checking it out myself a few months later.

None of the village people who lived in a heavily bombed (during the Ho Chi Minh Trail days) community next to the cave had ever been through it, as they feared the powerful spirits that were said to dwell inside, and before we could enter they insisted on making a pig sacrifice. To my delight the cave was absolutely massive, passing through tunnels that ranged between forty and one hundred metres in width and forty and one hundred metres in height. However, it was often hard to gauge the real size because our reasonably powerful lamps did not have the range to illuminate the great expanses. The Fai Cave is home to several large bat and bird colonies and is a thriving fish spawning ground, where an abundance of fish gather to feast on the bird and bat droppings.

I was so impressed by the sheer size of the cave after visiting it the first time that I mentioned it to some professional spelunkers (cavers) who my travel outfit later assisted to make an expedition through the area. Using lasers the team, led by British spelunker John Pollack, attempted to measure the dimensions of the cave. The expanses were so vast that they could not get accurate readings. However they believe we may have discovered both the biggest cave cavern and the biggest column formation on Earth. Another expedition is in the works to confirm this. It's a great feeling being on the cutting edge of discovery.

The Fai cave is one of dozens of river caves in the Annamites, some of which appear to pass through the mountains for up to thirty kilometres and many of them remain completely unexplored. As the Fai River disappeared from sight behind me I spent my lunch break floating down the mother of water as she shuttled me away from the limestone mountains that I'm convinced still contain some of the world's great unexplored wonders.

Unfortunately the presence of natural wonders could still not help me fully ignore the physical effects of such a long journey. After four months on the expedition my body was growing weary. Humidity regularly peaked at over ninety-five per cent as we continued into the heart of the rainy season and we would get caught in heavy downpours three to four times a day. Sweat would make us wet within minutes of taking to the river each morning but it was the sun's intensity between the storms that would inflict the most damage. The effect of the burning rays of the sun was dramatically increased with the reflection from the surface of the water. Sunscreen was insufficient to protect us from its relentless heat. Hutch and I lost so much skin from different parts of our bodies that we eventually started a kind of competition. Hutch would show me flakes coming off the back of his ears and a few days later I would surprise him with peeling shins. Feet, forearms, thighs, lips, backs, necks, stomachs, ankles and even ribs were all casting off layers of skin at one time or another as we passed through Laos.

Yuta and I had scraped every penny together that we could to keep the project going and we had nothing else to give. With the last of the money running out we were forced to move at a blistering pace, spending up to eleven hours per day on the river to cover the ninety-kilometre average distance that we deemed necessary to reach the South China Sea before the funds run out. One hundred days had passed since I took the first step down from the source and I found it harder each day to push my body to achieve the required distances. At night the lack of blood flow to my hands caused by repetitive strain would wake me up with pins and needles to interrupt my sleep. And with the South China Sea still around one thousand five hundred kilometres away I began to wonder if my body would pack it in before reaching that goal.

15 Secret wars and the settling of scores

We continued south for four days, encountering a series of short but powerful monsoonal downpours as we approached the town of Khong Chiam, which marks the last Thai settlement before the Mekong leaves the nation. Along the stretch the great river is sandwiched between a Lao and Thai national park where villages are few and far between. We were surprised to find a section of gorges where waterfalls plummeted from small cliffs directly into the mainstream.

We stopped briefly in Kong Chiam to cheekily grab a few cold Singha beers, or Beer Sing as the locals prefer to call it, from a Thai floating restaurant without actually being stamped into the country. Before long we entered the southern Lao province of Champasak and its capital Pakse. It was here that we bumped into Hans and Claude, who were employed by the Belgian government to assist the UXO (unexploded ordnance) Lao Project. They were technical advisors to Lao personnel who had the rather dubious job of locating and disposing of the millions of unexploded bombs left over from the US bombing of the countryside.

Hans was the cool and collected type while Claude was a little more outlandish and managed to get himself into a bit of trouble with the girls about Pakse. We went to the project office where we talked to bomb disposal teams and familiarised ourselves with the array of cruel ordnance that was illegally dropped across the countryside just three decades ago. Unfortunately between ten and thirty per cent of the tens of millions of individual explosives devices dropped across Laos did not go off on impact. Today around two hundred Lao people die per year as a result of these weapons of mass destruction.

I was already familiar with most of the items we saw at the UXO office. While waiting to talk with one of the project heads I spent a few minutes inspecting a defused MK81 rocket from the dusty display shelf. The sight of the rocket made my mind wander back to a particularly interesting conversation that played out on the afternoon of 12 September 2001 (it was 12 September in Laos but still 11 September in North America). While enjoying a cold beer with some friends in Vientiane, my mate Alan Boatman rushed in looking rather flustered, saying, 'The Twin Towers of New York and the Pentagon have been attacked, we've got to go somewhere where there's live TV.'

After we'd initially brushed him off, thinking that he was trying to play some type of prank, he said more urgently, 'I'm not fucking joking. I've got two friends who work in the Twin Towers.' The look in his eye left no doubt that he was serious so we rushed around the corner to the nearest bar with live news broadcasts. We arrived in time to catch the surreal scene of the second tower coming down and were all overawed by the gravity of the situation. No one spoke for the first twenty minutes as we took in all of the information that we could from BBC and CNN. Once things calmed down a little we started discussing the events amongst ourselves. Andy, an English friend and long-term resident of Laos, made the comment: 'It's tragic but they shouldn't be surprised that someone is trying to even the score.' Before we had time to respond, an American fellow from outside our group leaned towards our table and made his thoughts known.

'What the fu—! What do you mean?' He was visibly upset. 'Thousands of innocent civilians have been slaughtered like animals. How can they possibly deserve that?'

Andy calmly answered back, 'They don't deserve to be slaughtered at all, but if you're interested in figuring out why it happened, take a look at what you're sitting on.'

Everyone looked at the man's seat and despite the tense atmosphere, the timing and appropriateness of the example made it difficult not to burst out into laughter. The four legs of the chair the fellow was sitting on had MK81 US-made bombs welded into them. The bombs were collected from the tens of millions of similar items that were secretly and illegally flung from a great height by the US military across the internationally recognised neutral civilian areas of Laos for the best part of a decade, killing tens and arguably hundreds of thousands of innocent civilians.

The bar we had wandered into happened to be called 'The B52 bar', a theme bar made up of dozens of types of ordnance that had been collected from the Lao countryside. The tables were made of cluster bomb dispensers and the ashtrays were defused detonators. The American fellow was lost for words, his bottom lip quivered in frustration as he tried to think of a good comeback. He couldn't and was forced to sit and mumble into his beer.

It was an absolutely classic situation and I only wished that it could have been broadcast around the world to place the entire September 11 situation, and the questions it raised about the effectiveness of an invasive foreign policy, into a clearer perspective.

Christopher Robbins' insightful book, *The Ravens*, provides a fascinating account of how the United States managed their secret bombing operations in Laos. US military men volunteered to go to 'the other theatre', the code name for Laos, and were stripped of military uniform and recognition. The United States was knowingly breaking international law, so, in order to keep these illegal activities out of the public eye, the volunteers in Laos wore civilian clothes and 'Each pilot was obliged to carry a small pill of lethal shellfish toxin, created by the CIA, which he had sworn to take if ever captured by the enemy.' Four hundred of the American volunteers who carried out the secret CIA missions in Laos perished during the conflict while a further four hundred went missing in action. Many of these MIAs have still not been located.

I have often bumped into the Joint POW/MIA Accounting Command (JPAC) teams who currently operate from the US embassy in Vientiane in an effort to locate the remains of these secret servicemen. They are a nice bunch of people who are still picking up the pieces of a shameful piece of recent history that most Americans have absolutely no idea about.

From the dusty storage yard of the UXO Lao office we caught a ride to the Bolaven plateau. This plateau was formerly part of an extremely active volcanic area on the eastern side of the Mekong and it is now covered in dense forests that contain dozens of thundering waterfalls. The local people predominantly grow coffee beans there today and these have become some of the most highly prized gourmet beans in existence due to their unique aroma, flavour and the small quantities produced. Historically a tribal region inhabited by the Alak, Laven and Nge minority groups, the area was also once part of the Ho Chi Minh Trail.

Twelve kilometres along the road leading to the plateau we came across a blacksmithing village. It was an interesting speck on the map. The craftsmen made machetes and farm tools using the traditional large hammers and charcoal-fired ovens. The anvils were all made of bomb casings. The steel that was being forged included war scrap ranging from bomb casings to shrapnel and detonator housings. Even the manual air pump used to supply oxygen to the fire was customised from helicopter rocket launcher casings.

One of the most fascinating aspects of hanging out with the locals in these regions is chatting with the crusty old veterans who remember those dark years when they lived in constant fear for their lives and watched many innocent members of their villages die. Once lubricated with some Lao Lao, the old timers forgot their normal prudence and the stories would fly thick and fast. 'They came here and started killing us, so we fought back. We shot one of their planes down from this village and it landed over there,' said Toon, a fifty-five-year-old man, who showed me the numerous shrapnel scars on his back, arms and legs.

'They destroyed our crops, our homes and killed our people. We did whatever we could to get them back,' said Aon, a sixty-five-year-old farmer from Khammuane province.

Dozens of similar stories that came from hardy and surprisingly honest and friendly veterans from all over the trail area have left me in no doubt that almost none of them understands why America bombed their villages and agricultural lands for nearly a decade. They simply wanted to resist the aggressors who brought indescribable violence to their world.

We paddled south from Pakse, which is located just one hundred and ninety kilometres upstream from the Cambodian border. About four hours south of town by paddle power we parked our kayaks on the riverside to visit the World Heritage-listed ruins of Wat Phou. This ancient Khmer temple complex inspired the setting for the early 1980s film *The Jungle Book* and is evidence of one of the first major civilisations to flourish in the Mekong Basin between the sixth and eleventh centuries.

Wat Phou clings to the side of a mountain and commands panoramic views of the Mekong Valley. The temple complex has many rare examples of pre-Angkorian art and artefacts, characterised by a strong Hindu influence with sandstone sculpture of the gods Vishnu, Garuda and Ganesh featuring prominently. A unique feature of Wat Phou is that it has been built into a mountainside rather than on a plain or on top of a hill as most other significant Khmer sites are. When you are walking between the beautifully crafted palaces of the lower levels, which were used for ritual ablutions, and up through the frangipani-fringed staircases to the sanctuary overlooking the Mekong, it's easy to let your mind wander back to a time when the civilisations along the lower Mekong were some of the most powerful and advanced.

From Wat Phou we took to the river and entered one of the most beautiful legs of the Mekong, commonly referred to as the Four Thousand Islands. Starting from a point some one hundred kilometres north of the Cambodian border the Mekong begins braiding out into various channels separated by islands that make up a unique seasonal wetland habitat that can be found only in a few select places such as the Amazon Basin. The islands are fringed with coconut palms and thatched huts that seem to transport you back through the centuries. Yet the peace is soon interrupted by a scene of extreme violence. Immediately before the river crosses into Cambodia, at a breadth of over twelve kilometres, it tumbles off an expansive natural fault line, which has resulted in a vertical drop of some ten metres. Khone Falls is not as high as Niagara in America or Victoria Falls in Africa but it does have far more water tumbling off its edge, making it an extremely challenging whitewater obstacle at any time of year.

We paddled down to a large inhabited island called Don Khon located in the middle of the Khone Falls. With all the rushing to make our way south we had missed some important filming opportunities so we decided to spend a few days in the dramatic falls area to capture the fascinating region for the documentary. The Khone Falls are home to some of the bravest and most adept fishermen on Earth. The local fishermen have mastered the art of fishing around the perilous falls to catch the vast range of fish that shoal there. We decided we could allow three days with these wonderful and inspiring people to gain some insights into their intensely close relationship with the river.

'For as long as anyone can remember the fishermen of Khone Falls have harvested the fish like this,' said Mr Boon, the seventy-four-year-old owner of the guesthouse we stayed at. He pointed to a *lee*, or traditional bamboo fish trap, wedged into a black sulphide rock chute being sprayed with whitewater. 'The best time is during the first rains of June when the waters come up,' he continued. Mr Boon was happy to think of that special time because the annual fish run is the cash cow for several villages that are in close proximity to the falls.

The rising monsoonal flows of the Mekong send the fish of the great Tonlé Sap Lake and elsewhere in the Cambodian Mekong on a spawning migration upstream into the Khone Falls area of Laos. Hundreds of millions of fish undertake this journey and at peak times it is not uncommon for Khone Falls fishermen to catch over one hundred kilograms per day, using just the traditional wood and bamboo traps that are only five metres wide. The fish run highlights the cyclical nature of the river's ecology, which doesn't recognise national borders. There are six nations that lie along the Mekong—if the fisheries in downstream Cambodia deteriorate then the fisheries in Laos and beyond will suffer and so on down the line.

Despite being whitewater experts who often took significant risks around rivers, Brian, Hutch and I were amazed to see young men swinging across treacherous sections of whitewater using ropes and vines and setting up immense fish traps in sections of incredibly powerful water without so much as a life vest.

We decided to check the catch with one of the fault line fishermen and rose at 5 a.m. to go and inspect the *lees* and nets of Mr Phon, a wiry forty-five-year-old fisherman, who had set bamboo and rattan cane fishing traps in the powerful rapids of the Khone since childhood.

'A lot of people who come here from other places think we're crazy, but to the people from our village it's just the way we fish,' explained Mr Phon as he began paddling me in his six-metre-long, solidly built teak wood canoe towards a powerful eddy near where he had set his net. He skilfully read the current and eddy line with the precision of an Olympic standard slalom kayaker and carefully edged us upstream towards his net. I paddled to help him but the boat was so unstable in the surging current that it wobbled with every stroke and threatened to flip.

It took my full concentration to maintain balance and as we edged into position right on the whirlpool-studded rim of a powerful eddy line, I began cursing myself for not thinking to bring a life vest. The eddy line and whirlpools were so powerful that if we made even a minor mistake the result would almost certainly include us being tossed out of the canoe. Without the all-important flotation of life vests strapped to our bodies it would be a serious fight for survival, providing the whirlpools with the ability to hold us under for unpredictably long periods, perhaps as long as two or three minutes. When the adrenaline is rushing and your heart beating out of control you need at least twice as much oxygen as normal, so it only takes one to two minutes to actually die in these circumstances. I breathed in and out quickly in a deliberate attempt to aerate my blood in the same way I prepare for kayaking a particularly dangerous rapid. I gripped a small hardwood paddle, using it to keep the boat at the appropriate upstream angle to the current so that it would not get jerked and flipped over by the current broadsiding it. To my dismay, right at the point where I thought we seemed closest to flipping, Phon stood up and skilfully began walking towards the front of the bow. The adrenaline was surging as I attempted to counter the subtle instability this caused. From the tip of the bow Phon reached out and grabbed the net in one hand and with the other pulled the boat against a partly submerged branch.

With a certain degree of stability provided by this he looked at me with a reassuring glint in his eye, which made me realise that for him at least it was all just part of a day's work. After a fishing experience that gave me the same standard of adrenaline kick as I typically get from running a class V first rapid descent I was very pleased to feel my feet back on the island of Don Khon.

The boatmen of the Khone Falls area are by far the most skilled traditional boaters I have ever encountered. Even though we didn't catch anything that morning I was most impressed by the whitewater confidence and skills of Mr Phon. Lucky for us, some of the other fishermen returned with single fish weighing around four kilograms and they gave us one to take back for dinner.

On the same day, we were invited by some of my Lao friends on the island of Don Khon to attend the funeral of a fisherwoman who had passed away from a mysterious fever. In contrast to western funerals, Lao wakes are designed to be relaxed, enjoyable and even slightly jolly affairs that take place over the course of several days. It's quite acceptable to come to such events with friends even if those friends are not familiar with the deceased. From the moment Hutch, Brian and I walked in with a big fish as a gift we were immediately greeted like family and spent most of the day eating, talking and enjoying the company of the villagers. Hutch finally managed to say a few sentences in Lao without referring to his penis and Brian entertained everyone by displaying his distinct sunburn lines, a phenomenon that the dark-skinned southern Lao people found pretty humorous.

The Khone Falls presented the last major whitewater barrier for the Mekong First Descent Project and it was the single biggest rapid challenge of the entire journey, something I had been concerned about for weeks as we approached the falls. I had actually already run several channels of the falls previously, including taking part in the first full whitewater exploration of the Khone Falls area with a team of professional kayakers in November 2000. But all of my previous descents through the Khone had been at medium to low water flows. They were at the most extreme end of the scale, even at the moderate to low water levels, but now that we were approaching the end of July the river was full. By the time we finished capturing the footage we wanted, we were left with little time for scouting to locate a viable kayaking run through the falls. We had just one morning before we were scheduled to meet our logistical support team, who were sponsored by Asian Trails Cambodia and were waiting just downstream of the falls at the Lao–Cambodia border crossing.

We went to one channel, then another, then another—all of the runs we checked out were so extreme that there was a very significant chance of disaster if everything did not go perfectly to plan. The risks were huge. I was determined to take on the Mekong's Khone Falls from top to bottom but after hours of searching we just couldn't find her most accessible weak point where I could do so without placing my life at an unacceptably high level of risk. We searched until we were well past our appointed meeting time with the Cambodian support team, who would probably be getting frustrated, but we finally narrowed it down to one potential run. The falls of Liphi. The immense Liphi channel at flood water levels was about two hundred metres wide and flowing at around thirty kilometres per hour in the fastest sections. The safe point through the falls was in the middle of the channel and was perhaps ten metres wide. To the left and to the right of that survival channel lay holes and violence of such ferocity that I wouldn't expect to survive if I was not on course. The problem was that from above the falls it would be impossible to see whether I was on course for the ten-metre-wide safe zone before going over the lip or whether I was slightly off course and headed for disaster.

I mentally calibrated and recalibrated the actions and distances required, discussed the run in detail with Brian and Hutch and then reassessed it again and again, yet I struggled to reach a decision about whether I could pull it off. Successfully pulling off life-threatening whitewater runs that are at the extreme outer realms of one's abilities is an art form. Physical strength, technical ability and determination play small parts. Success or failure is hinged upon your ability to reach a point of Zen in your mind that allows you to combine absolute focus, coordination and collaboration between mind and body. I looked at the run and breathed in and out steadily. I knew what needed to be done in order to survive it, I just needed to reach my Zen point in order to make it happen in defiance of the river's overwhelming power and chaos.

I couldn't put my finger on it, but there was something not quite right within my subconscious. Something was niggling at me, a niggle that I just couldn't seem to shake and try as I might I could not reach a point where I felt everything was in place psychologically. Something was warning me not to place my life on the line at this particular moment in time. My mind flashed back to some of the greatest challenges of the expedition to that point and I realised that I could have avoided a lot of hardship and suffering if I had listened to my instincts more in the early stages of each journey. I made the call to portage a short section of the Liphi Falls and put in around halfway down the drop rather than at the top as I had already run Liphi several times in the past when things had felt right. I decided not to push my luck this time.

It was a slightly frustrating decision to have to make due to the fact that it was a major Mekong landmark but I know I made the right decision. The lower half of the falls still offered a challenging class V section to help me get my adrenaline-soaked whitewater fix. Hutch joined me for the run down the remainder of Liphi and managed to paddle himself straight into the centre of a particularly large hole, but luck was on his side and it spat him out about as quickly as it made him disappear under a huge mound of foaming whitewater.

Immediately downstream from the gorges is the bizarre habitat of flooded forest where the trees literally grow sideways due to the extremely powerful currents that surge against them throughout much of the year. Just as the turbulence subsided we entered the domain of the extremely rare Mekong Irrawaddy dolphin. The dolphins can be found in the deep pools that are up to forty metres deep near the base of the falls.

These shy, dark grey creatures usually hunt in packs in the deep pools at the base of the falls and they tend to spend most of their time hunting. The Mekong's waters are an earthy red that provides zero visibility for most of the year, so these Mekong dolphins rely on their sonars. Catching enough fish to eat each day takes far longer than it does for their seafaring cousins. The Mekong Irrawaddy dolphins' snub-nosed heads give them the appearance of a porpoise rather than the bottlenose dolphins that most people are familiar with and their skin colour possesses a smooth, moderately grey appearance. Finding the dolphins is usually done by listening for them as they make a distinctive 'shhhh' sound when they come up for a breath.

Today the dolphins can be seen at the base of the falls if you know where to look but the numbers have dropped off in recent years due to a mixture of decreasing fish stocks, explosives fishing on the Cambodian side of the border and getting caught in fishing nets. Highly informed biologist and Mekong fisheries researcher, Ian Baird, who lived on Don Khon for many years studying the dolphins and assessing the general fisheries outlook for the area, estimates the dolphins will probably cease to exist within ten to twenty years and has no doubt that, like the bulk of the mainstream fisheries, the dolphins will certainly be negatively impacted upon as more of China's mega dams come on-line.

As I paddled past the dolphin habitat on the last day of the expedition in Laos I watched the stunted dorsal fins of a mother and calf breach the surface followed by a momentary glimpse of the mother's head as the Mekong islands of Cambodia provided a beautiful backdrop. I felt a wave of energy sweep over me and the reason that the river captivated me seemed tangible, almost three dimensional. Yet my euphoria was interrupted as I thought about the precariousness of the Mekong Irrawaddy dolphins. I remembered a phrase quoted in a recent paper by Dr Milton Osbourne, one of the world's most distinguished authors and commentators on the Mekong situation, who cautioned, 'The river's future as a vital part of the life of mainland South-East Asia is on a knife's edge.' I couldn't agree more.

16 Cambodia and the beating heart of the Mekong

At the border of Cambodia we were met by our guide and translator, Chanta, a thirty-six-year-old Khmer national with a no-nonsense professional manner and dry sense of humour that soon earned our respect. Chanta was sponsored to assist us by Asian Trails Travel of Cambodia and didn't beat about the bush when it came to sorting things out.

'So tell me what you want to do and I'll arrange it,' Chanta said as I shook his hand for the first time. 'The water is strong, if you drown there will be trouble, can you handle it?' I liked his honesty and assured him that the locally famed Sambor rapids that we were heading for would be quite mild for whitewater kayakers.

After discussing the game plan we decided that Brian and Hutch should go ahead by speedboat to get some stock footage of a land-mine victim centre for the documentary while I was left to make my way downstream alone for the rest of the day. I continued through significant stretches of flooded forests and was astounded by the prolific birdlife I saw.

As the Mekong goes into flood, hundreds of square kilometres of old growth forest are inundated by the swift-moving waters, providing an important spawning ground for fish and a naturally protected nesting site for myriad bird species. The current moved me silently under the canopy of trees, allowing for close encounters with the different birds. In the sections where there were not too many obstacles I would lie on my back and look up through the canopy; watching the way the light shone through the foliage was mesmerising.

On the same afternoon I spotted three species of hornbill, two species of crane, woodpeckers, kingfishers, parakeets, fish eagles and at least nine other bird species. To the east of the flooded forests lie the remote and densely forested mountains of Dangkrek and the sprawling Virichay National Park, where tigers, gibbons and other wildlife roam.

Around the time of writing, two separate groups of bark-clothed people had wandered out of the park and into Laos where they were subsequently arrested. The group had been hiding in the forest for over two decades, still believing the Khmer Rouge were in charge of the nation. This particular incident highlights how remote the north-eastern regions of Cambodia are.

When I was travelling through this area I was curious to find out whether the villagers in the area could speak the Lao language, because of their proximity to the border. I attempted to question people I came across, yet the reaction I received was not quite what I expected. The first group of people I met were in small wooden boats. Before I could say anything, they screamed to one another then frantically paddled into the flooded forest to hide. A similar thing happened the next time when I approached a couple of ladies who were checking nets. They dropped everything to make a slightly panicked run for the forest. The stories told to me by Lao people living along the frontier before I crossed the border into Cambodia, which involved incidences of the former Khmer Rouge terrorising the locals of the region, suddenly seemed to have some foundation when I considered the unusual reaction of these locals.

As I paddled on alone the silence seemed to shroud the river with a slightly eerie presence and I imagined some armed bandits coming out from the forest to do as they pleased. On my third attempt at making contact with the locals, a cautious-looking fisherman stayed long enough for me to communicate with him. Fortunately, he spoke Lao and Khmer so I was able to ask him a few questions. According to him, most of the villages in the area were made up of bilingual ethnic Lao peoples. When I asked why people had fled when they saw me he said simply, 'They are scared.' When I asked why, he looked at me as if I was silly for asking an obvious question.

'They have never seen a foreigner paddle a red boat before.' I asked him if there were any current problems with the Khmer Rouge.

'It was bad here for a long time but they have left. It's quite safe now. There are still some people with black hearts, but it's not so dangerous.' I thanked him for talking to me and continued downstream where I met up with Brian, Chanta and Hutch just before sunset on the eastern channel. We headed towards a small village on one of the many islands that divide the river into separate channels.

People on this island had only recently begun to return to the area after the local population was decimated by the Pol Pot regime in the late seventies. Although extremely poor, they were proud to be honest farmers and cherished the peace that they now had living on the island. We chatted with an energetic old man called Tou, who was the first to return to the island since those terrible times. He told us that he could still remember the last group of foreign paddlers that had passed through his village—a group of Australians in 1969 on a bamboo raft. I asked how many foreigners had stayed in his village since then and he told us that none had.

We chatted with the charismatic and charming Tou for quite a while about life in the area and the changes he had seen, yet when we eventually came to the subject of the Khmer Rouge, particularly his thoughts about the movement, I noticed him clam up and change the subject back to more comfortable topics. Chanta, who was translating, told us that he was too scared of repercussions to talk about the Khmer Rouge—an alarming thought. I asked one more question before moving on: 'I don't need to know what you think about the Khmer Rouge but did the people of your village suffer due to their policies?'

Tou glanced at me for a moment but his gaze seemed to pass straight through me. He motioned to speak, but nothing came out. In the space of a millisecond, a bolt of anguished energy that felt like a physical pulse passed from his faraway gaze into my body. As Tou's thoughts seemed to return from the darkest memories of his life, he closed his eyes, shook his head slowly, still unable to speak and lowered his eyes to the ground without saying a word.

I felt I had learnt as much in that moment about the real effects of the Khmer Rouge and the second Indochina war than I had from over a dozen books on the subject and my wide-ranging travel through the region. It was a moment I will never forget.

The village was one of the poorest that we had stayed in and several of the children's stomachs were bloated from malnutrition. One concern that all the locals had was that they were forbidden to hunt wildlife for food and with fish stocks in rapid decline they were having a hard time replacing the animal protein in their diet. This problem was exacerbated by periodic raids on their crops by wild monkeys, deer, pigs and birds. They had already run out of rice stocks for the rest of the season and were left with no choice but to hunt wildlife again. The poor yields they had experienced in the previous year forced them to eat all of the rice seed that they needed for the next planting season so they had to borrow new seed from suppliers at extortionate interest rates, creating a vicious cycle of debt. This was the second year running that their rice growing efforts had produced a deficit. The outlook for the village was grim.

According to their estimates if they were fortunate enough to experience bumper crops it would still take them four years to pay back their debt. There are many people in similar situations along the various stretches of the Cambodian Mekong who can least afford to have their natural resources compromised by outside forces, however it is Cambodia that will be the most affected by China's dams.

I continued downstream towards the Khmer capital of Phnom Penh. As I got further away from the Khone Falls border it was interesting to see that the style of river craft changed completely. North of the Khone Falls, the landlocked people of Laos design their craft to be efficiently built, light and sleek, perfect for moving against river currents and dragging the craft around obstacles that they come across. On the other hand, the Khmer civilisation had flourished due in part to its proximity to the ocean. When the first westerners travelled up the Mekong over four hundred years ago the Khmer used craft that were river/ocean hybrids so that they were able to tackle the navigational challenges that both environments posed. Today it's still possible to see these craft in action.

The small 'V' hulled hardwood vessels have high gunwales to reduce the chance of swamping, significant hull 'rockers' (hulls that are angled like the curved base of a rocking horse) for efficient turning, and sails to reduce the human energy inputs associated with moving the craft. We were moving into another distinct cultural realm and it felt great to experience another aspect of the vast diversity of the Mekong Valley. I found it amazing to consider that all the different peoples we met, from the nomadic herders of the Tibetan Plateau to the Khmer fishermen of the flooded forests, shared the same, single continuous valley.

Chanta, Hutch and Brian took off in the speedboat to spend a couple of days in the floating villages on the Tonlé Sap Lake while I paddled onwards towards Phnom Penh. I had another three days on my own before joining up with them. I was paddling over ninety kilometres per day. In the middle of a two-hour paddle stretch two days after the guys sped off to the lake, I popped a tendon in my right elbow and with each stroke a slightly painful click occurred. It was time to get off the river for a few days but I was still eighty kilometres from Phnom Penh and we planned to spend five days off the river there, so I thought it best to keep going until then. As the pain got worse I decided that the best thing to do would be to rest on the kayak and let the Mekong's brisk currents take me the rest of the way instead of having to use my arms. With the current flowing around four to five kilometres per hour I estimated I would have to stay on the river until around midnight to cover the rest of the ground.

I had a couple of good books to get through and between reading and sleeping knocked off the first eight hours without too much trouble. As the sun set, a pervasive feeling of peace came over the river and from centre stream barely a thing could be heard except for the occasional wisp of wind over water or the sound of bats and birds flying overhead. I was surprised to see that there were hardly any large villages upstream of the national capital. I fell asleep at one point and awoke suddenly when I collided with a houseboat moored off a small island in the centre of the river. Fortunately there was no major damage to either boat and I was able to move on.

It was a moonless night and from twenty kilometres upstream I could see the ambient light of Phnom Penh approaching. A feeling of inner calm came over me as I sat there spinning in slow circles and arcs in the current, at the whim of the river. It occurred to me that the mother of water would bring me to the South China Sea whether I was able to paddle or not. Occasionally the voices of people living on houseboats came and went, as they chatted away, oblivious to my passing in the darkness. I felt at one with the river and the timelessness and tranquillity of her flow seemed eternal. More than one per cent of the world's people were sitting on or nearby the river and its tributaries that night, most of them finishing meals that, in one way or another, were gifts from the mother of water.

For a moment I could sense the enormity of her role, which seemed to be accomplished with peaceful grace and charm. I dozed off for half an hour and when I awoke found that the light of Phnom Penh was now to my west. I had overslept, which left a large area of island and swampland between me and the capital. I spent the next two hours struggling through spider's webs and swamps as I tried to cut right towards the downtown area of Phnom Penh. By the time I made it through the swamp I had already overshot the Siem Riep River, which marks the downtown area and was headed for Vietnam. I pulled into the southern suburbs on the outskirts of the city at around 1.30 a.m. and after spending forty-five minutes looking for a taxi or tuk tuk I decided to sleep on the kayak until morning.

After a restless night's sleep I waved down a passing boat, which took me upstream into the Tonlé Sap River to the colonial-style boardwalk area of the city. I went to meet the crew at Asian Trails Cambodia, who were helping us with logistics. The friendly crew soon had me on a large speedboat cruising across the great Tonlé Sap Lake en route to the floating village of Kampong Louang where Hutch, Brian and Chanta were staying.

The Tonlé Sap represents one of the most bountiful lakes on Earth due to its unique ecology which is based around the dramatic seasonal rise and fall of the Mekong. Between October and August the Tonlé Sap receives its water like most lakes, with the essential liquid entering it from the surrounding highlands before eventually exiting at a separate point—in the case of the Tonlé Sap Lake that exit point is via the Tonlé Sap River, which flows into the Mekong.

But the Mekong's highly seasonal flows cause an extremely unusual situation. When the mother of water approaches peak levels around June, she rises higher than the Tonlé Sap Lake and as a result gravity feeds immense quantities of water from the Mekong into the lake. The water causes the Tonlé Sap River to reverse its flow so instead of draining the lake it starts filling it. In the space of just a few months the Mekong contributes approximately sixty-two per cent of the lake's total water volume, increasing its size by around five hundred per cent to approximately eighty thousand square kilometres or forty-four per cent of the nation's total area. The lake in effect acts like a huge cistern, storing the Mekong's floodwaters during the peak flows then releasing them at drier times of year.

As the lake expands it floods thousands of square kilometres of forest, providing an important spawning ground for a wide range of fish species. The unique ecology of the lake, which is created by this phenomena, results in it being classified as one of the most abundant inland fisheries on Earth, with over two hundred and thirty thousand tonnes of fish harvested annually. The importance of this fishery to the two million people that depend upon it directly as a primary source of income, and to the entire impoverished nation as the primary source of animal protein, cannot be overstated. On an ecological level the Tonlé Sap contains the largest continuous area of savannah swamp forest and inundated forest (normal forest that is seasonally flooded) in Asia and is a habitat for hundreds of bird and aquatic species, hence its inclusion as a UNESCO World Biosphere Reserve.

The unique storage and flushing cycle and the vital role that these aspects play in the Mekong's ecology have resulted in the Tonlé Sap being nicknamed by various fisheries and hydrological experts as 'the beating heart of the Mekong Basin'.

When the massive Xiowan Dam on the Mekong in China becomes operational around 2012, the flood and ebb cycle of this great lake in Cambodia will be affected, permanently. The Mekong's natural flows will no longer reach the same flood peaks that annually inundate the forests surrounding the lake and in turn provide the key spawning habitat that is so important to the lake's ecology. Although the regions surrounding the great lake are already some of the most impoverished in all of Asia, it seems that the battle for subsistence is soon to become a great deal more difficult and, according to many experts, a widespread famine is definitely not out of the question if the fisheries collapse rapidly.

From the Royal Palace in Phnom Penh, a five-hour cruise took me across huge expanses of water through points where land was not visible in any direction to the floating village of Kampong Louang, where I met up with the rest of the team. We spent the next two days interviewing local fishing families about their lives on the lake for the film. With a population of over three thousand the village had everything a weary paddler could hope for, including floating pubs, grocery stores, restaurants, hardware stores and even a floating prison. The residents of Kampong Louang are a mixture of Khmer, Vietnamese and Cham, who live quite harmoniously in this waterborne community. Each dry season the village is floated out towards the centre of the lake to be closer to where the fishing action is and in the rainy season the village is moored near the edge where many fish accumulate to take advantage of the flooded forest habitats. Needless to say, fishing is the most popular pastime on the lake but after talking to the locals it became apparent that this might not be the case for long.

The building of upstream dams, rising population pressure, expanding agriculture, over-fishing and deforestation have all combined to decrease fish stocks in recent years. Many of the young men that we spoke to were looking for alternative ways of making a living because surviving off their declining catches no longer seemed viable; unfortunately making alternative livings in one of the world's most impoverished nations is easier said than done, especially for people with poor levels of education and restricted experience in anything besides the very specific subsistence skills that have allowed them and their ancestors to survive until now. The question is, how long will those skills provide for their sustenance?

Due to public awareness campaigns set up by the Cambodian government and foreign non-government organisations, the locals we spoke with appeared to be particularly well informed about events affecting the ecology of the Mekong and the Tonlé Sap, unlike most of those we spoke with outside the Tonlé Sap area.

The Cambodian government is in the process of implementing broad-ranging legislation and village-based projects to develop community fisheries management strategies, including stricter policing of illegal logging, fish size limits and other measures that stand a good chance of improving the situation. One of the arguments presented to us by the fishermen was that it seemed futile for the Cambodian people to work hard in an attempt to stabilise the resource base of the Mekong and Tonlé Sap while the Chinese could 'turn off the tap' in the north and destroy their way of life anyway. It was a valid point.

We spoke with fisheries expert Patrick Evans, head of the United Nations Food and Agriculture Organization's Tonlé Sap project in Siem Riep. Patrick has spent over seven years researching the fisheries of the great lake and helping the Cambodian authorities create and implement a sustainable management plan. Patrick is widely acknowledged as a leading authority on the Tonlé Sap's fisheries situation and like other authorities throughout the basin he is very concerned about the implications of China's dams. He pointed out that the road towards responsible management of lake's resources had been a bumpy one within Cambodia, yet recently great strides have been made with community-based management and usage now beginning to take precedence over large-scale commercial fishing concessions and unmanaged forest exploitation. The Cambodians are trying to do their part in responsibly managing the Mekong Basin's resources. Sadly, this alone may not be enough.

We asked Patrick, and other experts from agencies, such as the International Crane Foundation and the Cambodian government, if during their many years of working on the lake they had ever encountered Chinese scientists conducting detailed research into its ecology or the effects that their dams might have on the lake—none of them were aware of such studies.

We headed across the vast expanse of water to the most impressive historical site to be found in the Mekong Valley—Angkor. The temples of Angkor rate as one of the seven man-made wonders of the world. Built between the eighth and thirteenth centuries, during the peak of the Khmer civilisation, Angkor was the biggest city on Earth with a population of over one million. This sprawling empire of Angkor encompassed much of Thailand, Laos, Vietnam and Burma with the metropolis based on the edge of the Tonlé Sap Lake.

Hundreds of monuments dedicated to Buddhist, Hindu and god-king religions are spread throughout a huge area and are typically engulfed by tropical forest, providing a serene and mysterious ambience. The following day we had the pleasure of spending hours looking at the temples and vistas around Siem Riep from the air with Cambodian West Coast Helicopter Services, filming for the documentary.

On our last day in Siem Riep we paid a visit to the Land Mine Museum and it is here that we met a truly inspirational character in the form of Aki Ra, the museum's founder. An unassuming thirty-three-year-old man, Aki Ra sat cross-legged on the floor of a small wooden hut where we talked to him about how he came to be the founder and curator of the museum.

'Before I could tie my own shoelaces I was being trained to kill people by the Khmer Rouge,' he said. By the time he was in his teens, Aki Ra believed that violence, murder and bloodshed were normal. Eventually he was captured by Vietnamese forces and after discovering that the Khmer Rouge had murdered his parents, he fought on the other side of the conflict for several years.

'It was only when the United Nations came to Cambodia in the 1990s that I realised there were parts of the world where violence and killing were not a part of everyday life.' Aki Ra was employed by the United Nations to help locate and disable the mines that he and others had helped set during the savage conflict. It was through his experiences with people from the outside world and doing something positive for his fellow Cambodians that he realised his calling in life and eventually dedicated his existence to clearing as many of the estimated six million active landmines in Cambodia as he could, by hand. Even when the United Nations left and funding for mine clearance dried up, Aki Ra continued to clear mines in his own time and with his own money.

In 1990 Aki Ra assembled many of the thousands of mines that he had located and defused under a tin roof, opening up the landmine museum near Angkor Wat in an attempt to educate people about the horrors of war and the ongoing problem of landmines in Cambodia. A walk through his museum reveals the dozens of varieties of mines on display with 'made in' labels from the United States, Germany, Russia, China and Vietnam, all boldly advertised on the sides, and shows the sickening variety of ways that people can develop technology to hurt, maim or kill fellow humans. Bouncing betties, claymores, remote-triggered and timed devices along with a range of custom-made devices are on show. As we walked out through the museum gates about a dozen kids played football outside. A closer look revealed that it was not quite a standard game of football. Most of the kids had missing limbs. Aki Ra had taken it upon himself to adopt or semi adopt fifteen kids in a bid to provide them with an education that will ensure they have alternatives to begging for a living.

We chatted with these shy, bright-eyed kids who played football with amazing agility using crutches and artificial limbs. All the kids we spoke with were extremely grateful to Aki Ra for his kindness and when we asked them how they felt about the landmines in their country the responses were similar. 'They usually kill or maim civilians rather than the enemy,' answered Nong, a shy boy barely in his teens.

It is a sad fact that the current US administration completely failed to show concern for the millions of maimed civilians around the world when they blocked moves to join the one hundred and twenty-nine nations that had already ratified the UN Mine Ban treaty that would effectively ban the use of these horrific weapons. I wondered whether such leaders might see the downside of allowing these indiscriminate killers and destroyers of civilian lives to be manufactured and dispersed by the millions each year if they were forced to deal with three per cent of their own population being maimed by mines as Cambodia does. In the case of the United States, which has become the greatest driving force behind allowing the continued use of landmines, that would equate to around eight hundred thousand maimed American civilian victims and counting. I wonder what the chances of re-election would be then?

It was refreshing to meet someone like Aki Ra, who has the moral fibre to recognise the evil of such indiscriminate violence against humanity. In his own way, Aki Ra is undoing the mistakes of the past and making the world a better place to live in—a true hero of the Cambodian people.

We returned to the hustle and bustle of Phnom Penh where we rested up overnight. The city was completely depopulated under the Khmer Rouge in the late 1970s and it was during this period that the nation entered the darkest hour in its two thousand-year history. A particularly poignant reminder of the horrors inflicted under the auspices of the Khmer Rouge can be found at the Tuol Sleng torture and extermination facility. This former high school campus, which became infamously known as S-21, was transformed into a type of hell where some seventeen thousand men, women and children were mercilessly tortured and put to death in nearby killing fields. The graphic images inside the torture centre made me accept for the first time in my life that evil does in fact exist.

Today Phnom Penh is a vibrant and bustling city, a living monument to the courage of the Cambodian people who, despite suffering unthinkable hardships in recent decades, are striving to develop their nation in peace. We visited the Khmer classical dance school on the outskirts of town, where a small band of dedicated teachers are reviving the fine arts of Cambodia. For all of the hardship and struggle that one finds in Cambodia's recent history there is certainly no shortage of incredible people helping to rebuild the nation.

We had to bade farewell to Chanta, a character we had grown quite fond of during the thirteen days he accompanied us, and Brian, Hutch and I took to the river unsupported, en route for the Vietnamese border some eighty kilometres further south. We immediately discovered how valuable Chanta had been when we tried to ask the locals directions on which channel we were in, in less than qualified Khmer. We knew there were several channels to the Mekong just south of Phnom Penh but after some long discussions with fishermen we felt we had confirmed our location on the map. We were wrong and inadvertently cruised down the smaller eastern channel of the river rather than the main western channel. That afternoon we hit the Vietnamese border in a place where we couldn't cross.

For a while it looked like we were in for a six-hour drive to get into the right channel until, after some very interesting negotiations conducted almost completely in sign language, a boatman agreed to smuggle us through the no man's land between the two nations on a long-tailed boat. The Khmer lad was constantly on his mobile phone ringing one military outpost after the other to make sure that machine gun-toting border patrols knew who we were. It was obvious that lost paddlers weren't particularly welcome in this area and we were looked upon with deep suspicion by several guards who wanted to question us but could not speak a word of English.

Our hired negotiator was worth his weight in riel, the Cambodian currency, as he skilfully talked each one around with friendly candour and the occasional packet of cigarettes.

The route we took passed through extensive areas of swamps, reeds, canals, rice fields and half a dozen remote guard posts, the similarity of which created some interesting conversation.

'The sun's fried your peanut, man. We're back in the same spot!' yelled Brian as he tried to keep some humour in an increasingly heated argument with Hutch about where we were.

'Fuck off, dipshit, we have not seen that guard post before.' Hutch pointed to a group of thatched buildings where some roughly dressed and heavily armed Khmer soldiers hung out.

As the sun sank low into the afternoon sky, we were all starting to have doubts about where we would be spending the night and none of us was really sure where we were. I thought to myself what a drag it would be to make it all the way down to the Vietnam border from Tibet to be then inadvertently blown out of the water by an edgy young border guard who saw a suspicious looking vessel sneaking past in the failing light. The whitewater may have been behind us but the risk to life and limb wasn't.

There is a significant black market in people smuggling between Vietnam and Cambodia. Besides the young Vietnamese women and girls transported across the land routes to service Cambodia's thriving sex industry, the obscure wetland route we travelled on was also one taken by the Vietnamese boat people who wanted to take advantage of the lower population density and greater fish catches that could be expected in Cambodia. The number of Vietnamese people that have entered Cambodia along this route in recent history is quite astounding and a large percentage of all the houseboats we encountered throughout Cambodia were actually homes to ethnic Vietnamese.

We were all relieved when, just as the sun began to set, the swamps and forests finally opened up to expose the more travelled eastern channel of the Mekong where the official Vietnam/Cambodian border crossing was located. After more than four and a half months on the expedition only one nation and a paddle distance of around two hundred kilometres separated me from achieving the first descent of the Mekong and the realisation of my dream.

17 The nine-headed dragon: the Vietnam delta and beyond

The moment the border formalities of departing Cambodia and stamping into Vietnam were completed we were abducted by a delightful gang of young girls, who wasted no time in emptying our pockets of loose change by selling us everything from Pepsi to accommodation and even a kayak storage service.

'Mr Mr, what you need? Pepsi, smoke, biscuit, chocolate? Buy from me, buy from me!' said Lee, a pretty nine-year-old girl, as she thrust cold cans of Pepsi and several plastic bags full of sweets towards me.

'But I spoke you first, Mr,' yelled eight-year-old Trung through the gap in her front teeth as she hip and shouldered her way between Lee and me to present her own array of wares.

These amazing little entrepreneurs made sure that before Hutch, Brian and I even had time to finish asking for something it would turn up at our fingertips with a thirty per cent service charge. As they skilfully took full advantage of our inability to keep up with their slightly dodgy antics, we found it impossible to shake them off because they were just so damned cute.

Several meals—at restaurants where the girls received commissions to take us to—two hours of wizzy-dizzies, some magic tricks and a couple of bike chases around town later they finally set us free to go and crash, completely exhausted, at the only guesthouse in town. Getting ripped off had never been so much fun.

The next morning the entire pack was waiting at the front of our guesthouse and Hutch was reaching into his pocket before he had rubbed the sleep out of his eyes. Before I knew it I was commandeered into paddling around piles of kids in the village canals. I had so many giggling, screaming and bouncing kids on my kayak that it soon became a submarine and we all flipped off half a dozen times before I managed to get rid of the last of my abductors at around 10 a.m. and escape into the swift waters of the Mekong. The children waved us off excitedly and chased us along the river-bank, yelling their goodbyes at the top of their lungs.

We had entered the region known to the Vietnamese as 'The Nine Dragons', a metaphor for the nine major channels through which the Mekong is released into the South China Sea. We met our Vietnamese translator and facilitator, Phuoc, from Asian Trails Travel, the next morning and after some discussions about our filming goals in Vietnam Brian and Hutch took off with Phuoc to film some Vietnam War-era historical shots, including the sites of some major battles. I headed down a complex system of tiny canals that resembled a spider's web en route to the riverside city of Chau Doc. I vied for right of passage with river craft of every description that were motored, poled, paddled, pulled and swum by curious locals who were always surprised to see my little red boat passing by their villages.

I stopped at a small rural restaurant for lunch and seemed to bring the entire district to a standstill with my presence as over a hundred people came to check out what I could only assume was the first foreigner to visit their village by kayak. I couldn't help myself and decided to unleash my favourite water-splashing magic trick on the group. With so many people the vibe was electric as I built up the tension before the inevitable drenching. When it finally happened, chaos ensued as grandmas, fathers and toddlers made for the hills before putting on the brakes when they heard the belly laughs of the slightly braver onlookers, overcome with hysterical laughter. Their fits of giggles, which lasted for the rest of my lunch break, left me in a fine mood for the rest of the day.

The capacity of the Mekong people to forgive and forget never fails to amaze me. Due in large part to America's military engagement in the lower Mekong many hundreds of thousands of people died in the region, yet with very few exceptions, the people I met were genuinely friendly and curious. I thought back to the course of the journey and realised that I had turned up, unannounced, in dozens of small and remote villages and I was treated respectfully on every occasion. The world could learn something from this remarkable cultural characteristic that allows societies to move forward, relatively unburdened by the burning hatred and resentment that war typically ignites.

Nowhere is the bounty of the Mekong River so aptly displayed than at the lively floating markets that seem to appear throughout much of the delta, precisely as the first rays of morning light start to dance on the surface of the river. From canals big and small, the rural people descend on these designated points of commerce with every kind of Mekong-related food you could care to imagine. The live food section, with toads, eels, snakes, shrimp, crabs, fish, beetles, grasshoppers, crazy crabs (small crabs that employ empty mollusc shells to protect their soft and vulnerable behinds) and dozens of other species, is always an eye-catcher as the captives vigorously fight for freedom from their bindings of vine, string and bamboo.

With skill and precision, conical hat-wearing delta ladies manoeuvre their hardwood craft with a paddle in one hand and their wares in the other. Flowers, fruit, vegetables, rice and sugar cane harvested from the Mekong's silted riverbanks add splashes of colour to the fringes of these fresh food department, while the soft drink and hardware vendors, in outrageously overloaded boats, remind onlookers that they are indeed witnessing a scene from the twenty-first century. Apart from this, delta life seems to go on much the same as it has for centuries.

That night I met the team in the bustling upper delta town of Chau Doc, some thirty kilometres south of the Cambodian border. This small city, which is currently experiencing a dramatic boom in aquaculture production, has long been a trade centre associated with the movement of goods up and down the Mekong River. Roman coins, dating from the second century AD found upstream in Angkor, provide an indication of the range of the ancient trade routes that brought goods, philosophies and religions from throughout the world to the people of the Mekong. Today the different religious faiths found in the Chau Doc area is testimony to the diverse cultural heritage that exists. Mosques, churches, and Buddhist, Taoist and Hindu-influenced shrines can be found in and around a town with a population of around one hundred thousand.

As we continued south we made a point of visiting major battles sites of the Vietnam War. This was of particular interest to me as my late father was conscripted into the Australian Armed Forces and served in Vietnam as a machine-gunner with the 8th Royal Australian Regiment from 1969 to 1970. The horrors of that conflict left terrible scars on many of the infantrymen who saw action. But as is always the case with war, it is the civilian population who ultimately pay the most terrible price. We asked some of the locals about their involvement in the war and why they chose to support either side in the conflict. There was one particular answer that seemed relevant to current world events.

A former Vietcong guerrilla called Phuoc (a different Phuoc to our translator) summed up the sentiments of so many Vietnamese when he stated, 'I didn't care too much for the ideology of either side, I was just a farmer, but eventually I went to war because we had foreigners from the other side of the world over here killing my countrymen by the thousands. I just wanted to support whoever opposed them.' It sounds remarkably similar to the response that so many Iraqis would give today.

Standing as a monument to the courage and veracity of the Vietnamese people, the delta has evolved into a rich agricultural region, created by countless hours of toil and the nutrient-rich earth replenished by the meandering mother of water. Despite the widespread use of defoliants during the second Indochina war, which destroyed vast tracts of previously arable land, the delta still produces around half of Vietnam's rice, making the country the world's second largest rice exporter. We stopped at various locations to chat with rice farmers and to learn about how these farmers produce such bountiful crops. Surprisingly, besides the ploughing of the fields and the husking of the grain, which increasingly employs machinery rather than buffalo and traditional rice pounders, the majority of farming and processing still follows time-honoured techniques that have been passed down through many generations.

From Chau Doc, Hutch and Brian took off with Phuoc, leaving me to paddle solo for a couple of days. For the first time it really started to hit home that I would soon reach the South China Sea. As the sun was setting that evening I pulled up at a small delta market village that was not marked on my map. I hauled my kayak up on to a hardwood long-tailed boat and walked into the market. I was soon surrounded by dozens of onlookers. I tried to ask whether there was a guesthouse in town but before anyone could understand my phonetically awful attempts at Vietnamese, a shy student was shuffled by others to the front of the group. 'Good evening, I am Trung, to where you go?'

It soon became apparent that there was no guesthouse in town so I began asking if it would be possible to stay at a village temple rather than to paddle off into the night. Trung was initially quite intimidated to be talking to a foreigner but her curiosity soon got the better of her and she started asking questions about life in the west. Before I knew it I was whisked across the village by a band of children to Trung's sister's house, where I was warmly welcomed by her sister, Chee, and a large gathering of brothers, cousins, uncles and aunts.

The family prepared a tasty meal of tiny fried fish and a separate dish of frogs' legs with rice. I showed them a map and traced the Mekong descent and I received my first congratulations for the achievement in the form of several thumbs up with the comment, 'Number one, you number one.'

After dinner, and my polite refusal of Trung's hand in marriage a couple of times, I was led by Trung and a band of around twenty kids on an hour-long twilight tour of the village. I was happily displayed as the token item of interest for the evening to various friends and relatives who greeted me with smiles and offers of food. The people of the delta were great and the village was a clichéd picture of rural harmony, everyone seemed to know everyone and by and large they seemed very happy. This perception was soon shaken when we returned to Chee's sister's house and were summoned to report to the local police station.

The cement tin-roofed building sat off to the west side of the village and was staffed by two cops who appeared no older than eighteen. They spoke sternly to Trung about a matter I could not quite understand and when her relatives tried to cut in to make a point they were abruptly silenced. Through Trung, who was quite nervous, they asked me a series of seemingly pointless questions before telling me that I was not allowed to stay in the village and that I had to go to a town some twenty kilometres inland.

When I asked why, Trung told me that the pair had apparently decided that because they had not had a foreigner stay in the village before that they might get into trouble if they let one stay this time. The policemen wanted me out of the village but they had no way of transporting me to the next town. I offered to paddle out to save Trung and her family any further trouble but this offer was refused.

It was a stalemate and as the hours passed I started to get grumpy. I desperately wanted to vent my frustration at the officers' indecision but with all communication going through Trung I didn't want to get her into more trouble so I was forced to grin and bear it. Two-and-a-half hours later a plump English-speaking captain arrived on a motorcycle. He introduced himself as the boss and came across as being calm and polite. Within minutes of sharing a cup of tea with him and telling him what I was doing in the village I was amicably released and returned to Chee's house.

The experience reminded me of various other similar situations I had encountered in other communist countries, where government employees were absolutely mortified by the prospect of using initiative to resolve a problem.

The next morning I bade farewell to Trung and her family and paddled down to the last significant stop of the descent, the port town of Cantho. Large ocean-going cargo vessels of up to five thousand tonnes lined up under gantry cranes waiting to be loaded with produce ranging from rice and fish to fruit and vegetables. It was the largest river port I kayaked into on the journey and I was amazed at the amount of traffic. The sight of sharks, stingrays and other seafood being offloaded from boats at the riverside markets helped drive home the reality of just how close I was to the South China Sea. I floated past industrial areas and large grain storage facilities and couldn't help but think about the sheer diversity of all the cultures and environments I had traversed. I had come a long way from the yak-hair nomad tents of Tibet. I was looking forward to reaching the mark. One hundred and forty-one days had passed since I flew into China en route to the source and a lot had come to pass in the interim. I was excited and ready to claim the prize.

On 8 September 2004, the day of reckoning arrived. I set out by kayak that morning while Brian, Hutch and Phuoc were driven in a thirty-seater speedboat by a driver whose name I didn't catch. We were forty kilometres from the South China Sea. My standard two-hour morning paddle burst was not needed on that fine day and I casually floated and occasionally paddled towards the ocean while discussing the experiences of the previous one hundred and forty-one days with Hutch and Brian, who relaxed in the speedboat. I realised how lucky I was to have these professional and cool companions with me for so much of the trip.

By three in the afternoon the swells started to stir our hulls and I soon had to separate from the speedboat to avoid being slapped against its side with the rise and fall of the waves. The size of the swell increased over the next two hours as the mother of water silently propelled me towards the realisation of my dream. I began to feel excited and felt like paddling off into the ocean but we were trying to time our arrival with the sunset so I held back.

At around 5.30 p.m. I noticed the distant palm- and mangrove-covered banks that had flanked me for the entire day gradually fading into the water. Ahead of me lay the great expanse of the South China Sea. My body surged with adrenaline as swells from the ocean began to pick up my kayak and slam it down into the troughs between each wave. Brian and Hutch were all smiles as they knocked back some cold Heinekens in between filming this major milestone. I almost powered out into the swells but the guys sensibly asked me to hold back until the sun was setting perfectly on the horizon in front of us. I finally got the prompt I had been waiting for from Brian: 'Paddle into the sunset and don't look back.' I have never been so happy to follow instructions in my entire life.

The feeling of paddling into those swells and realising I had conquered the Mekong was like a great celebration. After around five minutes I looked back to see where the crew were and they had completely disappeared. I found out later that while they were following me the speedboat powered a little too fast down the backside of a large wave and pitched its bow into an oncoming wall of water, taking in hundreds of litres of water through the front hatch in seconds. Brian and Hutch had to frantically bail with whatever they could find. The captain wisely hightailed it back up into the estuary before they sank. I was left to finish the journey of my lifetime as I had started it—solo.

I continued out for another three kilometres until I was well beyond the axis of the two points of land that marked the river's southernmost mouth. I had wondered several times what would go through my mind once I reached my goal, the point where, after one hundred and forty-one days, I would turn my kayak around to paddle against the natural flow of the mother of water. Now I had reached the invisible finish line.

As I lay my paddle to rest across my lap, taking in the perfect sunset, a feeling of peace and content enveloped me. This was a sensation beyond words or thoughts and I had no urge to rush it. As the darkness descended I surrendered myself to the deep sense of harmony that seemed like it could go on forever.

I made it!

Epilogue

I paddled back up the estuary where Brian and Hutch cheered me in with sprays of cold beer, hugs and a little dancing on the back of the boat. We were euphoric after pulling off an epic challenge and tears of happiness welled up in my eyes as I came to terms with the fact that I had defied the odds and succeeded in living out the dream.

As the weeks passed and the euphoria of successfully making a small mark in the historical records and achieving a personal dream subsided, I started coming to terms with what had really been achieved over the course of the descent and the year of planning. On a personal level I had lived out a dream and succeeded in exploring incredible wilderness areas that no other person had seen before. I became the first person in history to explore the entire course of one of the world's great rivers, and managed to prove something that various inspirational characters had instilled in me throughout my life—we all can achieve anything if we believe in ourselves and put in the hard yards. However, I soon came to the conclusion that besides being personally satisfying, these achievements and realisations amounted to little more than being trophies of one's ego.

There were always two main inspirations for mounting the challenge. There was my unquenchable desire for exploration and learning through experience, but I was also motivated by the desire to reveal this incredible region and some of the issues facing it to the world. It is this second inspiration, this achievement of publicising the fate of the Mekong, that I hope will leave the most enduring legacy.

One of the largest and most destructive damming projects in human history is currently underway on the Mekong mainstream in China. The ability of the great mother of water to sustain the basin she has nurtured for fifty million years is being severely compromised in the name of profit and her ecological vitality will go into decline over the coming years as a string of new dams come on-line.

It is the Mekong subsistence peoples and its natural environments who will pay the greatest price for cheap hydro-energy being produced by the cascade, yet more than fifteen years after construction began on the dams, China still hasn't allocated a single dollar towards compensating those affected downstream. Recent increases in global energy prices ensure the anticipated profit margins of the US$10 billion plus cascade have more than doubled since my descent of the Mekong commenced. So the dam builders do possess the financial resources and also have a legal and moral obligation to compensate the losses faced by the Mekong peoples. The only thing currently lacking is the will of China's dam builders to respect the basic human rights and resource rights of those affected. It is time this situation changed.

Half of all my benefits from the sales of this book will be donated towards establishing The Mekong First Descent Foundation, an organisation with the primary goals of creating greater global awareness of the concerns of the peoples and environments of the Mekong and to rallying international support to put pressure on China's dam builders to address these international human rights' and resource rights' violations. If you would like to learn more about these efforts to protect the resource rights and human rights of the Mekong subsistence peoples then please visit the project website: <www.mekongdescentfoundation.org>.

Acknowledgements

I'm delighted yet at a loss for words to express my sincere gratitude to all of the individuals and organisations who assisted in bringing the first full exploration of the Mekong River's mainstream from a dream into reality.

The expedition team: I would like to thank our documentary director of cinematography and co-paddler Brian Eustis and assistant cameraman Hutch Brown, who both reminded me that with the right team anything can be achieved; Alan Boatman, whose extensive knowledge of the Mekong Basin and contributions in the early stages of the project helped get things off the ground; Hoopy Letsunyane, who contributed her time and effort at a critical crossroad in the pre-expedition preparations; Abe Phimmasorn, whose footage contributions are a credit to his abilities. To our local guides and translators: Jimmy Doujie, Young, Jan, Phonsai, Chanta and Phuoc for bringing their unique perspectives into the fold. To the most important ladies in my life: my mother Lyn Scarlett and my wife Yuta O'Shea who were pillars of strength when adversity came knocking—I love you guys!

For financial support: I would like to thank Dick Smith and the Australian Geographic Society whose support of young Australian adventurers is unrivalled; Sky Telecom of Thailand and Laos who believed in our vision; Andreas Reinhard from the Volkart Foundation; Jeff and Jackie Nyhart who financially assisted Abe's involvement in the expedition; our good friends Marcus Gilmore, Sooki, Karantarat Kimyuan, Sombat Meeboon and Piti Pitaphat, who were all there with financial and moral support when we most needed it. Finally to my parents and parents-in-law Lyn and Don Scarlett, Paw Sombat and Mae Buntoung, your boundless support never wavered.

For logistical assistance: I would like to thank Asian Trails Travel Cambodia and Vietnam for providing faultless logistical and permit support throughout those countries, Lao Airlines who provided broad-ranging flight support throughout the Mekong region, the management and support staff of Wildside Asia and Green Discovery Laos for exceptional logistical assistance through Laos, and Lao West Coast Helicopter Service and Siem Riep Helicopter Service for sponsored filming flights that provided unique perspectives of the Mekong Valley.

The equipment sponsors: Feelfree Kayaks of Thailand; Wasit from Equinox Extreme International; Rob and Rick from Bomber Gear Paddle Gear Accessories USA; AT Paddles USA; Green Discovery travel for use of a support Zodiac in Thailand and Laos; Wildside Asia Travel for supplying a wide range of outdoors equipment; Abdul Halim from Sumatra Savages for providing a kayak which turned out to be the coolest 'pot plant holder' I have ever had; and Carl Traeholt of Tracks Outdoors Malaysia for Kayak Sponsorship. Without the right equipment I never would have made it, thank you.

For technical assistance: I would like to thank Andy Dennis and Azadee Sarayev from Sabaidee.com for sponsored web page design and support; Dr Milton Osborne for being there to steer me in the right direction in various areas; David Gillbanks and Ken Scott from the Pacific Asia Travel Association for their guidance and assistance; Khun Satit from the Tourism Authority of Thailand for his support of the project; Chris Bohren and Todd Leong from Admotiv Thailand who bent over backwards to help us keep things on track; Raffa Manuel from Raffa Laos Productions for creating the project promo video; and Mr Souraxay and associates from Lao Mekong River Commission.

Other friends and associates who lent their support in various invaluable ways include: Eric Southwick; Johan Gabrielson; Michael Lake; James Little Johns; Rattapoom Youprom and the 2000 Miles team; Sit, Phonsai, Lee, Janet and Toei from Wildside Asia, Patrick Evans, Steve Vanbeek, Frank Wolf, Philip from outdooreyes.com; Tim from wetasschronicles.com and Natasha from wetdawg.com.

Special mention needs to be given to my stepfather, Don Scarlett, and the Legacy Organisation of Western Australia; without either of them my highly evolved sense of adventure and the practical skills, confidence and experience to live out those adventures probably would not exist.

Finally, to all those people from the Mekong and beyond who gave of their time and energies to assist our descent to the sea, thank you.

Bibliography

Asian Development Bank, *Greater Mekong Subregion (GMS) Atlas of the Environment*, Asian Development Bank Publications, 2003.

Australian Mekong Resource Centre, Mekong Update and Dialogue Newsletters, 2002–06 cited at <www.mekong.es.usyd.edu.au>

Chandler, David, *Brother Number One: A political biography of Pol Pot*, Westview Press, Boulder: Colorado, 1992.

Chazee, Laurenze, *Atlas Des Ethnies et des Sous-Ethnies du Laos*, Bangkok, 1995.

Gargan, Edward A., *The River's Tale: A year on the Mekong*, Vintage Books, 2001.

Garnier, Francis, *Further Travels in Laos and Yunnan: The Mekong Exploration Commission Report (1866–1868)*, vol. 2, White Lotus Press, Bangkok, 1996.

——, *Travels in Cambodia and Parts of Laos: The Mekong Exploration Commission Report (1866–1868)*, vol. 1, White Lotus Press, Bangkok, 1996.

Hayden, Sterling, *Wanderer*, Sheridan House, 1963.

Hilton, James, *Lost Horizon*, Grosset and Dunlap, New York.

Osborne, Milton, 'River at Risk: The Mekong and the water politics of China and Southeast Asia', paper published by LOWY Institute of Australia, 2005.

——, 'The Paramount Power: China and the Countries of Southeast Asia', paper published by LOWY Institute of Australia, 2006.

——, *Mekong: Turbulent Past Uncertain Future*, Allen&Unwin, Sydney, 2000.

——, *River Road to China: The search for the source of the Mekong, 1866–73*, Atlantic Monthly Press, 1999.

——, *Southeast Asia: An introductory history*, Allen&Unwin, Sydney 2004.

Oung, Loung, *First they Killed My Father: A daughter of Cambodia remembers*, HarperCollins, New York, 2000.

Resistance and Reform in Tibet, Bloomington Press, Bloomington: Indianna, 1994.

Robins, Christopher, *The Ravens*, Crown Publications.

Rooney, Dawn, *Angkor*, 4th edn, Odyssey Publications, 2003.

Stuart Fox, Martin, *A History of Laos*, Cambridge University Press, 1997.

——, *Buddhist Kingdom Marxist State: The making of modern Laos*, White Lotus Press, Bangkok, 1996.

Winn, Pete, First Descent Expeditions in Western China, cited at <http://www.shangri-la-river-expeditions.com> in 2004.